Counting Books Are
More Than Numbers

Counting Books Are More Than Numbers:

An Annotated Action Bibliography

Patricia L. Roberts

Library Professional Publications
1990

First published in 1990 as a Library Professional Publication,
an imprint of The Shoe String Press, Inc.,
Hamden, Connecticut 06514

Printed in the United States of America

The paper used in this publication meets the minimum requirements of
American National Standard for Information Sciences—Permanence of
Paper for Printed Library Materials, ANSI Z39.48-1984. ♾

Library of Congress Cataloging–in–Publication Data

Roberts, Patricia,
    Counting books are more than numbers : an annotated
action bibliography / Patricia L. Roberts.
        p.   cm.
    ISBN 0–208–02216–3 (alk. paper).
    ISBN 0–208–02217–1 (pbk. : alk. paper)
    1. Counting—Bibliography. 2. Children's books,
Illustrated Bibliography. I. Title.
    Z6654.C69R63   1990   [QA113]
    016.5135'5—ds20   89–19936
                                              CIP

To James Roberts,
James M. Roberts,
and
Jill Frances Roberts

Contents

CONTENTS

Acknowledgments

Since I received assistance in preparing this book, I owe sincere acknowledgments to the following people:

Virginia Mathews, Vice-President and Editor of The Shoe String Press, Inc., for her thoughtful suggestions and fine editorial skills;

Dr. Edward Arnsdorf, Professor of Education, California State University, Sacramento, for his review of the manuscript;

Dr. Patricia Marshall, Associate Professor of Education, California State University, Sacramento, for her interest in teacher education;

Dr. Ann O'Neil and Dr. Ruth Hartley, Professors of Education, California State University, Sacramento, for their tireless search for books;

Dr. Robert J. Whitehead, Professor of Education, California State University, Sacramento, for his support and interest;

Roz Van Auker and Marilyn Merritt, curriculum librarians, California State University, Sacramento, for their aid in bibliographic research;

Ms. Kathryn King, who serves in the inter-library loan department, California State University, Sacramento, for her unfailing searches for selected material;

Anke Carstensen, Katrin Seig, and Birte Hogel, three friends from Germany, for their interest in children's books;

Marie Lopez, one friend from Galt, for her interest and help;

and James E. Roberts, James Michael Roberts, and Jill Frances Roberts, for their support at home while the information for this book was found, reviewed, thought about, and typed.

Introduction: Counting Books are More than Numbers

A Child's Books: The Values

A parent, librarian, teacher, or teacher's aide can find many authoritative opinions about the value of introducing counting books to young children. Examples of good reasons for doing so and values therefrom are included below:

- Babies need books and children need books (Butler, 1982). Adults need books, too, for reading aloud from quality literature is one creative way for an adult to teach a child (Coody, 1983). Counting books can stimulate interest in numbers of objects, encourage interaction with the text, and may influence a child's language development (Norton, 1987). Counting books also offer one-to-one correspondence and other simple math concepts (Huck, Hepler, and Hickman, 1987). As part of this stimulation, teachers may help young children to develop an understanding of one-to-one correspondence between clusters of objects and a particular number by using objects to count along with the books which will provide a bridge to concepts of counting (Bell, 1988). The accuracy of direct experiences may be confirmed with counting books; the pages give a viewer some proof in pictures of these experiences in colorful, diverse, and imaginative ways. Moving from manipulative experiences to proof in pictures, the child's progression from concrete objects to picture to numeral is pedagogically and developmentally sound (Burke, 1986). As part of the progression to pictures, counting books may be used for teaching number concepts when the concept and the symbol is clear (Tiedt, 1979). A variety of numbers, numerals, words, and names of objects are to be found in counting books. In addition to introducing numerals, counting books offer clarification about sets, grouping, and place value (Burke, 1986), and large numbers

of things (Sutherland and Arbuthnot, 1986). Counting books also contribute to the learner's cognitive structure by reinforcing a grasp of
seriation (Cullinan et al., 1981) and by offering clarification about mass,
position, and size (Lickteig, 1975; Sutherland and Arbuthnot, 1986).

• Counting books may focus ability to identify simple objects; to describe
  pictures; to count sequentially; to recognize themes; and to develop
  cognitive thinking skills (Whitehead, 1984). To meet some children's
  abilities, selected books may show the sequence with counting up and
  counting down as well as the operations of addition and subtraction
  (Sutherland and Arbuthnot, 1986). Other books may present higher
  order thinking skills (Brown, 1986) and reinforce understandings in
  mathematics (Radebaugh, 1981; Harsh, 1987; Fischler, 1988). As an
  example of one reinforcement activity, the beginning reader can develop the skill of time-order sequence and write a math sentence with
  the numerals and signs representing the sequence of events found in a
  simple word problem (Wilson and others, 1983).

• Supporting language development, certain counting books can be the
  center of storytime sessions (Bauer, 1977) or introduce stories for discussion (Glazer and Williams, 1979; Huck, Hepler, and Hickman,
  1987). The young reader may identify Mother Goose or counting
  rhymes containing numbers and then make up individual word problems for friends to solve. Other counting books will hold interest with
  a counting song to sing, an introduction to another culture, or a puzzle
  to solve (Cullinan and Carmichael, 1977). Further, some counting
  books contain works of art and offer aesthetic experiences (Burke,
  1986). A counting book may lead to a wide variety of experiences in
  other books. Books with enumeration may be a valuable component in
  a beginning reading program, for several of them have patterns that are
  predictable for a child and show the time, days, months, and cardinal
  numerals (Hall, 1985). Additionally, books in math series may stimulate
  investigation and may sharpen a youngster's mathematics vocabulary
  by presenting a single concept in depth. Indeed, the vocabulary and
  concepts of some modern math programs for students in the primary
  grades would seem to encourage viewing and reading selected trade
  books about mathematics (Sebesta and Iverson, 1975).

A Child's Math: The Understandings

What understandings and appreciations for mathematics can counting
books promote? According to a recent state mathematics framework
(California State Department of Education, 1982), a girl or boy, at the

completion of the primary grades, should have developed understandings about number, measurement, geometry, patterns and functions, statistics and probability, and logic, including the following content:

Number

- counting by ones, twos, fives, and tens

- using cardinal numbers to compare quantities

- using ordinal numbers to order quantities

- understanding the meaning of the four basic operations: adding, subtracting, multiplying, and dividing

- using basic addition, subtraction, and multiplication facts

- estimating answers to computation problems

- adding and subtracting whole numbers with two-digit and three-digit numbers

- multiplying a two-digit number and a one-digit number

- dividing a two-digit number by a one-digit number

- choosing an appropriate basic operation for a selected situation

- interpreting word problems with models, pictures, and role play

- writing math sentences using symbols to represent a selected situation

- using the understanding of commutativity ($a + b = b + a$ in addition)

- using the understanding of associativity ($[a + b] + c = a + [b + c]$ in addition)

- using the understanding of the identity property of zero (e.g., zero when operated on with another number results in the other number in addition)

- using the understanding of the identity property of one (e.g., one when operated on with another number results in the other number in multiplication)

- using concrete materials to recognize, represent, and compare halves, thirds, and fourths

- using money to recognize, represent, and compare decimal values

- recognizing decimal and fractional equivalents for halves, fourths, and tenths

Measurement

- using nonstandard, metric, and customary units of measure to estimate and measure length, volume, and weight

- using digital and traditional clocks to tell time reading and interpreting Celsius and Fahrenheit temperatures on thermometers

- choosing an appropriate unit of measure and using a variety of measuring instruments

- recognizing and counting money used in the United States

Geometry

- using visual attributes (characteristics) and concrete materials to identify, classify, and describe common geometric figures and models: circles, cubes, rectangles, spheres, squares, and triangles

- using correct vocabulary about geometric figures and models

- using several geometric shapes to make other geometric shapes

- deciding when figures are congruent and when they are similar

- covering an area with repeating geometrical patterns so everything fits together with no spaces unfilled

Patterns and Functions

- identifying, verbalizing, and extending a pattern in a sequence

- using a concrete model to create a pattern

- representing a pattern symbolically in a table

- describing a relationship given in a selected table or shown by a sequence of objects

- determining a location by using ordered pairs of numbers on a rectangular grid

Statistics and Probability

- collecting and organizing data obtained from surveys and experiments
- representing and interpreting data received from surveys and experiments
- conducting surveys and experiments
- creating and interpreting concrete, pictorial, and symbolic graphs
- predicting outcomes
- carrying out simple activities involving probability.

Logic

- classifying and sorting objects
- using one or more attributes by observing relationships and making generalizations
- making reasonable or logical conjectures and conclusions about situations with concrete materials
- using such words as *all, and, if-then, none, not, of, or,*and *some*

In addition to the number concepts having been identified by California's mathematics framework, common number concepts for young children have been identified in the Huei-Joyce Hsu's study (1987) which focused on the critical early years when mathematics interest is often neglected. Hsu identified several common number concepts for young girls and boys that were emphasized in fourteen mathematics textbooks used in the education of preservice elementary teachers. Integrating the results into a model curriculum for developing a child's number concepts, Hsu found these major concepts: classifying; ordering; matching; comparing; rational counting; and recognizing and comprehending cardinal numbers. Marshall (1988), too, worked with preservice materials. She classroom-tested and edited a collection of math plans developed by preservice elementary teachers which emphasize some of the major areas of mathematical understanding: probability and statistics; geometry; and measurement. Other math plans which support understanding in additional areas are in the process of being developed. In considering the skills listed above, the interested adult realizes that some counting books go far beyond the rote counting of numbers to offer opportunities for learning several of the listed skills. Specifically, counting books offer:

> discrete objects to be counted
> math language
> number-numeral relationships
> numeral shapes
> objects to be classified
> patterns that match
> problems and ways of solving them
> relations of numbers and their order
> relative size
> sequence of numbers and numerals
> spatial relationships
> visual forms to be identified

A Child's Math: The Difficulties

What are some of the problems a child may encounter in achieving understanding of these math concepts? Information from research is available about the problems girls and boys may have during their early interactions with mathematics. As a result of these studies, there are guidelines which may be used to extend mathematics experiences for children. These recommendations offer help for adults who work with this age group (from two or three years old through the primary grades) daily.

1. Children need time to use language about math and to talk about mathematics. Since there is a link between syntax and semantics, young girls and boys should have opportunities to talk about math (Webb and Webb, 1982; Liedtke, 1988), to extract meaning, and to restate the problem in their own words (Thomas, 1988). A good way to teach simple arithmetic is to build on the young learner's informal knowledge (Ginsburg, 1977; Carpenter and Moser, 1983), and learning to count everyday objects is an effective basis for these early lessons (Gelman and Gallistel, 1978; Fuson, Richards, and Briars, 1982; Resnick, 1983; U.S. Department of Education, 1986). At two to three years of age, a child may count and use object correspondence rather than number correspondence or sort objects according to size or color (Carlson, 1985). Counting also may promote number-concept relations such as those found in: patterns of arrangements of objects; recognition of two or more parts of a number that make up

the whole number; and relationships of each number to other numbers and in considering such patterns as *one-more- than* and *one-less-than* (Van de Walle, 1988).

A preschooler needs exposure to numbers and to the abstract symbols that will come to have meaning with the passage of time and experience (Carlson, 1985). Girls and boys arrive at kindergarten with a varied collection of acquired number skills, concepts, and strategies (Katz, 1986). However, some of these children may have difficulty with counting rhymes, riddles, and time rhymes if they are unfamiliar with the Mother Goose nursery rhymes (Hall, 1969) and be unable to identify basic shapes such as squares and circles, recognize primary colors, sit still to listen to a short story or tell a simple story with a beginning, middle, and end (*Sacramento Bee*, 1988). Children who have developed certain mathematical concepts are ready for a curriculum program of mathematics (Hsu, 1987; Bauch and Hsu, 1988) that includes grouping to reflect individual differences. In such a program, mathematics can be exploring materials, graphing, sorting, and classifying—all to develop concepts (Wolfinger, 1988).

Generally, five-year-olds recognize sets of three or four objects and can write or recognize numerals up to five or ten but do not develop concurrently the concepts of cardinal and ordinal numbers (Rea and Reys, 1979). Some kindergarten children recognize halves, fourths, and thirds, and others are familiar with the ideas of time, liquid measurement, and money (Ginsburg, 1980; Hollis, 1981). Still other kindergarteners can solve simple addition and subtraction examples in a verbal story problem. When their math lessons include physical objects, children in the early grades generally learn mathematics more effectively (Piaget, 1965; Hamrick, 1980; U.S. Department of Education, 1986).

Given the importance of physical objects in lessons, emphasizing symbolization too early in mathematics should be avoided (Hamrick, 1980; Matthews, 1983; Hyde and Bizar, 1989) and emphasizing homework in arithmetic computation should be considered carefully (Marshall, 1983; Cooper, 1989). Meta-analysis shows that homework in arithmetic computation is not consistently beneficial: only 33% of twenty-one comparisons of studies shows that homework is superior to no homework in this area. However, problem solving achievement shows a much more consistent benefit from homework for 90% of twenty comparisions of studies show homework superior to no homework (Marshall, 1983).

As girls and boys develop their concepts of number, the ability to count is not a reliable sign that a preschooler has a concept of number (Hollis, 1981). Before asking the learner to consider such ideas as *one more, one less, addition,* and *subtraction,* the extent to which the child can *think* about numbers should be determined (Kennedy, 1984). Before considering addition and subtraction, girls and boys should be able to think about numbers as a correspondence between the elements of two groups (or sets) even when the configurations of the groups are changed (e.g., the number of toys in a box does not change when the toys are poured into another box or when the toys are rearranged).

Older boys and girls also should be given time to talk about math and be encouraged to discuss their procedures in addition and subtraction, in mapping, in the writing code, and when ready, in the base system (Resnick, 1983). It seems that older children, who work and talk in small groups, seek to understand verbal mathematics problems through the function of constructing mental representations or physical displays of the problems and the function of evaluating the constructions (Duncan, 1985).

2. Children should be encouraged to talk about what they think about when using a number-word sequence, counting on, counting in a descending sequence, double counting, and when using a set or group approach (Steffe, Von Glaserfeld, Richards, and Cobb,1983). For one topic, girls and boys may discuss using a number-word sequence to solve simple addition problems (Resnick and Ford, 1981). First, the number-word sequence is learned as an unbreakable sequence (Fuson and Hall, 1983), and later, as a breakable sequence into which the counter can move mentally and tell the number *after* a given number in the sequence. With this knowledge, it is possible to say that the number four comes after three. After many opportunities to review the number-after relationship, a boy or girl may be ready to recognize the number that comes *before* another given number in a familiar sequence (Fuson, Richards and Briars, 1982). Still later, one may be ready to think of addition or subtraction involving one quantity such as four crocodiles plus one crocodile or four crocodiles minus one crocodile (Resnick, 1983).

    Without understanding the principle of commutativity, some girls and boys invent labor-saving strategies in addition that include spontaneous counting, counting all beginning with the first addend, counting on from the larger addend, or counting on from the first addend that is selected by the child (Baroody and Gannon, 1983). In counting all, when given an addition situation such as three cookies plus two cookies, a boy or girl may count *one, two, three*, then say *four* and think: *That is one more;* then say *five* and think: *That is two more. The answer is five.* Using counting all as their first strategy in addition, some young counters make a transition from counting all to counting on in later addition situations (Secada and others, 1983). In counting on (rather than counting all) in a situation such as three plus two, a girl or boy will move mentally into the number-word sequence at a selected addend, usually the largest number, *three.* Then the child will count on from three, say *four* and think: *That is one more;* then say *five* and think: *That is two more. The answer is five.*

Several studies analyze the performance of girls and boys in the early grades. One type of ability possessed by first-graders who performed better than others in addition problems was the ability to conserve number: that is, to recognize that if two sets are matched one to one, the number of objects in each is the same regardless of the arrangement or rearrangement of the two sets. If a learner matches five collars to five puppies (placing one of the collars on each of the puppies) and recognizes there are five collars for five puppies (one collar on each), then the number of collars and puppies remains the same regardless of how the puppies rearrange themselves as they play. Kindergarten and first-grade children may be instructed in matching two sets in one-to-one correspondence activities (Kennedy, 1984), an instruction that may continue through elementary school. Students in the sixth grade may receive lessons on the one-to-one matching of a set of counting numbers with a set of even (or odd) numbers (Cordeiro, 1988).

Participating in activities with cut-out shapes of Zorkies, (natives of the imaginary planet Zorka), who differ in color and number of eyes, legs and arms, some girls and boys in the primary grades may be successful in learning one-to-one correspondence and in recognizing equivalent and nonequivalent sets (Lettieri, 1978).

3. Children also develop informal subtraction strategies that include the counting down strategy. In subtraction, some girls and boys have problems when counting in a sequence and when double counting (Baroody, 1984). Using the counting down strategy, one considers, for instance, a situation of four crocodiles minus one crocodile, and moves mentally into the number sequence at the larger number four and gives as the answer the number before four, *three.* To consider addition or subtraction involving more than one crocodile or quan-

tity, another girl or boy may use concrete objects and enact a take-away action (Carpenter and Moser, 1983). To do this, objects such as markers, tally marks, all fingers on two hands, or one-handed finger patterns, may be used to show the larger number (Fuson, 1988); the items equal to the smaller number may then be removed and the items remaining in front of the student counted. Some may also use a counting down procedure without concrete objects for subtraction. In this counting down procedure, the student says the larger number, counts back the number of times equal to the smaller number, and says the last number counted as the answer. As an example: considering four crocodiles minus two crocodiles, the boy or girl may think of four, move mentally to three, and consider: *This is one that is taken away.* He or she then moves mentally to two, and thinks: *This is two that is taken away, so the answer is two.* This counting down procedure involves three tasks: counting back from any number in a number sequence; counting back a certain number of times; and counting forward to keep track of the certain number of times that are being counted back. Thus, the student is involved in counting back as well as forward during the period of thinking about a subtraction problem. For some, counting back in a subtraction situation makes the situation more difficult; the degree of difficulty of counting back in a problem depends on the number given as the smaller number. As another example: given a problem of ten crocodiles minus six crocodiles, a student counts back from ten six times to reach four as an answer. In this procedure, the learner will also count forward to keep a record of the six times. Using these steps over and over to solve subtraction problems may make subtraction problems with two-digit numbers suddenly become too much for the counter's concentration and mental record-keeping. For still another example of the difficulty encountered, one could complete thirteen steps of counting back (and forward) to consider thirteen crocodiles from sixteen crocodiles—a long task for some children.

To introduce subtraction, the decomposition method of subtraction (taking away) is favored for certain primary grade children (Kennedy, 1984). For some third-grade students, the use of the decomposition method in subtraction provides greater accuracy and understanding (Sherrill, 1979). For other students, a counting up procedure in subtraction is introduced through the school curriculum: one begins with the smaller number, counts forward until the larger number is reached, and keeps a count of the steps in this counting up procedure. For instance, to respond to a two-digit subtraction problem of fifteen minus thirteen, a girl or boy will begin with thirteen, move mentally to fourteen, and then consider: *That is one,* then move mentally to fifteen and think: *That is two. The answer is two.* However, if this procedure involves many moves, a young counter may feel rushed, lose the place in the counting up process, lose the count, or forget the number of steps needed to move up this mental number line.

With an awareness of some of these problems, an adult will be concerned about introducing ways for a child to see the number sequence, with presenting the numbers as words and symbols, with offering opportunities to break into the sequence at different numbers, and about giving time to review counting back as well as forward in a selected sequence.

4. Children need materials to move and manipulate, and often enjoy playing with markers used as math aids or in math games. Interacting with objects in the environment, a young girl or boy uses numbers spontaneously. Values contributed by math games (Suydam, 1983) and by manipulative aids to early math experiences should be considered as part of this spontaneous use of numbers (Slaughter, 1981; Slaughter and Chilcott, 1981). These early math experiences can be more enjoyable when there is access to books, stories, rhymes, and interesting game activities at home, in the classroom or in the school or public library. "Bo Peep Count to Ten," "Numbers in Literature," and "Number Stumper" are just a few of the many games available (Whitehead and Van Scoy, 1971), and many of the books will be described in later sections.

Materials for a girl or boy to manipulate include parent-made, teacher-made, and commercially-made materials. *Family Math* is a series of sessions for parents and children with content that follows most elementary school math programs. Parent-made or parent-collected materials may support lessons in such areas as measurement, time, money, and geometry. Teacher-made materials generally are as effective as purchased materials (Ashlock and Washbon, 1978), but the question of whether making them constitutes the best use of increasingly valuable professional time should be asked in each case. Two examples point out the value of materials: kindergarten and first-grade children used geoboards to make designs and patterns, to explore figures, and to learn about open and closed figures (Holcomb, 1980); second-grade children received dice and paper grids as an introduction to the concept of probability and graphed the outcomes of multiple rolls of the dice (Woodward, 1983). Additional supplementary materials may include number lines, instructional programs with clocks for time-telling, journal writing, calculators, and selected software for the computer. Two separate studies focused, for example, on journal writing and calculators. One study investigated the relationship between journal writing and achievement in mathematic measurement and place value/regrouping among primary school children, and showed that third-grade children lowest in prior achievement in place value/regrouping scored significantly higher gains when they received mathematics instruction with journal writing (Wells, 1986). The effect of minimizing computation load through the use of calculators by students in grades three through eight also was assessed with one finding, among others, that the three experimental groups of low-achieving students using calculators in this study showed significant improvement in problem solving (Babbitt, 1986). Reports on the use of computer software by educators indicate Logo Writer and computer games have been valuable tools in the classroom. Logo Writer allows students to make clock faces and write stories based on what happens at different times of the day, as well as preparing supplemental bar graphs, numerical values, and descriptive text about the graphs (Newman, 1988). Considering the effect of computer-assisted instruction (CAI) on first-grade phonics and mathematics achievement computation, the results from a criterion-referenced mathematics test showed all CAI experimental group students scored significantly higher than control group students (Abram, 1984).

5. Children need time to dramatize story problems and to create original problems, particularly story problems based in their home environment. Results from one of the few studies to focus on this indicated that math problems with a common name for the groups such as cats (group 1) and cats (group 2) appear to be easier for first-grade children to solve in a verbal story problem than those with different names for the groups such as apples (group 1) and bananas (group 2) (Steffe, 1967). Children may bring these problems into the classroom to discuss (Kahn and Wirtz, 1982). After discussion, a current class file of individually created story problems may be kept on index cards (Ferguson and Fairburn, 1985), and interpreted through role play (California State Department of Education, 1982). Puppets, including those made by the children, may be introduced to dramatize selected story problems (Ferguson and Fairburn, 1985). Also, visual equations in picture form can be prepared and a story problem may be duplicated for a take-it-home experience of showing and discussing it (Ferguson and Fairburn, 1985). Techniques for improving a

child's problem-solving abilities include: using drawings and dia-grams on an overhead transparency; games and practice activities (Ashlock, 1971); writing an original problem (Muller and Kurtz, 1982); solving original problems by friends; using problems without numbers; using problems presented orally (Thompson and Van de Walle, 1980); reviewing vocabulary in the problem; writing math sentences about the problem; sequencing problems from easy to hard; receiving assistance in correcting problems; and receiving praise (Hutchinson and Hutchinson, 1978; Riedesel, 1985). Using a learner's own creations, an adult can model simple computational problems for remediation experiences (Ferguson and Fairburn, 1985).

6. Children benefit from peer assistance in appropriate groups. For third-, fourth-, and fifth-grade students, peer support for learning verbal problem-solving in arithmetic generated positive attitudes to-ward arithmetic. Further, and most noticeably in the fourth grade, this peer support increased students' positive comments about their classmates (Snethen, 1975). In addition to same-age tutoring, cross-age tutoring may be encouraged also (Peterson, 1981; Sharpley and others,1983). Within this tutoring arrangement, a small heterogene-ous group approach to cooperative learning brings together students of differing abilities to work on tasks with reward and recognition based on the group's performance. In each cooperative learning group, a leader reads the questions and gets the reading, the prob-lem solving, or the task, started. The recorder writes down the group's answers. The checker makes sure that everyone understands each question and its answer. The encourager sees that all students participate in the work of the group (Nelson-Herber, 1988). In coop-erative learning groups, low-achieving children benefit from the in-teraction and the support from the better students and high-achiev-ing children benefit from maintaining a high level of performance while still contributing to the knowledge of others.

For several years, studies have shown that a learner's number concepts are associated with factors of previous experience, educa-tion, and socioeconomic status (Almy, 1966). Recent findings indicate that girls and boys who enter first grade with marked differences in number abilities continue to be quite markedly different in these abilities as they proceed in their formal arithmetic programs. Those who enter first grade with higher number abilities perform better than those who enter with intermediate number abilities; and those children, in turn, perform better than those who enter with low number abilities (Charles, 1984). High achievers are usually girls and boys who, because they have been exposed to reading and to other cultural experiences before they begin to go to school, generally have a better chance of success in formal learning than those who do not have this experience (American Library Association, 1984).

The cooperative learning group activities can include meaningful experiences in number knowledge and in number concepts and integrate language and mathematics learning. Such experiences appear to be needed by most children. One finding indicated that first-grade children interpreted pictures of addition and subtraction situations within a range from no understanding to full understanding (Campbell, 1981), while an earlier finding indicated that culturally disadvantaged children at the elementary school level generally did not attain as high a level of understanding of the number concepts presented as did advantaged children (Dunkley, 1965).

7. Children need experience with mental mathematics. From kindergarten on, the habit of estimating before calculating an answer should be encouraged and the activities about estimation should focus on the *range* of a reasonable answer rather than on formal calculation procedures (California State Department of Education, 1982). For one example, estimation and counting can take place on a regular basis as large play blocks are used for construction in a classroom corner, cleared away, and brought to a circle of young kindergarten conversationalists who respond to questions such as "Did our estimate of the number of blocks to take away from our corner clean up our construction corner?" and "If not, what should our estimate be this time?" (Singer, 1988). After improvement through developmental practice, a learner's pattern of error may occur again later even with reinforcement activities for calculation (Sadowski and McIlveeny, 1984) for certain systematic errors seem to arise from a learner's failure to represent mentally the arithmetic procedures on quantities (Resnick, 1983). When students' error patterns are contrasted, low-achieving students generally tend to make systematic errors while high-achieving students seem to make more nonsystematic errors (Owston, 1981).

8. Children benefit from time and opportunities to think about their own thinking. Metacognition principles—thinking about one's thinking—will improve some children's performance on a range of academic tasks (Reeve and Brown, 1984). In solving problems, a girl or boy needs to see that a problem exists, develop an understanding of it, analyze it, consider alternative solutions, choose the best solution,

and then evaluate the results—all steps that overcome obstacles to problem solving (Cook and Slife, 1985).

In every discipline, including mathematics and its intrinsic challenge to solve problems, reading and writing are tools for learning. Writing, including journal writing, is a significant life skill and students should use writing and reading frequently. Writing about mathematics in a personal journal appears to reinforce a student's mathematics instruction (Davison and Pearce, 1988). As an example of the value of writing as a problem-solving experience (Ganz, 1983), the writing of one second-grade student demonstrates that some of life's crises can be successfully worked out through the writing process and points out that writing appears to aid in cognitive, as well as social and emotional, development.

9. Children benefit from certain books that support understanding about numbers which may also lead to resolving some difficulties with word problems. In counting books, written number words may be anticipated by a girl or boy and quickly learned visually. The illustrations, along with other clues, aid a viewer's memory (McCracken and McCracken, 1986). Illustrations may help to make the printed word more concrete and extend the text. Illustrated books may help the young reader to form more mature and adequate concepts of self as well as the ever-expanding world.

In the primary grades, a girl or boy may have difficulties of various kinds with word problems. There are the difficulties in understanding a problem that include use of language, vocabulary, and conditions of the situation, which require interpreting the facts, relationships, and goals of the problem and involve much more than ordinary reading skill. Math reading, after all, uses specialized vocabulary and forms rarely encountered in normal discourse or in other subject areas (Thomas, 1988). There are the difficulties in preparing a plan of attack for solving the problem; difficulties in carrying out the plan; and difficulties in reviewing the plan to see if the answer or solution "fits," e.g., to see if the answer is reasonable or logical (Hyde and Bizar, 1989). Further, the concepts and relationships involved in the problem may not be fully understood; the strategy employed for working the word problem may be incorrect; a single step may be used to solve a two-step word problem; or the order in the procedures for solving the problem may be mismatched with the order of the presentation of information in the problem (Quintero, 1984). A direct instruction approach—in which reading skills considered necessary for the content area of mathematics were taught and developed apart from the regular mathematics curriculum—appeared to be effective in teaching problem-solving skills and metric skills at the third-grade level (Sower, 1980). Considering the use of certain aids—including pictures—to remediate difficulties with word problems, investigators have looked for an answer to the question, "Would changing the format of a problem to a rebus or telegraphic (drawn) format or mapping a subtraction algorithm help remediate difficulty with word problems?" While illustrations, along with other structures, may aid a young child's memory, it seems that using a drawn format or mapping of a word problem is not always helpful to older children. For example, mapping instruction with regrouping has not always been successful for some fourth, fifth, and sixth graders because some of the students miss the trade-borrow analogy that is central to some of the problems (Omanson and others, 1983).

For other boys and girls in grades three through seven, the drawn format was not helpful because: the format lacked the words to help bring a mental image to the ideas; the format lacked needed context and became confusing for some; and the translation from the long verbal format to the short picture format was too difficult for others to grasp easily (Threadgill-Sowder and others, 1984). For still other girls and boys in grades three through eight, an abbreviated format of story problems—use of pictures—did not result in better performance once the pictures were removed from sight (Sowder and others, 1984). For example, students from grades four and five saw pictures as providing a strong sense of the structure of a problem but could not recall the information given in them once a picture problem had been removed from view (Moyer and others, 1983). This inability to recall on the part of students in the intermediate grades may have meaning for adults who assist students in the earlier grades.

In one recent study, findings indicated that the prerequisite skills needed for fifth-grade students to read and solve arithmetic word problems depended most on the skills of vocabulary meaning, computation, and determining the correct operation (Brenner, 1981).

10. Children need assistance with math remediation through language activities. An adult's assistance with math often extends to language development when the adult realizes that effective reading in math is closely associated with the development of math skills and concepts. With the guidance and the diagnosis of the school's math specialist, one may ascertain that a student in a primary classroom may be unable to read math symbols, to designate math terms ver-

bally, or have difficulty in understanding certain math ideas and relationships.

In the interests, therefore, of helping a girl or boy become a better math reader, an adult will be interested in these values and varied opportunities offered by counting books beyond the rote counting of numbers:

- Counting books offer children math readiness activities.

- Counting books offer children language about math.

- Counting books lead children to supplementary materials.

- Counting books lead children to create original problems.

- Counting books give children a focus for peer assistance and mental arithmetic, and discussion of math concepts.

- Counting books offer children activities and opportunities for thinking about thinking.

- Counting books offer children word problems and opportunities to solve them.

- Counting books offer children page formats useful in solving problems.

A Child's Counting Books: The Variety

If counting books can be of value to a young child, then what are the types of counting books that are available, what is in them, and how do they implement the above listed opportunities? These counting books may be grouped as ABC-123 books, rhymes, and as topics with related or unrelated objects to count. In the ABC-123 group, there is a number sequence as well as the familiar alphabet. In the books with rhymes, there are rhymes for counting and counting-out, for enjoying humor and nonsense, for learning, and for singing. In the number stories, a viewer sees animals, insects, personified numerals, monsters, and other creatures as the main characters. Settings for these stories include the carnival, circus, farm, family, school, and community life. In the books that focus on topics with related objects, the reader finds a relationship among the objects found in similar settings. Leading a boy or girl through these topics may be characters similar to the ones found in the number stories—animals, insects, monsters, and other creatures. There are mysteries, puzzles, and books about transportation, too. In the counting books that feature the work of the artists and their collections of unrelated items to count, the objects are arranged in groups that show numbers fewer than ten, up to ten, and greater than ten. All titles are given and fully annotated in the body of the book.

Counting Books Offer Children Math Readiness Activities

Given time to use language about math and to talk about it, young girls and boys open counting books to find activities such as reviewing ABC-123 sequences, chanting rhymes, singing songs, and listening to stories. They may, with this stimulus, want to talk about mathematics.

ABC-123 books offer Hindu-Arabic numbers along with English letters in the alphabet. Some titles include animals to count, a sequence of groups or sets from one to ten, the numerals, and the names of animals. This review is a possible readiness activity for the reading and interpretation a girl or boy will need in later charts, graphs, and tables filled with information and found in other books. In another book, numbers of personified foods introduce language play as they are counted: up to eighteen bananas with appeal, nineteen wealthy muffins made of dough, and twenty vegetables in a stew. Riddles in another book contain puns (e.g., "What's more wonderful than a counting dog? A spelling bee"), and are about animals (e.g.,"What part of a fish weighs the most? The scales"), and the sounds animals make (e.g., "What would you have if you put four ducks in a box? A box of quackers"). Finger plays include "The Counting Lesson," "I Have Two Eyes to See With," and "Five Little Chickadees."

In one book, rhymes for boys and girls interested in Roman numerals offer information and show the placement of *V* and *I* together as figures to symbolize the number six, the use of *L* for fifty and *M* for a thousand. For other titles of books for children that contain both the ABCs and the 123s, consult *Alphabet Books As a Key to Language Patterns* (1987) by Patricia L. Roberts. This reference book discusses the role of books in supporting a young child's developing language, literacy, and learning, and identifies patterns found in alphabet books, and including some with numbers and numerals.

Rhymes are available for counting, counting-out, playing games, enjoying humor and nonsense, for learning information, and for singing aloud. The rhymes about counting and counting-out offer activities in daytime or nighttime settings for a young listener. Most go from one to ten, but a few demonstrate numbers and numerals up to twenty. To add to the enjoyment of rhymes, some are accompanied by games, finger plays, or a counting-out activity. One may begin with finger movements, play games, and then continue with other number games accompanied by the rhythmic beat of music.

Humor and nonsense rhymes about gnus who wear shoes, whales with curly tails, and baboons who hold balloons are found as well as internal rhymes about one dragons pulling wagons and twenty fishes juggling dishes. Some titles feature animals and numbers in nonsensical situations: one whale wears a veil, an eight-tentacled octopus eats oatmeal, and twelve swans twirl batons.

Rhymes for other learning are available, too. Word-symbol associations are found, for instance, where an accumulating number of crows represent the use of numbers in folklore and superstitions: two crows stand for mirth, three for marriage, four for birth, and on up to ten with each group of crows symbolizing a saying. A rhyme found in several books teaches the number of days in the months of the year beginning with the line, "Thirty days hath September, April, June, and November." Used as memory devices by some children, other short rhymes give instructions for forming the shapes of numerals up to 9 (shaped like a balloon on a stick). One story in rhyme is designed so the reader can supply some of the rhyming words.

In addition to rhymes for counting, humor, and learning, some counting books have rhyming songs to sing. Most girls and boys like to sing and will respond to a bouncing rhythm in a counting song, and several versions of a traditional counting song offer animals to recognize, information to discuss, large and small illustrations to compare, and a script to act out with the song. Another popular numerical song about animals, "The Twelve Days of Christmas," is available in several versions that show parallel plots, have movable flaps, accordion-style pages, variety in the illustrations, and variations of the song.

Counting Books Lead Children to Supplementary Materials

Counting books offer girls and boys experience with materials to move and manipulate and may lead them to supplementary materials that include computer-assisted learning. Counting books have math activities, games, and information that encourage the moving and counting of concrete objects. After many opportunities to move or rearrange numbers of real objects, and to talk about what happens in the moving of objects and their rearrangements, a boy or girl may turn to the movement seen in a counting book. These are created by die-cut flaps, flip-over pages, and unusual page shapes.

Movement of objects also can occur without any physical movement of the paper on the page of a counting book or the movement of actual objects in one's environment. This movement of objects occurs with the movement of the eyes as the viewer notices the artist's message presented in the changing placement of objects. In another book, to show the passing of time in sequence, one sees only one event on each page of thirteen picture stories. The page must be turned to see the second event in the sequence of each of the picture stories, and so on.

Some books introduce follow-up materials such as software for the computer. After seeing one such book, a girl or boy, with the help of an adult, may turn to a computer disk with accompanying activities based on this story. These activities are brightly colored, show the illustrations from the book, and should hold the attention of a primary-age child.

Counting books and their illustrations also serve as resources of supplementary information for girls and boys. An interested adult looks for a book in which the illustrations are rich, extensive, and give help in seeing an existing problem or its setting.

Counting Books Lead Children to Create Original Problems

Counting books help children to dramatize and create their own original story problems. Counting books may provide the characters, settings, titles, and formats from which plots (presenting problems) may be selected by a girl or boy for role play situations. If desired, the introduction of masks and puppets may help young boys and girls act out the story problems they create. Characters from the books are often the stimulus for creating one's original masks or puppets—or even characters. Stories in counting books often include animals and insects as characters—often popular mass market ones. Personified numerals, monsters, and other creatures also serve as characters.

Stories in counting books have many settings which may encourage the use of original words and the creation of problems arising from the settings. Children may think of a short story problem for a friend to solve or act out after hearing number stories with settings at the carnival and circus. Sister-brother relationships are portrayed in several books, as are other family relationships and events, such as birthday parties. Some counting books offer numbers in a city setting; others are in the country, where picnics are a favorite topic.

Word-symbol associations as well as ideas about relationships can come from the pictures and the words in certain books. A numeral-word-object arrangement follows a mouse who chases an escaping red balloon through the air and past ten objects through the pages. Some counting books offer information about other countries, are valuable additions to a social studies unit and can serve as references for reports. One illustrator's diverse illustrations show pandas and maps of China as well as its zones of vegetation, and in other illustrations, a viewer finds Fujiyama, chopsticks, and other objects in panels that reflect a Japanese art style on the pages. In the work of a Russian artist, one sees the onion domes on churches, the Kremlin, and the colorful Matryoshka dolls, the wooden dolls that nest one inside of the other all the way down to the smallest one.

For older children at school, different ways of counting and the usefulness of numbers may be discussed as it is in the classroom setting in another title. Information about various ways people recorded numbers of things is offered in other books; thirteen different ways that show how people have recorded numbers of things are seen in one title; and, in another, a shepherd invents symbols to count his sheep.

Boys and girls also find information about the farm and country life in some counting books. Food needed by a bunny, an animal often found on a farm, is seen on the sturdy pages of a board book, and there are numbers of fruits in another—the produce from farms and orchards. In the clear, colorful photographs of another title, items on the farm (eggs, horseshoes on a barn wall, and bright red strawberries) are counted. One-to-one correspondence also is shown as a viewer matches the number of cats on the farm to their bowls of milk.

Fantastic creatures such as monsters demonstrate math relationships— among them one-to-one correspondence, seeing parts that make a whole, and the adding and subtracting of numbers. Subtraction is shown in one book in which the young reader pulls the tabs and monsters hide behind shutters, get shut in a cabinet, and play games. Above the monsters on the pages, number sentences record the subtracting operation while rhyming lines tell about the subtraction situation. The answer appears in a cut-out window when the tab is pulled. Among the monsters in other books, creatures are met such as humorous little devils, dragons, goblins, and even personified dinosaurs.

Still other books offer mysteries, puzzles, and activities. In one, two bird detectives, dressed in trench coats, move about the pages to find ten of something. To keep interest high, the young viewer will not discover what the detectives are searching for until the final page. In another counting book, the mystery of "Sherlock Hemlock and the Mysterious Stranger" is just the right joke and just the right length for young listeners. Puzzles also intrigue girls and boys in different ways. In one type of puzzle, strip pages are turned to locate different scenes and objects. In one book, to emphasize the *one-more* idea, one of the objects in each group is separated from the others. Objects increase and decrease their number in the review groups. The numbers of objects in the groups on the review page are different from the ones seen on the previous pages.

For instance, a child saw nine buckets, eight rabbits, and three pigs on the strip pages but now on the review page sees ten buckets, nine rabbits, and five pigs. In another book, a girl or boy will puzzle over the meaning of *more,* and the increasing number of wacky objects up to twenty that are out of place. After seeing a shoe on the wall and another on the ceiling, a reader sees three wacky things (bananas growing on an apple tree, a worm chasing a bird, and a cut garden hose spraying water), and then three more wacky things (two doorknobs on a door, a red-and-white striped candy cane for a table leg, and a broom leaning in the hall). Still more wacky things are found and counted while going to school, studying at school, and returning home through the park.

Puzzling over a prediction about what may be seen next may be discussed as a result of viewing a book which specializes in unexpected sights. The reader classifies, considers the unusual (something-is-out-of-place) pictures, and notices the one object that is odd (or wrong or identified as unrelated and hence should not be there). Later, a young learner may use this ability to transfer problems on paper and notice what is odd, wrong, or out of place in a problem currently being calculated.

To assist numeral recognition, there are numerals to locate hidden in the illustrations of several books. For older girls and boys (8–9), there are books with animals to find hidden in detailed drawings and several missing items to locate. Also for older readers, there are riddle questions and a numerical search.

In books about transportation, there will be contrasts to discuss between the daytime driving that presents ten objects on trucks to count and the daytime racing in which one encounters twelve bicycle racers to identify. In the first one, a girl or boy counts familiar objects found on trucks. In the second one, the racers, wearing numerals, are sometimes in sequence and other times, out of sequence, so the presentation requires numeral recognition rather than counting in a sequence. Further, one may classify the order of position of the racers with the ordinals of first, second, last, and so on. If appropriate, the viewer may use numbers to identify the racers in the order of their positions (e.g., Racer number one is third in the race).

With still other counting books, a girl or boy also sees the work of several illustrators in collections of unrelated objects to count on the pages. These books show groups of unrelated objects to count that are fewer than ten; up to ten; and greater to ten.

In one book, as the numbers increase, the pages become wider. There are objects and squares to match in a one-to-one correspondence activity. At a selected number, a viewer identifies the numeral, counts the objects, and matches each of the corresponding squares to one of the objects on the page. The ways in which one basic shape—a cube—can measure objects are explored. One places cubes beside an illustrated object (such as a tree) to determine that the tree on the page is the width equal to a certain number of cubes. Another book offers oversize numerals which hold the appropriate number of objects within each numeral shape. Predictions of objects to come are made by peeking through die-cut openings on the colorful pages of still another.

The titles of certain counting books ask questions and encourage a counting response to numbers of objects greater than ten. The title of *How Many?* is used for books by two different authors. One offers the concept of *one-more-than* with number sentences to fifteen while the other book leads the count up to twenty without showing number sentences.

Other books demonstrate increasing numbers and other concepts. A girl or boy counts to fifty in one title and sees each page with the number, numeral, word, and object name. The counter is taken to one hundred and nine in a final matrix in one book and to a shower of one thousand raindrops in another. Then, fifty thousand spectators in a sports arena are found in a book, and finally, the idea of one million of something is discussed in another. The concept of infinity is considered in the number of stars in the sky on the final page of one book, and another book offers rhymes and a variety of ways to count with tools such as calendars, clocks, cups and spoons, rulers, scales, and thermometers.

Along with objects to count, numbers to sequence, number words to read, and numerals to recognize, counting books contain activities that include matching patterns, classifying objects, and noting relative size. Looking at counting books with these activities gives a girl or boy time to engage in a range of possible actions and to think about his or her own thought process. For instance, a young learner can review the numeric symbols of math with some favorite 123 books just as the alphabetic symbols are reviewed with certain ABC books. One book has photographs of candles, cookies, and friends from one to one hundred to count as well as the one-to-one correspondence activity of matching numbers of things to dots in patterns. One hundred peas are shown in groups of ten within ten pea shells, a sight that may lead to the inquisitive opening of pea shells to verify the number of times ten peas may be found inside of the green shells. One author-illustrator team shows one-to-one correspondence with the pattern of using one page for the number one, two pages for the number two, and so on, a pattern that may be extended by a young illustrator in an original counting book. Some books present colorful small pictures—or rebuses—along with the rhymes. With other counting books, one will learn to read words in lists and to locate numerals in a top-to-bottom direction, a direction that prepares a boy or girl to recognize vertical notation forms just as learning to look at things in a left-to-right direction prepares for beginning reading. For instance, one activity is introduced for mentally combining parts of a pictured object into a total picture in a top-to-bottom notation.

Some children may have problems seeing mentally the arithmetic procedures on quantities. To show operations on quantities, certain counting books visually show procedures with numbers of things. In one book, one finds the arrival and departure of unwanted guests with ascending and descending numbers.

The sequence of the procedures in a counting book may help some children to understand the order of the book's presentation. This, in turn, may help them to transfer that understanding of order to a similar understanding of the order of procedures in solving problems, thus thinking about their own thinking. With one book, one may classify animals and identify their silhouettes from their full-color shapes in a one-to-one correspondence. In another, the relative size of zoo animals traveling to their new home by train as well as increasing numbers and one-to-one correspondence may be seen. With another book, a young girl or boy counts objects, recognizes the sequence of numbers and numerals, the pattern of the days of the week, and the life cycle of a butterfly.

One title presents an introduction to the concept of grouping and to the idea that some problems take two or more steps to solve. Hunters are chasing the dogs who are chasing the foxes. The foxes in turn are chasing the cats. The cats are chasing the mice. For discussion, one may ask, "What could happen first to stop this chase? What could happen second? Third?" For a young girl or boy, this understanding of order or the understanding of the steps to be taken in the story to stop the chase may transfer later to an understanding of order in solving another one-step word problem or in solving a yet-to-be-met two-step problem.

For a child who is ready for simple word problems, one looks for illustrations that will tell something about the problem, that may help overcome some initial obstacles in seeing a problem, and that offer information to help in solving it. Discussing the problem and how it is resolved may engage the viewer with the meaning of the word, *problem*, and later, help a child identify problem situations found in other places. In a discussion with others, the young problem-solver considers personal solutions as well as the possible solutions proposed by others. Considering points of view of others, one can select a "best solution" for a particular problem. Taking turns with a friend, a problem from another favorite counting book may be considered. Problems may be initiated by an adult, too, and considered from the child's point of view.

Also, there are illustrations that may provide a sense of the structure or the organization of a problem. One example is that of Harriet, the elephant, who is shown as first in line for the circus act, but when the door to the circus tent opens, it is near the last animal in the waiting line. The animals now turn around to face the open door and Harriet is not the first customer in line—she is last. Another book shows Barnaby taking accumulating numbers of passengers on board his raft. What problems does Barnaby face? How does he resolve the problems? Is there an alternative to consider for resolving the problems? Such illustrations will help the viewer to remember important information, see that problems exist and introduce possible solutions.

Counting Books Offer Children Page Formats Useful in Solving Problems

Returning to the discussion of California's mathematics framework earlier in this introduction, the reader will recall that young children are expected to have certain understandings about mathematics by the time they complete the primary grades. Within this framework, areas of mathematics were identified and included number, measurement, geometry, patterns and functions, statistics and probability, and logic. Counting books support these areas by offering girls and boys mental images about content through the format of the pictures and print.

Books which provide information about the *concept* of numbers are important as boys and girls begin to read math materials at home or in a primary classroom. Counting by ones may be introduced in a number of titles and reinforced by such activity as sorting buttons from a collection by color, size, and number of holes in the buttons. Using cardinal numbers that can be read as words, a viewer sees one yellow bear on a trampoline who introduces a single word, *one*, and the corresponding symbol, 1. This pattern continues as the bears increase in number while dancing, swinging, and falling.

Some counting books help to compare quantities. In one, accumulating numbers of bears are found on unicycles and bicycles, while another begins with one bear and adds one more bear in successive events up to ten bears. Still another bear book begins with ten and introduces groups with one less bear in each event down to one. For seeing greater numbers, there is a variation on the story of Goldilocks and the three bears, in which the three bears see as many as thirty, forty, and fifty objects to count around Goldilocks's house.

Counting by twos is only one of the challenges in a title in which a viewer is asked to find one animal among many animals, to count to one hundred, to count by twos, and for an extra-visual discriminating activity, to locate the cat who is hiding somewhere on each page. Counting by fives is encouraged in a title in which numbers increase to one hundred, and perspective is seen in three-dimensional numerals.

Other counting books offer ordinal numbers to show how quantities are ordered. One has cardinal numbers as well, and a cause and effect situation which gives a reader an opportunity to make predictions. In a second, the ordinals go up to thirty—one for each day in the month of April. The rabbits can be counted, and on the last day in April, a prediction can be made for this story's ending.

Counting books also present the arrangements and rearrangements of large and small members of groups to show how a number is conserved (recognizing the same number of objects in different arrangements). One, for instance, shows the same number of apples in two different arrangements, in a circle and in a straight line, and demonstrates the information that location does not affect the members of a number group. In a second example, both large and small tomatoes are arranged in two groups, conveying the information that size does not affect the members of a number group.

Reviews of numbers may consist of various arrangements in counting books. Some reviews show objects only, others show numerals only, and still others show objects in various patterns. Objects in graphs may be offered in pairs, in a vertical pattern, and in a horizontal arrangement.

Still other counting books offer readiness for the four basic operations: adding, subtracting, multiplying, and dividing. In some counting books, a viewer sees the operation as well as the written math symbols representing a selected situation.

Number sentences in a counting book may be discussed and read just as they are in a beginning reader. Several books provide number sentences as models and give a format for manipulating math markers as groups, showing the pattern of *one-more-than* up to ten and sums greater than ten.

The operation of subtraction is found in a wordless book in which, beginning at the left, the illustrations are "read." Only the symbols for numbers and for the subtraction operation on the numbers are seen in the corners of the illustrations as the action takes place, and five children slide off a runaway horse one by one. For older children, a wizard finds groups of objects, waves his magic wand and makes some of the objects vanish from each group. Words about these disappearing objects are in rhyming lines beneath the illustrations. In another one, a "mean machine" with its laser-like zap ray mounted on the top of its purple cab, roams the countryside to find groups of objects and zap several from each group. Words about the subtraction operation, and the large machine as it rolls by the objects, are read in rhyming lines beneath the illustrations. Both addition and subtraction are shown in a number of other counting books. A girl or boy who has developed writing skills may write a math sentence which retells the series of events that take place in a verbal problem and rebuild a time-order sequence for it.

Readiness for the basic operations of multiplication and division is found, too. One big book makes it possible for large groups of children to see the idea of addition leading to multiplication. Readiness for the meaning of division is shown, too, as two children divide a batch of cookies to give some to an increasing number of arriving friends and the concept of division becomes meaningful as the cookies are shared. This can be accompanied by an ever-popular shared (divided) food activity in the classroom or school library media center!

These books also offer an opportunity to select an appropriate math operation. Given a favorite book with a mask over the math sentences, a child may be asked to select an appropriate math operation for a certain situation. The listener may be encouraged to state the problem in original words aloud, estimate a solution, compute it, and then talk with the adult about the question, *Does this solution appear to be right (logical)?* Each child should have an opportunity to estimate an answer to a problem before calculating it. With every number story, a girl or boy may continue the habit of estimating before seeing the author's calculation of an answer. An adult may guide the estimation with the question, "Will there be fewer or more than five (ten, twenty)?" or "How did you "figure out" your guess?" By covering up with "post-it" tape a sum in a number sentence on the page, the adult may ask for an estimated answer before the tape is removed and the answer found.

Some books stimulate readiness for using two-digit numbers in addition and subtraction. Adding whole numbers with two-digit numbers takes place as Babar teaches Alexander to add on numbers to a group of ten in a final review. Another title tells of one hundred hippos marching in their annual parade and about the ones who drop out with exhaustion from the heat. These counting books, and others, show math sentences with the symbols that represent a certain situation. They may, for some children, bring a mental image to a selected idea, provide context, and help eliminate confusion about relationships of objects.

Still other books offer models of simple word problems to be interpreted in different ways with pictures and role play. Described with alliterative words, the young guests in one book arrive for the party dressed as one fairy, two capering clowns, three merry musketeers, and on up to ten royal rulers (kings and queens). After all of the guests are counted, the refreshments shown on the large page are counted again and questions considered: "Are there enough glasses of orange juice for all children to have one each? Are there enough (gelatin desserts, dough-nuts, cupcakes, and balloons) for all to have one each?"

One title informally reviews the concepts of commutativity and associa-tivity (grouping in addition). Its rhyming verses tell about the accumulat-ing groups of imaginary animals who join the little girl in her tub. The animals continue to rearrange themselves in groups and subgroups through the pages and may require an adult's guidance in finding them all.

One counting book offers readiness for measurement with coins. The reader is asked to recognize and compare values among coins used in the United States. Amounts of money represented by coins may be discussed after seeing the coins that are arranged and rearranged on the pages. Another title teaches a young counter how coins can add up to a dollar and how numbers of dollars can increase, too. One day, Harriet sees something she wants to buy that costs five dollars in a toy store. When she empties her piggy bank, she counts one hundred pennies, shown actual-size on a sky-blue page. Harriet thinks of a way to earn four more dollars, and each time she earns some money, the amount is shown by the coins in the illustrations. This makes it easy for a young counter to establish a one-to-one correspondence between the pictured representa-tions and actual coins.

A wordless presentation about "time" uses traditional clocks instead of digital ones to tell the time during the day as members of a family get ready for a little girl's birthday party. Each page reveals the clock in a particular room of the house, and gives an opportunity to identify the numerals on the clock faces or to show skill in time-telling.

Illustrations in a few other counting books offer readiness for geome-try. One offers a one-to-one correspondence with dots, and ends with a review of the creative ways dots are used in the illustrations. Others show the uses of colors and shapes accompanied by numerals, and visual char-acteristics of other geometric shapes to identify, describe, and classify. Colorful shapes are used to form such objects as an owl and an engine—a creative task that makes each object a collection of several geometric shapes.

More counting books offer readiness for patterns and functions. Some provide an opportunity to identify pattern, to talk about it, and to extend a selected pattern in a sequence. One may repeat aloud the verbal pat-terns in the ending rhymes about the five little chicks who are on a search for their breakfast. The reader of another book may engage in an imaginative venture, and see a changing landscape that shows the different times of day, the changing of the seasons and the passing of a year. The adventure begins with a winter scene which illustrates zero, with nothing visible on a snowy landscape. It ends with the last month of the year and a Christmas holiday scene. The relationship of numbers is shown as the men, women, and children live in their village from day to day. In the margins are colorful blocks stacked in patterns to show the numbers one through twelve. With similar colored blocks, or beads, a participant may recreate the pattern and then extend it over and over.

Other books may lead to early experiences in statistics and probability. A girl or boy may conduct a simple survey, collect data, represent the data with concrete objects, pictures, or symbols, and interpet the information. After surveying other children to determine how many of them can count to one hundred, the reader collects data and records them with tally marks in two columns marked with headings, *Yes* and *No*. With these tally marks representing the data, one can tell what was learned.

Still other books offer a readiness for logic, the opportunity to classify, sort objects, observe relationships, and make generalizations. Reasonable conclusions about situations can also be drawn and such words used as *and, or,* and *if-then.* One title shows a musical concert planned for people who gather around the bandstand to see the accumulating numbers of musicians in groups with all members of the same group wearing the same color. With this information, classes of musicians—by size, by instrument, by color of uniform—can be made. On the pages of two other books, one finds photographs of flowers that can be classified and sorted in various ways (color, size, number of petals, and so on). With flowers from the yard or cut-out paper replicas, a child may sort them in various ways and begin to realize through this activity and others, that mathematics can be found outdoors. Another title asks the reader to notice which objects are monsters and which objects are *not* monsters. Self-checking information is provided at the foot of each page, and math terms are used. For *all* and *not: All* are *not* monsters. For *and:* I see three monsters *and* three that are not monsters. For *if-then: If* these are not monsters, *then* they must be mailboxes disguised as monsters. For *none: None* of these are monsters. For *of:* Out *of* all *of* these, only two are monsters. For *or:* These are monsters *or* they are not monsters. For *some: Some* of these are monsters. Other counting books have pictures and accompanying words that introduce other terms, such as *pair, single,* and others.

Counting books offer children an opportunity to interpret illustrations and to make conclusions about the situations pictured. Using one circular story as a pattern, an interested girl or boy may take a pencil and draw a second number story which also ends back where it began—with a single pencil. This story, and others, may be shown to friends along with a challenge to create still another pencil-number tale.

In summary, counting books offer children time and the tools to develop the understanding needed to solve problems. Stimulated by these books, girls and boys may use math language and talk about mathematics as they get involved with materials to move and manipulate, as they use supportive aids found in illustrations, and as they interact with materials to extend certain concepts. Understanding grows as children dramatize and create their own story problems, engage in peer assistance, focus on mental arithmetic and think about their own thinking. Understanding needed to solve problems may be supported by some of the page designs, and other arrangements may help one build mental images about the content presented through print and pictures. Math language may be developed through the activities of chanting rhymes, listening to and discussing stories, and singing songs.

Indeed, counting books offer far more than the rote counting of numbers. As a personal possession, or on loan from the library, counting books are enriching, reusable, and individualized number presentations. The following annotated bibliography offers opportunities for teachers, parents, or other adults to introduce aspects of mathematics to a young girl or boy. It includes more than 350 counting books selected by researching standard review materials in the field of literature for children, noting published recommendations about counting books from specialists in the field, and first-hand examination. These, considered along with the author's experience as a teacher and consultant in the field, resulted in a "recommended" in the annotations. Within each section, titles are entered by the author's last name with suggested grade/interest levels, and some entries have a suggested activity to follow the book. References and an index with titles, authors, and illustrators are included.

What Specialists Say about Counting Books

Counting books can help introduce and deepen such mathematical concepts as number sequence, one-to-one correspondence, grouping, place value, and sets. Some are works of art and aesthetic treasures rather than simple concept books; some tell the number story via a merry, rhyming tale.

Eileen M. Burke,
Early Childhood
Literature:
For Love of Children, p. 232

A reliable way to make each cooking experience a cohesive learning unit with interrelated steps is to have it spring naturally from an excellent piece of children's literature. Since authors are aware of children's interest in food, many good books have been written in which food and the acquiring of food is the main theme. . . . Cooking experiences are rich in science and mathematics learnings. The children count, measure, estimate, add, subtract, multiply, divide and learn about fractions.

Betty Coody,
Using Literature with Young Children
(3rd ed.), pp. 120–21

Counting books contribute to children's cognitive structuring by reinforcing their grasp of number and seriation. Like alphabet books, counting books are used for much more than learning to count. They may also help children learn to add or subtract, or just to enjoy the visual portrayal of numerical concepts. Children delight in pointing to the objects displayed and checking to see if the illustrator presented the exact number of items for each numeral. The best illustrations for young children avoid distracting clutter so that the objects can be identified and counted without confusion. With such books children rehearse counting until it is learned by heart.

Bernice E. Cullinan,
Literature and the Child, p. 76

Books that develop mathematical concepts, specifically counting and size of sets, are available with vivid illustrations and photographs. Some present an increasing number of objects with a unifying theme or story, whereas others follow the counting sequence only. Bright, clear illustrations or photographs of easily discernible groups are best for conveying numerical concepts.

Bernice E. Cullinan and Carolyn W. Carmichael, editors,
Literature and Young Children, p. 8

Counting books, too, can develop themes, tell stories, introduce numerals—the written symbols for numbers—or provide pictures for young children to discuss. The concepts conveyed by these books are not always as simple as 1, 2, 3.

Joan I. Glazer and Gurney Williams III,
Introduction to Children's Literature, p. 127

Since time immemorial, . . . we have been providing children with counting books, substituting pictures for real objects. The young child can make this transition from the concrete to the visual representation if he or she first experiences the real and the visual illustrations are clearly presented.

Charlotte S. Huck, Susan Hepler, and Janet Hickman, *Children's Literature in the Elementary School* (4th ed.), p. 168.

Books to help children learn number concepts have as much variety as alphabet books. Some counting books have the numbers from one to ten, some have numbers to twenty, and there are books that even present the number 1,000. A good counting book for young children should present the numeral clearly written and the number word written out with the number of objects clearly shown in the illustration for ease in counting.

Mary J. Lickteig,
An Introduction to Children's Literature, p. 62

We use lots of counting books—books that count up and books that count down. The written numbers are anticipated and quickly learned visually. Usually some other structure aids the child's memory as well as the illustrations.

> Robert A. McCracken and Marlene J. McCracken,
> *Stories, Songs, and Poetry to Teach*
> *Reading and Writing: Literacy*
> *Through Language*, p. 48

The counting books can be readily used for teaching children number concepts because there is no conflict between the concept and the symbol. Children who are fascinated by these new concepts pore over the attractive books as they count repeatedly the figures in each illustration. Encouraged by parents and their own sense of accomplishment, they learn naturally in this way.

> Iris Tiedt,
> *Exploring Books with Children*, p. 45

Counting (number) books introduce number names (e.g., one), numerals (e.g., 1), and a few basic computations (e.g., $1 + 1 = 2$) to very young children. Simple examples of sets and the metric system may be developed and offered in book form to the very young child, but more commonly these mathematical learnings are reserved for school-age children. In addition to providing the cited learnings, counting books may develop the idea of one-to-one correspondence; develop the ability to count sequentially—primarily 1 through 10; develop cognitive thinking skills; teach about themes; offer the opportunities for simple object identification; provide pictures for discussion; and tell stories.

> Robert J. Whitehead,
> *A Guide to Selecting Books for Children*, p. 67

Like alphabet books, counting books range from those that present numbers, usually numerals from one to ten, in the simplest way, to books that have continuity, tell a story, or are used by an artist as a base for elaborately imaginative shapes or situations.

> Zena Sutherland and May Hill Arbuthnot,
> *Children and Books* (7th ed.), p. 96

Counting Books:
An Annotated Action Bibliography

ABC and 123

Arnosky, Jim. *Mouse Numbers and Letters*. Illustrated by the author. New York: Harcourt Brace Jovanovich, 1982.

In the numbers section of Arnosky's counting book, Arnosky introduces a gentleman mouse carrying his umbrella who visits a beach and counts nearby objects. Gentleman Mouse bumps right into one mushroom, climbs two sandy hills, then joins nine red outlined fish, and is considered the tenth fish in a meal for a hungry shark. These adventures are all quick-paced ones for the small mouse and for the young viewer. A viewer counts along in sequence from one up to ten as each page shows the appropriate numeral, number, and corresponding activities. The mouse's actions have a humorous, even slapstick, flavor (e.g., he steps on three turtles instead of stepping stones to cross the water). Slipping from one turtle's high shell, the mouse falls in the water, gets soaking wet, and before he can dry off, trips and falls over into the water again. One counts in the *one-less-than* sequence when the mouse escapes from a hungry shark's group of fish and hurriedly retraces his steps away from the water. Mouse runs past nine swimming fish, eight ocean waves, and skips on top of the water like seven water-skips of a thrown pebble. Mouse's anxiety to escape the shark and his dash to return to a mushroom is shown on a double-page spread with the events sketched across two pages in a cartoon-style format. Bordered in rusty-red, Arnosky's illustrations are easy to see and present a likable character to girls and boys.

Gentleman Mouse is an appropriate character for a story-in-a-box presentation. To prepare this story for play and further learning, cut-out shapes of Gentleman Mouse and the objects to count are needed. A small square opening is cut in one side of a cardboard box for the "stage." One curtain rod (round, small in diameter, longer than the length of the box) is slipped through openings punched in two opposite sides of the box. Cut-out shapes of objects are suspended from the curtain rod with pipe cleaners and pushed along the rod past the stage opening to stay out of sight in the wings or behind curtains on the rod until needed in the sequence of the story. As the story is retold in original words, the young performer pushes or pulls the objects along the rod to the opening for showing and counting to others.

"Molly the Monkey and the Crocodile" is a story that is similar to Arnosky's "Mouse Numbers" and is found in *Fold- and-Cut Stories and Fingerplays* by Marj Hart, a book that includes easy-to-cut illustrations for girls and boys in preschool up through third grade. One piece of green paper is the path through a big jungle. Molly falls into a hole (the hole is cut in the green paper in front of the audience), crosses the big mountains (also cut with jagged peaks), and meets the crocodile. The green paper path is unfolded to show the head, teeth, and jaws of a green crocodile. K-2.

Features: numeral-number relationships with objects one up to ten and back.

Bennett, A., compiler. *Picture Dictionary, ABCs and Telling Time, Counting Rhymes, Riddles, and Finger Plays.* Text by Lilian Moore and others. Illustrations by Nettie Weber and others. New York: Grosset and Dunlap, 1977.

Saying counting rhymes aloud, performing finger plays, and listening to short anecdotes can provide early enjoyment in mathematics. From this book, youngsters can chant about young rats with felt hats, eight cherries on a plate, and ten bluebirds who perch on a tree branch. In another section, "Telling Time," one sees how a clock helps Billy and his family. What is the time for each one of Billy's activities? Billy gets out of bed, eats breakfast, assists with household tasks, and goes shopping with Mother. After lunch, Billy takes a nap, plays at a nearby playground, and enjoys a snack of cookies and milk. After supper, Billy listens to a bedtime story before he falls asleep. To the tune of "Here We Go 'Round the Mulberry Bush" different words may be sung: "What did you do at eight o'clock, eight o'clock, eight o'clock? What did you do at eight o'clock, eight o'clock this morning?" The singer is invited to tell what was done, to sing what was done, or to mime an action. A real or simulated clock face may be labeled *in daytime* or *at nighttime* and the current time may be changed to different times to reflect the ones mentioned in other musical questions. Pre-K.

Features: numeric rhymes, narrative, time-telling.

A Book of Children's Rhymes and Verses. Illustrated by Janet Johnstone and Anne Grahame Johnstone. London: Dean and Sons/Playmore, n.d.

In one section, "Nursery Rhymes Old and New," the use of numbers is heard in phrases about four and twenty ladies, Betty Blue who walks in two shoes, and Gregory Griggs with twenty-seven wigs. One penny is spent for white cake, a twopenny for a pie, and a donkey has one ear up and one ear down. Paper replicas of nursery rhyme characters can wear the numerals and a cut-paper object associated with each character can present a corresponding number of dots for a number-numeral match activity. Pre-K.

Features: numeric words in traditional rhymes.

Bradbury, Lynne J. *My Honey Bear Big ABC and Counting Book*. Illustrated by Lynn N. Grundy. New York: Modern Promotions/Unisystems, 1981.

In this oversize book, Bradbury introduces numbers from one large frog to ten oversize buttons and gives practice in matching, sorting, and counting. Grundy's numerals and objects are colorful. Vegetables for a stew are counted (two onions, three carrots, six green peas), the number of legs on chairs, stools, and insects is identified, and then each number is matched to a numeral. Every page offers something about numbers to see and talk about with an adult. The viewer sees a milkman deliver one bottle of milk to each illustrated house for a one-to-one correspondence activity; the one ball that is different is located among the juggler's objects; and a sequence of odd numbers in groups is seen. In another activity, personified animals wait in line at the bus stop to present ordinal words and their numeral forms, 1st through 10th. K up.

Features: numerals and numbers of objects up to ten, ordinals, and activities.

Cloke, Rene. *My ABC and Counting Book*. Illustrated by the author. New York: Exeter Books, 1974.

In Cloke's illustrations, the foot of each page is devoted to a numeral and an appropriate object. From one airplane and two books to eleven colorfully decorated yo-yos and twelve black and white zebras, the members of each group may be counted. At home or in a classroom, familiar toys and objects such as an airplane, a yo-yo, and books can be counted as they are selected for play or returned for storage. K-1.

Features: numerals, cardinal number identification from one to twelve.

Delaunay, Sonia, collector. *Sonia Delaunay Alphabet.* Illustrated by the
collector. New York: Thomas Y. Crowell, 1972.

Numbers, and ways they can be used, are found in several of the
rhymes Delaunay collected for this alphabet book. On verso pages, traditional English rhymes are found about the bird's nest with five eggs in it,
the twenty-three *T*'s Thomas a' Tattamus took to tie a top to two tall
trees, and the four-and-twenty hairs that make a wig when a barber
shaves a pig. After reading the rhyming response to the question, "How
many miles to Babylon?," there are number situations: two corporals
with twine line up thirteen people; and groups of animals and people
increase from one old Oxford ox up to twelve tremenduous talebearers
telling the truth. Useful information is given in two rhymes about Roman
numerals: *V* and *I* are placed together as figures to symbolize the number
six; *L* is used for fifty (represented by soldiers who hide in a cave); and
M is for a thousand (represented by soldiers brave). Vocabulary develops
through responses by saying remembered words from rhymes and discussing such questions as, "How many eggs were in the bird's nest?" and
"How many hairs to make a wig after a barber shaves a pig?" Pre-2.

Features: numeric words in traditional rhymes, Roman numerals.

Gruelle, Johnny. *Raggedy Ann and Andy's Alphabet and Numbers.* Illustrated by the author. New York: Bobbs-Merrill, 1957.

In the second section, "Raggedy Andy's Numbers," a reader finds
rhymes about numbers one to nine and large colorful number words in
capitals. Each numeral, also in color, is found in different places on the
page (e.g., on the side of a green ball, near a toy wagon, or in Raggedy
Andy's hands). Rhymes give information such as "One is a single thing,
Two is one and one, you know," and "five are all the fingers on one
hand." After nine, the reader is introduced to zero, a concept to be
discussed as the number in an empty group or set. Zero is shown beside
other numerals to form ten, twenty, thirty, and so on. Colorful illustrations of Raggedy Andy in his blue trousers, red and white striped stockings, plaid shirt, and white hat are near the rhyming text on each page.
Playing a game, such as "Where is Ann Now?," with toy Raggedy Ann
(or Andy) doll characters may lead to an initial understanding about spatial relationships. One can take the doll *around* the bush, *through* the
doorway, or place the doll *under* the table and *on* the chair. To answer
such questions as, "Where did Raggedy Ann come from?" or "Where did
she get her 'I love you' heart?," an adult may want to relate an anecdote
about the beginning of Raggedy Ann:

In 1917, young Marcella Gruelle found a faceless rag doll in the family attic. Her father, political cartoonist Johnny Gruelle, sewed on button eyes and painted on a smiling face and the "I love you" heart. A year later, Gruelle wrote, illustrated, and published *Raggedy Ann Stories*, the first of over forty books about the doll. Gruelle's wife and mother made some Raggedy Ann dolls to display in bookstores with the stories, and in 1920, Raggedy Andy appeared when young readers wanted a brother for Ann. During that time, interest in the dolls became high (and remains high for some children today).

The doll characters are available in large toys stores and from the Smithsonian Institution, Department 0006, Washington, D. C., 20073–0006. For a true fan, sister and brother rag doll costumes are available from theatrical costume outlets. Pre-K.

Features: numeric narrative and rhymes.

Hoban, Tana. *26 Letters and 99 Cents*. Photographs by the author. New York: Greenwillow, 1987.

Whichever end of this book a viewer opens is its beginning. At one end, one sees brightly colored numerals and shiny coins on the endpapers. After the title page, there is a page divided into fourths that show the numeral *1* and one shiny penny, then *2* and two pennies, and so on. At the number five, there are two ways to group coins: five pennies in one framed illustration and a nickel in a second framed illustration. For six, there are six pennies in one insert and a nickel plus one penny in a second one. At ten, one dime is seen. At twenty-one, there are two dimes and one penny, and at twenty-five, one finds three ways to get to this number with coins: five nickels; two dimes and one nickel; and one quarter. The amount of coins continues to ninety-nine cents. At the other end of the book, color photographs show letters and common objects to teach the alphabet. The pattern of the coins in each photograph can be introduced as simple patterns to repeat with coins on a table top. Further, a set of pennies may be matched one-to-one with a set of other coins to determine that there are as many pennies as there are coins in the second set, to count the number of pennies, and to count the number of coins in the second set. Recommended. 1-2.

Features: counting with coins up to ninety-nine.

McNaughton, Colin. *Colin McNaughton's ABC and 123*. Illustrated by the author. Garden City, N.Y.: Doubleday, 1976.

In the section, "123 and Things," McNaughton illustrates ridiculous situations to introduce the numbers from one up to twenty and writes that this book is "for all ages for reading alone or together." Rhyming with the number words are end words found in lines which describe the situations: one, cream bun; two, marabou; three, giant's knee. Some of the situations require prior knowledge (e.g., recognizing adders as snakes in a game of snakes and ladders; realizing why young men might be in a lion's den, and identifying the number of blackbirds flying from a hot mince pie). After twenty, McNaughton jumps to fifty thousand and eighty-four spectactors in a sports arena. In the alphabet section, traditional sentences begin with the letters and the familiar phrases of" X is for. . . . " In contrast to these traditional sentences, ridiculous situations occur with X marking the spot on an athlete's forehead, Y introducing a yawning gap on a giant face, and Z showing people zipping along by pulling open a giant zipper on a grassy meadow. Humorous situations with internal rhymes in lines offer interest and develop vocabulary as the rhyming phrases are repeated. 2 up.

Features: sequential and numeric rhyming lines from one up to twenty in humorous situations.

Mazzarella, Mimi. *Alphabatty Animals and Funny Foods: Alphabet and Counting Rhymes*. Illustrated by the author. Cokeysville, Md.: Liberty Publishing, 1984.

Mazzarella, a former English teacher, wrote and illustrated this small book as a gift for a friend's child. There are four-line counting rhymes that bring foods to life in a humorous way. Each funny food takes on a personality of its own. For instance, most girls and boys enjoy reading about eggs that have bad tempers because they are in hot water and get boiled, about lemons who sing with a sour note, and about cashew nuts with colds who sneeze, "CASHEW!" Some will notice the creative use of print when the play on words is shown in capital letters. To provide an opportunity to count up to twenty, twenty unbreakable objects or twenty sturdy vegetable items (potatoes, onions, radishes, ears of corn) may be selected and dropped one at a time into a brown bag or other container. 2 up.

Features: numeric rhymes from one up to twenty about personified foods.

My ABC of Nursery Rhymes. Illustrated. New York: Derrydale/Crown, 1974.

These nursery rhymes have numbers of things including three men in a tub; three bags full of wool; and a man with seven wives who had seven sacks each filled with seven cats who each had seven kittens. Numeral use is shown on the clock face as the clock strikes one and the mouse runs down and information about Roman numerals is presented in "X Stands for Playmates Ten." Pre-2.

Features: numeric words in traditional rhymes, Roman numerals.

O'Callaghan, Karen. *Share with Us . . . Letters, Numbers, Words, Animals*. Illustrated by Eric Rowe, Bob Hersey, Robert Norton, and Tim Hayward. Newmarket, Eng.: Brimax Books, 1984.

"Count with Us—Numbers" is one of the four sections in this book. In the illustrations, one counts toys at home, items at the market, forward from one, and from ten to one in a descending sequence. There are number rhymes to listen to about trains and engines. An additional rhyme is "10 in a Bed" illustrated with ten toys in a small child's bed. One by one, as the words are repeated, the toys are pushed out of the bed by the nighttime counter. Call your reader's attention to the words of this bedtime countdown and say it together as the illustration is reviewed. K-2.

Features: numeric rhymes, counting one up to ten and back.

Polak, Johan. *True-to-Life ABC Book Including Numbers*. Illustrated by the author. New York: Grosset and Dunlap, 1952.

Polak includes number-numeral relationships in this ABC book with numbers and devotes one large double-page spread to objects to count. From the numbers one up to ten, there are labels for the objects. The viewer counts from one brown pony and two red squirrels to nine yellow chicks and ten birds with outspread wings. The illustrations show the sequence of increasing numbers in groups. Polak's objects are clear and distinct. They are easy ones to touch on the page and to count aloud.

Showing this page, an adult may point out a different row of animals several times and ask, "How many?" Pre-K.

Features: numerals-numbers relationships one up to ten.

Stevenson, Peter. *ABC 123*. Illustrated by the author. New York: Exeter Books, 1986.

Followed by buzzing wasps, a worker starts out to mow a meadow and sees numbers of things. First, there is a rabbit in a burrow, two swans are in the reeds of a nearby pond, and three tractors are used for work. Can a viewer always find the figure of the man in the illustrations? Can one find a numeral in the shape of an animal or on an object that is shown in each illustration? For example, the rabbit's ears stand as straight as the numeral 1, the curved necks of the swans form the shape of 2s, and the tractors cut the shape of a 3 in the meadow. Can the increasing number of wasps on the pages be counted as the wasps buzz around the man's nose, head, and legs? On each page, there is the appropriate numeral and an accompanying phrase to explain the illustrations, some of which are challenging because not every object is pictured completely. On the page for the number six, for instance, five frogs are seen along with the legs of another jumping out of the scene. At seven, six moles are found among the seven molehills. The seventh mole is running out of the scene and is identified only by its tail. This mole turns up again to peer out of another molehill in the next illustration. After ten, the question, "How many?" is asked. One may count birds on a wire, flying ducks, and apples on a tree. In this book, more mathematics can be discussed. For example, one question might be, "What shapes are there for us to see in the illustrations?" (space). "Is anyone interested in making a map to show the walk to the meadow and in recording what was seen with labels or stick drawings?" (measurement). "Who is interested in counting paper apple-shapes or in classifying them (big apples, small apples, red ones, yellow ones, green ones)?" These shapes may be displayed on a paper tree by color, by shape, or by size (classification). The trunk and limbs of the tree may be created by placing crumpled pages of a discarded newspaper into small brown paper bags. The bags then are aligned to form the trunk and the limbs of a tree and attached to a bulletin board or other display area (alignment, symmetry, balance). If desired, the bags can be painted with streaks or dabs of black or brown to give the effect of textured bark, arranged in different ways, and counted. K-1.

Features: numerals, numeral shapes, number phrases, and objects up to ten.

Todd, Mary Fidelis. *ABC and 123*. Illustrated by the author. New York: Whittlesey House/McGraw-Hill, 1955.

Todd offers rhyming lines about occupational choices from *A* to *Z*. A young reader also counts along to twenty-six. *A* is for an artist by the sea who paints a picture of one tree, *B* is for a baker who has two gingerbread men, and *C* is for a clown with three bright balloons. Each letter is accompanied by an increase in number: *X* is for the x-ray nurse whose machine shows someone's twenty-four ribs and *Y* is for the yeoman who sees twenty-five sea gulls through his binoculars. At *Z*, a zoo keeper throws twenty-six fish to the bears. Todd asks, "Which one would you most like to be?" This question may lead to a graph of small pictures pasted under headings of: *Would Like To Be* and *Would Not Like To Be*. Black-and-white illustrations have highlights of red. Capitals are introduced as oversize letters in bright red with the key words in capitals. Corresponding lowercase letters are found in a red frieze at the foot of each page, and beginning with *a*, accumulate through the book. Oversize numerals also are in red. Occupations to discuss, among others, are homemaker, inventor, judge, keymaker, and librarian. K-1.

Features: oversize numerals, rhyming lines about occupational choices from *A* to *Z*, and counting to twenty-six.

Walt Disney Company. *Adventures with Letters and Numbers*. Illustrated. New York: Bantam, 1985.

In this book from the Begin-to-Learn series, Minnie (one) prepares a surprise birthday party for Mickey and greets the guests (two, three). Packages arrive (four), party signs are made (five), birds (six) and squirrels (seven) and butterflies (eight) watch. Louie, one of the guests, blows up balloons (nine) and Mickey opens his presents (ten). Numerals and number words in bold type are found in the corners of pages. The reader may be interested in contributing his or her own original words to the story. The listener may announce the numeral as it appears. On the title page for this section, "Numbers *1-10*," are ten brightly wrapped presents for Mickey with numerals assigned to them. The young counter is invited to say each numeral as it appears out of sequence. If interested, one may assign numerals to real objects—small boxes wrapped as presents, to cone-shaped party hats, or to inexpensive party favors or noise makers. Further, the objects may be lined up in sequence in a row. If ready to order objects in position, one may identify a starting point and point out which present, hat, or favor will be first, second, third, and so on. Number names may be assigned as object names, as well as the order of position, to talk about the positions of objects with, "Party hat number one is first," or "I want to put the present numbered ten as second in the row." or "First, I want to make noise with noise maker number three."

If the Disney characters and parties are favorite topics, *Mickey's Counting Book* (Walt Disney/Random House, 1983), shows Minnie preparing for a party, too. An interested young viewer may compare the parties in these two books to see similarities. Jane W. Watson's *Disney Numbers Are Fun* (Los Angeles: Walt Disney Studios/Western, 1977) also may interest a young viewer and entice one to count again with additional characters, to recognize numerals, and perhaps to say the numeral name as each page is shown. Pre-K.

Features: numeric narrative up to ten with numerals and number words in bold type for easy reference.

Rhymes

For Counting and Counting Out

Chambless-Regie, Jane, illustrator. *The Real Mother Goose*. New York: Rand McNally, 1984.

Tall, thin, and shaped like a slender grandfather clock, this version of Mother Goose focuses on some rhymes with numerals that help a girl or boy tell time. One verse, "Tick-tock, It's 1 o'clock," and others, present use of numerals on a clock face. For each verse, a girl or boy may create an original game and show the time by moving the pointers on the clock face included in the book. Pre-K.

Features: use of numbers with numerals on clock face, traditional rhymes.

Delmar, Gloria T. *Children's Counting-Out and Rhymes, Fingerplays, Jump-Rope and Bounce-Ball Chants and Other Rhymes*. Illustrated. New York: McFarland, 1983.

As an example of one of the rhymes, "A Zigzag Boy and Girl" is included: "If you are not / A zigzag child, /You'll have no cause to say /That you forgot. / For you will know / Where things are put away." If used as a chant while jumping rope, the jumper counts the number of successful jumps. Pre-6.

Features: rhyming lines for counting out and other chanting games.

Grayson, Marion F. *Let's Count and Count Out!* Illustrated by Deborah Derr McClintock. New York: Robert B. Luce, 1975.

Grayson's selected rhymes are organized into key number concepts with number-numeral relationships from one up to twenty. There are jingles to say, rhymes to chant, and number names to read along while recognizing the symbols. Several activities are suggested for an interested beginning counter. Pre-1.

Features: numeric rhymes from one up to twenty.

Grice, Mary, selector. *One, Two, Three, Four: Number Rhymes and Finger Games.* Illustrated by the selector. New York: Warne, 1970.

Number rhyme fans will find lots to choose from in this book. There are 123 rhymes for counting in a *one-more-than* sequence, in a *one-less-than* sequence, and for reviewing cardinal numbers and ordinals. For some girls and boys, there are several favorites: "The Twelve Days of Christmas," "One, Two, Buckle My Shoe," and "This Old Man." In addition, finger games accompany several of the selected poems and rhymes. For more rhymes and rhythm, *Counting Games and Rhythms for the Little Ones* (Scholastic Records), a recording by Ella Jenkins, offers counting nursery rhymes and includes rhythmic counting exercises to go with them. K-2.

Features: numeric rhymes, sequences of one up to ten and back, cardinals, and ordinals.

Gutman, Bill, editor. *Favorite Counting Rhymes to Read Aloud.* Illustrated by Ellen Dolce. New York: Modern/Unisystems, 1988.

Page corners hold the number words in colorful capitals and selected counting rhymes are featured for the numbers and numerals. The appropriate number of objects is taken from the rhyme or illustration and shown at the foot of each page. As an example for the number five, a viewer sees a girl and boy fishing to the words from "One, Two, Three, Four, Five, / I Caught a Fish and It Was Alive." The numeral 5 stands near five fish at the foot of the page. After the number ten, there is a frieze of numerals up to ten and a recap of the number sequence with the rhyme, "1, 2, Buckle My shoe." For a second review, numerals up to ten are shown again in a vertical format in the margins with "I Caught a Hare Alive." One final illustration shows ten teddy bears wearing numerals, 1–10, on their night shirts to accompany the words of "Ten in a Bed." Pre-1.

Features: traditional counting rhymes, sequence from 1–10, numerals, objects, number words.

Haley, Gail E., selector. *One, Two, Buckle My Shoe: A Book of Counting Rhymes*. Illustrated by the selector. New York: Doubleday, 1964.

Haley offers rhymes about each number from one up to ten, about the terms big and little, and odd and even. Familiar characters met include Old King Cole and Gregory Griggs. Word patterns, unfamiliar to some girls and boys, are heard in such phrases as "ten trombones in a sitting-standing-marching-running Big Brass Band" and "There Once Was a Sow . . . . " Rhymes offer a review of numbers with such choices as "Over in the Meadow," "The Twelve Days of Christmas," and "One, Two, Buckle My Shoe." Oversize numerals are inserted near the rhymes and color illustrations are alternated with ones in black and white. Green endpapers show white outlines of numbers of objects to identify (one apple tree, six snails, and ten eggs) and to match to the rhymes which can be recalled and told again. Pre-K.

Features: rhymes about each number from one up to ten.

Horton, Mary. *ABC and Counting Rhymes*. Illustrated by the author. New York: Grosset and Dunlap, 1980.

Horton's small pages show pale illustrations around these counting rhymes. There are several well-known ones and most girls and boys will enjoy repeating "Birthdays," "Days of the Months," "One, Two, Buckle My Shoe," and "Ten Little Bluebirds." Pre-K.

Features: rhymes showing use of numbers.

McGee, Shelagh. *One, Two, Button My Shoe*. Illustrated. New York: Derrydale/Crown, 1987.

Playful mice are found in each illustration and lead the way through this familiar rhyme. The mice knock at the door, knock down bricks, and shut the gate. At the number ten, the mice encourage the reader to "begin again." Pre-K.

Features: familiar rhyme, board pages, and sequence up to ten.

Montgomerie, Norah. *One Two Three: A Little Book of Counting Rhymes with Pictures*. Illustrated by the author. New York: Abelard-Schuman, 1967.

Montgomerie gives children some untitled rhymes to say aloud. Pen-and-ink sketches with touches of blue-green and orange surround such lines as "I Caught a Fish Alive," "Ten Little Mice Sat Down to Spin," and "This Old Man." Boys and girls see the old man coming from St. Ives, notice Old Davey Jones, and guess some of the answers to the riddles in "How Can There Be a Chicken without a Bone?" K-2.

Features: rhymes showing use of numbers.

Pierce, June, editor. *Wonder Book of Counting Rhymes*. Illustrated. New York: Wonder Books, 1957.

Because the illustrations are bright and colorful, a boy or girl may be attracted to it and find several rhymes that are familiar ones—traditional words which can be repeated over and over to learn the names of the numerals (language about numbers). In addition, there are songs to sing and jingles to chant. K-1.

Features: rhymes showing use of numbers.

Scales, Dora. *Read and Count 1, 2, 3*. Illustrated by Heather Potter, Mark Jackson, and Rich Amor. Crystal Lake, Ill.: Rigby, 1987.

In a big-book format, approximately seventeen by thirteen inches, eleven rhymes about the numbers one through three are presented with full-color illustrations. "Diddle, Diddle, Dumpling, My Son John" begins the selections and "Out for a Walk" is the final choice. In this verse, three bears walk in the woods with "Father Bear first, / Mother Bear last, / and Baby Bear in between." The rhymes are brief (usually four lines) and contain the number words instead of numerals. As another example, one little girl plays outside after a rainstorm has ended and counts the chickens in the yard who have ventured outside to search for food. The girl says there is "nothing to do" when along comes a playmate to make "two." Other books by Scales in this series include *Read and Count 4, 5, 6* and *Read and Count 7, 8, 9, 10* (both Rigby, 1987). In the first book, illustrated by Majory Gardener, Margaret Power, and Geoff Hocking, a beginning reader finds six rhymes—some short, others long—about the numbers four through six. To show the number four, four fish are in groups in a fishbowl: three swim at the bottom and one swims at the top. At the pet shop, Tom's grandfather buys the four fish and takes them home in a plastic dish. In the second book, the illustrations by Ester Kasepuw, Robert Avitabile, and Tony Oliver, show nine rhymes for the numbers seven through ten. A viewer sees monkeys playing tricks and groups them together to count to six. For more to count, there are 7 little dwarfs and the numbers of objects they find, 8 jolly sailors, 9 seagulls, and 10 bears in a den. On a page, a counter may group a set of tigers together by touching each one while counting. A listener is asked to clap and count up to ten. Both the adult and young counter may clap together as the process of counting is shown in print. To accompany these big books, small editions (six inches by eight inches) are also available from the publisher. Pre-1.

Features: rhyming lines, number words in text, and process of counting shown in print.

Schell, Becky. *Mother Goose from 1 to 10*. Illustrated by the author. Los Angeles: Price/Stern/Sloan, 1988.

With a shawl over her white feathery wings and a hat tied on her head, Mother Goose stands surrounded by numerals. Favorite nursery rhyme characters in full-color illustrations are found in rhymes with words that may be new to a listener's ear. Each rhyme is a variant of a familiar one in this small board book (approximately six inches square) and focuses on one of the numerals from one up to ten (language about math). Pre-K.

Features: numeric variants of rhymes for use of numbers from one through ten.

Seiden, Art, selector. *Counting Rhymes*. Illustrated by the selector. New York: Grosset and Dunlap, 1959.

These selected rhymes use cardinal numbers to compare quantities such as numbers of blackbirds, to show use of numbers with clocks, to identify the months of the year, and to determine which friend is "it" with a counting-out rhyme. Seiden's book offers several familiar rhymes, such as "Four Little Blackbirds," "Hickery, Dickery," "Eenie, Meenie," and "Thirty Days Hath September." Pre-K.

Features: numeric rhymes showing use of numbers, days of the months, and counting-out.

Seymour, Brenda M. *First Counting*. Illustrated by the author. New York: Walck, 1969.

Seymour uses descriptive couplets in this one. Seymour's words describe such objects as one red engine for a train, wet weather boots, nighttime stars and twenty bright, shining candles. Can a young viewer determine if all of the illustrations match the numerals being presented in these numeric rhymes? Does anyone notice that four boys and girls are seen in the illustration for ten fingers? (number-numeral correspondence). This could cause confusion so adult guidance may be needed. K-1.

Features: numeric rhyming lines and variety of objects to count up to twenty.

Stobbs, William. *One, Two, Buckle My Shoe*. Illustrated by the author. London, Eng.: The Bodley Head, 1984.

With the familiar words of this verse on the lefthand pages, the double-page spreads show the texture of the canvas and several animals to count in the watercolors. At the words "One, two," a horse is shoed. For "Three, four," the goats butt at a door. Dogs pick up sticks, squirrels lay twigs straight, and a hen has nine chicks to show the viewers. At "Nineteen, twenty," a plate is empty and cats yowl to be fed. Is any young viewer surprised by the different sized pages that are interspersed at needed places in this book? The actions of the animals may be mimed as the counting increases. If a girl or boy is interested in another version, several editions are available. As one example, *One, Two, Buckle My Shoe: A Book of Counting Rhymes* (Simon and Schuster, 1988) is a version for preschoolers retold and Illustrated by Rowan Barnes-Murphy. Included are such rhymes as "Gregory Griggs," "One Old Oxford Ox," and "This Old Man." Pre-1.

Features: numeric rhymes from one up to twenty.

Tudor, Tasha. *1 Is One*. Illustrated by the author. New York: Rand McNally, 1956.

Tudor's original verses present numerals and numbers of objects to count. Most girls and boys enjoy the short lines when the lines are read aloud. Number words in lines refer to how many objects are presented. Beginning with one duckling swimming in a dish, Tudor's illustrations in color are delicately bordered and alternate with black and white sketches. To represent ten, the number sequence of ten numbers is seen on a slate. If a beginning counter counts eleven numbers on the slate, it is because the two-digit number ten is not written as compactly as it should be written for counting purposes. With the exception of one illustration, all of the sketches show realistic scenes (e.g., four sheep nibble rye), but at twelve, a young viewer sees a feathered songleader with a music chart leading a choral group of twelve baby birds (cardinal numbers). The birds sing to a musical accompaniment of a mouse's stringed instrument. Reviewing the book with a youngster, an adult may consider the question, "Is the numeral on the same page as the objects to be counted?" If not, the appropriate numeral may be indicated where it is found. On the endpapers is a flower centerpiece which carries the concept of nature found in these illustrations. Recommended. K-1.

Features: original numeric rhyming lines and objects to count from one through twenty.

Ward, Dorothy D. *Teddies' Counting Rhymes*. Illustrated by Chrissie Wells. Designed by Graham Brown. New York: Larousse, 1984.

In this book, Ward offers counting rhymes about teddy bears. One bear plays with Christine, a doll, and prepares for a tea party. Two bears, Peter and Sally, go to the zoo and see the animals walk two by two. Rhymes go up to ten and tell the reader five bears plus five bears make ten bears and then show a subtraction situation where five bears minus five bears leave "no bears at all." K-1.

Features: number words in rhyming lines about bears up to ten and down to "no bears."

Wildsmith, Brian, selector. *Brian Wildsmith's Mother Goose*. Illustrated by the selector. New York: Franklin Watts, 1964.

Counting-out rhymes are found in various versions of Mother Goose, including this one by Wildsmith. To take a counter up to ten, Wildsmith offers "One, two, three, four, five, / Once I caught a fish alive. / Six, seven, eight, nine , ten, / But I let it go again." An older reader (ages 9–12) may go on a search through this book and other versions of Mother Goose rhymes to find other number rhymes to teach to younger girls and boys. Two versions published in the '80s to consider are Lilian Obligado's shape book, *Nursery Rhymes* (Western, 1980), for toddlers and *Tomie de Paola's Mother Goose* for preschool children (Putnam, 1985).

Paper Stories by Jean Stangl features more easy-to-cut paper illustrations to accompany selected rhymes. The words of "The Little Orange House" surprise girls and boys with a jack-o-lantern for the ending. "The Disappearing Snowperson" could complement words describing play on a snowy landscape; "Five LIttle Snowboys" may be counted as they are unfolded in front of an audience listening to words about winter settings; twelve eggs can demonstrate some of the words of "Hickety Pickety"; and rows of different cut shapes can be counted (trees, tulips, and pumpkins) when added to an unusual garden for "Mistress Mary" on a display board. "I'd Like to be . . . ," one of Stangl's paper stories with a cut-out display of shapes, offers an introduction to another book by Wildsmith, *Brian Wildsmith's 123s*. Pre-1.

Features: numeric words in traditional rhymes.

Williams, Jenny, selector. *One, Two, Buckle My Shoe: Counting Rhymes for Young Children*. Illustrated by the selector. New York: Dial, 1987.

Williams offers familiar nursery rhymes in this one. One single rhyme with accompanying illustrations appears on each page or on the spread that crosses two pages. A favorite counting rhyme of young children, "The Animals Went in Two by Two" (groups or sets), is included. Williams uses watercolors highlighted with marking pens and shows a young viewer some artistic variety in the illustrations. Pre.

Features: numeric rhymes, groups.

Withers, Carl, collector. *Eenie, Meenie, Minie, Mo and other Counting-Out Rhymes*. Illustrated by Elizabeth Ripley. New York: Dover, n.d.

In this republication of a 1946 edition, Withers has chosen one hundred variations of different rhymes and verses—enough words for a different rhyme or verse for every school day for five months. Some of the short counting-out rhymes may be appropriate for selecting the one to be first to collect a lunchbox at noon, to repeat to select the leader as boys and girls get ready to line up for recess, or to chant to identify the helper who will be responsible for returning the play equipment to the classroom after an outside play period. K-1.

Features: rhymes for counting out, use of numbers.

For Enjoying Humor and Nonsense

Bayley, Nicola, reteller. *One Old Oxford Ox*. Illustrated by the reteller. New York: Atheneum, 1977.

No one captures these numeric tongue-twisters better than Bayley whose version offers alliteration and shows dignified animals. For instance, one very dignified animal, an old ox warmed by a blue plaid laprobe, sits in a wheelchair and opens an oyster from a picnic collection of bread, drink, fruit, and oysters. Different animals are discovered as this collection is presented on the pages: resting green toads, tea-drinking tigers, and fishing penguins. A girl or boy may enjoy repeating the alliterative sentences about the animals from the numbers one to twelve and engage in identifying, verbalizing, and extending an alliterative number pattern in a sequence. With two-digit number use, place value is reinforced. Recommended. Pre-up.

Features: numeric alliteration up to twelve, place value.

Eichenberg, Fritz. *Dancing in the Moon: Counting Rhymes*. Illustrated by the author. New York: Harcourt Brace Jovanovich, 1955.

Eichenberg's humorous book offers some nonsense about animals and their numeric antics. His illustrations introduce one raccoon who dances, two moose who scare something, five dragons who pull wagons, and ten cats who model hats. Eichenberg's book is large, full of bright colors, and includes internal rhymes in lines about these unusual events and others. The illustrations may suggest miming the action for a review of the numbers in groups (using cardinal numbers to compare quantities). Numerals go up to twenty so place value is reinforced. In numbers after ten, an adult will notice that groups of ten are not seen or separated for recognition and counting purposes. If there is interest in more nonsense, Eichenberg's book may be compared with Beau Gardner's *Can You Imagine?/ A Counting Book*. Recommended. Pre-K.

Features: original, humorous, numeric lines with internal rhymes, and real and fanciful animals to count up to twenty, place value.

Gardner, Beau. *Can You Imagine . . . ? A Counting Book*. Illustrated by the author. New York: Dodd, Mead, 1987.

Gardner's rhyming text introduces animals and numbers in nonsensical situations, too. To answer the title question of "Can you imagine . . . ?" a viewer turns the pages to find colorful double-page spreads with large numerals and number words in the top corners and rhyming phrases below the featured objects. Gardner's witty words and imaginative situations include a whale who wears a veil, ducks who drive trucks, and giraffes who take photographs—all choices that may bring some giggles. Gardner's illustrations are bright with backgrounds of bright blue, green, orange, and red. Word rhymes (patterns to extend by supplying the rhymes) are heard: armadillos-pillows; raccoons-balloons; otters-teeter totters; squirrels-pearls; and swans-batons. There is a numeral-number words chart up to twelve so place value is reinforced and a rebus presentation of the silhouette shapes of animals for one-to-one correspondence. Recommended. Pre-2.

Features: numerals to identify, number words from one through twelve, matching, place value, and one-to-one correspondence.

Holl, Adelaide. *Let's Count*. Illustrated by Lucinda McQueen. Reading, Mass: Addison-Wesley, 1976.

McQueen's bright and cheerful endpapers give visual clues about the words to come. Holl's rhymes are light with words about one bear who rocks in a rocking chair, two elephants who swing, and three gnus who wear shoes. Bordered in a variety of styles, the illustrations are double-page spreads with eye-catching colors of orange, pink, red, and yellow, and show animals in action: there are four apes eating grapes, five whales with curly tails in a tree, and six silly dodo birds having toast and tea. A young viewer may count numbers forward to ten (the *one-more-than* sequence; place value reinforcement) and then count back in sequence to one (the *one-less-than* sequence) with different groups of animals. The decreasing sequence begins with ten baboons holding ten balloons and ends with one silly octopus on a high trapeze. K-1.

Features: humorous, numeric rhymes about animals from one up to ten and back in nonsense situations.

Irons, D. *Ten Silly Sheep.* Illustrated. Crystal Lake, Ill.: Rigby, 1988.

Written in the form of the traditional rhyme pattern moving back from ten to one, this oversize books shows sheep in the meadow, and as events happen, the number decreases. At the number three are the words, "three silly sheep were having fun. Two ran away. Then there was———?" This pattern continues: *Two silly sheep were having fun. One ran away. Then there was———?* This pattern links words in rhymes to-gether—a writing technique to discuss with a young author—and always identifies and repeats the number of sheep who ran away in the previous rhyme at the beginning of each following rhyme (verbalizing, extending a pattern). Pre-K.

Features: numeric rhymes from ten down to one, *one-less-than* se-quence.

Lear, Edward. *The Complete Nonsense of Edward Lear.* Illustrated by the author. New York: Dover, 1957.

Some of the nonsense verses from Edward Lear in this republication of an 1857 edition can be included in several counting sessions in a primary classroom. Favorite verses may be chanted with the boys and girls as they count and name objects. For instance, one kindergarten teacher presents "There was an Old Man with a Beard" with accompany-ing felt shapes on the classroom felt board to review a group of eight. The teacher recites the verse and mentions the names of the birds who built their nests in the old man's beard, then asks the students to count the birds and to remove the shapes one by one (*one-less-than* sequence) from the board (interpreting word problems). A second verse that the children enjoy repeating with the teacher is "There Was an Old Man on Whose

Nose . . . . " For this verse, the girls and boys select their own groups of birds to repose on the old man's long nose—a nose that extends the full width of the felt board. K-1.

Features: Lear's rhyming verses linking language to math.

Merriam, Eve. *You Be Good and I'll Be Night: Jump-on-the-Bed Poems.* Illustrated by Karen Lee Schmidt. New York: William Morrow, 1988.

One of the offerings in this one is a counting rhyme featuring a train at the station. In repetitive words, a young reader finds similar sounds in the second line of each couplet. The number words identify the times the train leaves: one-oh-one; two-oh-two; three-oh-three; and so on ending at ten.

Features: repetition, rhyme, and time-telling numbers from one up to ten.

Oechsli, Kelly. *Too Many Monkeys! A Counting Rhyme.* Illustrated by the author. Racine, Wis.: Golden/Western, 1960.

Additional monkeys are the topic for more counting and reading with the brief text in large type that makes this book easy to read. Large, colorful numerals with key words in capitals are above Oechsli's text that is inserted in the illustrations. On the pages one sees monkeys looking for something to do (two), playing in a tree (three), and knocking on the door (four). For girls and boys who listen for the pattern of words and can extend the pattern (*one- more* sequence), there is a repetitive phrase on each page with words of "One monkey joins them. Now there are . . . " Here the viewer turns the page after making a prediction, and with the page turn, verifies the next number and numeral. The monkeys find ticks (six) in their coats, meet Brave Kevin (seven), and skate (eight). At ten, the *one- less* pattern is introduced and the monkeys decrease by one on each page. With each decrease, there is another episode: after ten monkeys dine, nine feel great, eight see Kevin, and seven play tricks. Finally, one goes home, and then there are none (empty group or set). K-1.

Features: humorous, numeric rhymes about playful monkeys from one up to ten and back to none.

Samton, Sheila. *The World from My Window: A Counting Poem.* Illustrated by the author. New York: Crown, 1985.

Who would like to take a peek through a bright paper window in this book? Who would like to listen to the poetic words about the moon rising, the pale clouds drifting, and the black hills seen against the sky? Verses invite the listener to count along from one up to ten and learn about the natural world. An increasing number of animals and objects are seen as they are presented in the verses and found in the enlarging window shown in the illustrations. As each numeric view enlarges, a viewer counts such animals as blackbirds, cranes, fish, and horses. At the foot of each page of objects is a contrasting band that shows the number and the object word. At the end, the window returns to its original size, a first ending. For a second ending, the next two pages bring everything together in a review for a final look and another counting. Collage and paint form the full-color illustrations. Pre-1.

Features: number words, object words from one through ten, poetic phrasing, and a review as ending.

Sazer, Nina. *What Do You Think I Saw? A Nonsense Number Book.* Illustrated by Lois Ehlert. New York: Pantheon, 1976.

In Sazer's counting book, a young viewer meets Ehlert's bright pink rhinoceros as the rhino goes to town and counts along from one up to ten with numbers of other nonsense animals and objects. On double-page spreads, the animals are seen along with the numerals and the text in rhyme. For example, a count of two shows two pink llamas dressed in purple pajamas who dance around on their tiptoes. At six, there are six shiny machines on the page. However, a young viewer also sees a rhinoceros and a basket so the counting may reach more than six when considering all the objects on this page and adult comments may be needed when discussing them. At ten, a listener hears about ten kangaroos with striped tennis shoes and may count six big kangaroos as well as four baby kangaroos who are carried in their mothers' pouches (with no shoes showing). On the last two pages, there is a second review of the numbers (possible early experience in reading tables and graphs). Here, one counts the colorful nonsense animals again and sees the numerals 1 through 10 (using cardinal numbers to compare quantities). K-1.

Features: rhyming text, numerals, and numbers of animals in nonsense situations from one up to ten.

Vogle, Ilse-Margaret. *One Is Fun but Twenty Is Plenty.* Illustrated. New York: Atheneum, 1972.

For number play nonsense, Vogle's pages introduce the humorous antics of Lion and his companion, Hippo. There are numerals to be found within the text and nonsense action to see in the pictures (e.g., going for a drive while mixing a cake), as well as to read about (using cardinal numbers to compare quantities). Hippo (one) jumps off a sled and begins her adventures with Lion (two). The two animals search for pirates, find them, prepare 18 meatballs, and dance together to a 19-piece band. After a 20-day visit, the pirates sail off in a lavender haze leaving Hippo to say, "twenty is an enormous number." Most young girls and boys will enjoy the rhymes including the words about clocks that never run and always show the same time—five o' clock. Pre-K.

Features: numeric narrative in rhyme and numbers one through twenty.

For Learning

Aylesworth, Jim. *One Crow: A Counting Rhyme*. Illustrated by Ruth Young. New York: Harper and Row, 1988.

In full-color illustrations, Aylesworth presents a contrast of two seasons, summer and winter, as objects from one crow up to ten children are counted. Beginning with zero and an empty summer meadow, a young boy or girl sees one crow on a telephone wire, three puppies playing in the farmyard, and ten children playing together on a summer day. During winter, the same scenes and objects are shown again: an empty meadow is covered with snow; the crow perches on the wire above a snowy farmyard; and as they play with their sleds, all ten children wear boots, warm clothing, and hats. For one follow-up activity, drawing numbers of things in a winter setting may include the addition of dry, crumbled egg shells. As numbers of snowballs, snowpeople, snowflake patterns, or snow-covered roofs of farm buildings are drawn, white glue may be painted on with the tip of a toothpick or cotton swab dipped in glue. Crumbled eggshells are sprinkled on the glue and left to dry. Corresponding numerals may be included in the drawings. Pre-K.

Features: numeric rhyme linking language with math, use of numbers in seasonal changes, and numerals from 1 up to 10.

Holder, Heidi, reteller. *Crows: An Old Rhyme*. Illustrated by the reteller. New York: Farrar, Straus and Giroux, 1987.

Holder's retelling interprets her grandfather's memories of sayings associated with the number of flying crows seen in the sky at one time. Holder's research about these sayings goes back to English and Scottish folklore and a belief that crows (magpies) are intelligent, social birds and symbols of future events. With crows as the central motif, this book presents twelve sayings. Large pages (nine by twelve inches) show the setting and the animals on recto pages while the verso pages present a selected number of crows and a related saying. The pattern is repetitive, with framed illustrations of crows, the setting, and a capital letter beginning the number word. Words always appear on verso pages with the number word inside a decorated frame. On the recto pages in full-page illustrations, Millie the Mink and Willie the Weasel, the main characters, are seen as well as the crows who tell the events in the plot. Three crows, a symbol of a wedding, are found when Millie and Willie meet and marry. During the wedding procession of the animals, Willie, the groom leads one of the crows on a leash. In this scene and others, objects and textures, e.g., details in the costumes from an earlier time, are easy to see. The colors in each double-page spread are attractive blues, beiges, and corals. Each painting is a setting showing minks (fearless hunters), weasels (sly but not mean), and other animals and plants related to the sayings. As one example, flowers related to superstitions are found: at the numeral *1* for bad news, a viewer sees meadow rue, a symbol of regrets; at *2* for mirth, the saffron crocus represents gaiety; and at *3* for a wedding, there are several pink carnations, a symbol of love and marriage.

There is misfortune in the story but a satisfying ending as Millie and Willie are shown together again in a final illustration. Best suited for one-to-one discussion, this book is for pairs of readers so interested children and adults can talk about the illustrations, the symbols taken from folklore, and their meanings. Discussion may be needed as viewers connect the words with the actions. The reader may turn to the informative pages at the end and read the facts about the symbols and the habits of crows, weasels, and minks. 2–3.

Features: numeric folk sayings up to twelve and visual narrative.

Jacobs, Allan D., and Leland B. Jacobs, editors. *Arithmetic in Verse and Rhyme*. Illustrated by Kelly Oechsli. New York: Garrard, 1971.

Verses and rhymes may bring math language into daily math lessons in an entertaining way. Jacobs and Jacobs offer clever riddles, verses, and counting rhymes as examples of language about math to incorporate into appropriate lessons. All of the selections relate to numbers in some way. The arrangement makes this collection easy for a teacher to review for promoting numbers and numerals in the classroom (observing relationships through rhyme). 1 up.

Features: numeric rhymes and riddles to link language to math.

Marmaduke Multiply's Merry Method of Making Minor Mathematicians. Illustrated. New York: Dover, n.d.

Originally published in Boston in 1941 by Munroe and Francis, this book is a facsimile of that early edition. A special girl or boy who is quite adept with addition and subtraction may want to move toward the multiplication tables and review the rhymes about them. While this reproduction may not appeal to every one of today's children, the math couplets may serve as models for a creative review of some of the multiplication facts (understanding the meaning of the basic operation). If interested, a boy or girl creates his or her own math rhymes from the models. For instance, the words, "Twice 2 are 4," become "Two times two is four" or another original line very quickly. A rhyming second line may reflect a current interest, a fad, or a popular item to bring the couplet up to date. Words might be said aloud or written about patch-type dolls, members of music groups, or computer language. Here is one short math couplet quickly chanted aloud by an interested third-grade student: "Two times three are six./Are you playing tricks?" 3 up.

Features: rhyming couplets link addition to multiplication.

Scales, Dora. *Our First Big Book of Numbers.* Illustrated. Crystal Lake, Ill.: Rigby, 1986.

In a big-book format, number-numeral relationships are shown in a sequence from one up to ten. One child getting dressed begins the sequence that continues up to counting ten big bottles. An accompanying big book is Scales's *Our Second Big Book of Numbers* (Rigby, 1986). In this one, a viewer counts the objects at a sidewalk sale, those seen in a train-track layout, and others up to twenty. Objects are shown in graphs. Dots to count for objects are found in the different scenes and offer a viewer one-to-one correspondence. 1–2.

Features: variety of objects to count in number-numeral relationships from one up to twenty, one-to-one correspondence.

Scales, Dora. *Time for a Number Rhyme.* Illustrated by Randy Glusoe, David Pearson, Heather Philpott, Donna Raulins, and Jane Tanner. Melbourne, Australia: Thomas Nelson, 1983.

In a big-book format, seventeen inches by twenty-four inches, there are pages of full-color illustrations and rhymes. Including "One, Two, Buckle My Shoe," and others, the text offers the use of numbers in the descriptive lines. *Time for a Number Rhyme* also is available in a small edition with an accompanying audio cassette (language about math). There is a variety of Mother Goose rhymes accompanied by large, full-color illustrations. An interested viewer may select a favorite to chant along with the reader. Pre-K.

Features: rhyming lines, use of numbers.

True, Louise. *Number Men*. Pictures by Katherine Evans. Chicago: Children's Press, 1962.

True devises short rhymes for instruction to help one write the 123s. The rhymes may serve as memory devices since they give clues about the shapes that are needed to write the numerals. For example, when a young girl or boy wants to write the numeral 2, True's words about each person having two ears may bring a memory picture of an ear, and the shape of a beginning line that makes the numeral 2. The curve of the ear at the top may guide a young writer in starting the shape of the numeral 2. In True's illustrations, the numeral 3 becomes a ruffle; 4 takes the shape of a garden gate; and 6 is a monkey's tail. A flag waves for 7, a snowman appears for 8, and a balloon on a stick is made from the shape of 9. While there are a variety of objects to count in the large black and white illustrations, an adult will notice that at times the numbers refer to how many objects are shown on one page, and at other times, on two pages, and will want to indicate to the young viewer which page or pages of objects should be counted. K-1.

Features: instructive rhymes for writing numerals, 0 to 9.

For Singing

Adams, Pam. *There Were 10 in a Bed*. Illustrated by the reteller. Restrop Manor, Eng.: Child's Play, 1979.

To illustrate this traditional rhyme, one die-cut half-circle opening allows a girl or boy to see all ten children (then nine, eight, and so on with different ethnic representations) in one large bed. Verso pages hold the words and as the command, roll over, is given, one tumbles out. The number of children in the bed decreases and the number on the floor increases each time the sturdy full-colored pages are turned. For a final review, a young counter finds a paper-engineered wheel to turn to reveal the faces of the girls and boys again in a sequence from one up to ten or ten down to one.

Features: traditional rhyme from one through ten, die-cut openings, paper-engineered wheel to manipulate, sequences of *one-less* and *one-more*.

Adams, Pam. *This Old Man*. Illustrated by the author. New York: Grosset and Dunlap, 1974.

Adams's work is a single version of *This Old Man*. The familiar sequence in this rhyme helps make the numbers predictable for young children. The repetitive pattern helps some boys and girls feel comfortable about what comes next in the sequence and encourages them to repeat the words of the text (predicting outcomes). Another single version published in the '80s is *This Old Man: The Counting Song* (Putnam's Sons, 1988) and is illustrated in full color by Robin Michal Koontz. K-2.

Features: repetition, *one-more* number sequence through ten in rhyme.

Brett, Jan. *The Twelve Days of Christmas*. Illustrated by the reteller. New York: Dodd, Mead, 1986.

In Brett's full-color version are one plump partridge among green leaves, golden pears, and other elegant gifts given by a gentleman to his ladyfriend (cardinal numbers) on the days before Christmas (ordinal numbers). Central scenes, with ethnic themes, show details, and are framed. For examples, the seven swans wear crowns from Russia and the eleven ladies dancing are Spanish senoritas. Additional small scenes show the family's preparations for Christmas (choosing and decorating the tree). There are personified creatures (e.g., the French hens wearing French gowns), and the holiday greeting, "Merry Christmas," is shown in twelve languages. Words for each verse in this carol are found at the foot of each double-page spread and can become the basis of the counting song or an indoor game (identifying, verbalizing, and extending a pattern in a sequence). K-up.

Features: visual story, alliterative number verses, and objects one through twelve.

Brierley, Louise. *The Twelve Days of Christmas*. Illustrated by the reteller. New York: Holt, Rinehart and Winston, 1986.

Setting on an estate with statuary and barren trees, these twelve days present a different mood from Brett's version. Similar to the surrealistic work of Dali, the work of Brierley shows the characters elongated or out-of-shape in some way. In keeping with this approach, the characters for the twelve days are shown from different points of view. For instance, the viewer looks down from an overhead perspective to an inside scene and sees nine drummers marching around the dining table. Outside, the viewer looks down again to see the cows being milked. 4 up.

Features: surrealistic scenes, alliterative number verses, and objects up to twelve.

Count Me In: 44 Songs and Rhymes about Numbers. Illustrated. New York: A and C Black/Sterling, 1985.

In this songbook, one of the forty-four songs is "Over in the Meadow," a children's favorite, with only three verses included. This traditional rhyme, and other counting songs, are accompanied by original music and suggestions for the use of rhythm instuments. Piano and guitar accompaniments are included. Pre-1.

Features: numeric rhymes with original music and traditional counting songs.

Duke, Kate. *Seven Froggies Went to School.* Illustrated by the author. New York: E. P. Dutton, 1985.

While there are no sequential numerals to show the count from one up to seven, an interested viewer may focus on a group of seven and may count seven frogs in each illustration (recognizing quantities). Duke's text is adapted from a lullaby the author's grandmother learned as a child. The original version is *Twenty Froggies Went to School,* by George Cooper; however, Duke's version is about seven young frogs who are under the instructional eye of Master Bullfrog who teaches them the wisdom needed to survive by the pond. Since this book was not designed originally as a counting book, the reader follows the story-song as the frogs study, play, and keep the Bullfrog's rules, (i.e., learning the tricks of the muskrat and keeping away from cats, birds, and boys with sticks). The frogs swim, dive, and ride upon a newt. They dance and play the flute. When the froggies grow up, they in turn take their places on the logs to teach other young frogs the wisdom of the bog. No music for the lullaby is included. Pre-2.

Features: recognizing groups of seven in narrative.

Emberly, Barbara. *One Wide River To Cross.* Illustrated by Ed Emberly. Englewood Cliffs, N.J.: Prentice-Hall, 1966.

"One Wide River to Cross," a popular folk song, is adapted by Barbara Emberly in this number book. Ed Emberly illustrates the adaptation and provides pictures that help boys and girls count as they see the animals come into Noah's ark. Counting two by two, three by three, and on up to ten (groups or sets) takes place while looking at the illustrated wood-block prints of groups of animals (understanding addition and its link to multiplication). Pre-2.

Features: numeric verses about animal groups from one up to ten.

Galdone, Paul. *Over in the Meadow: An Old Nursery Counting Rhyme.* Illustrated by the reteller. New York: Prentice-Hall, 1986.

Galdone's version of this old counting rhyme is an appealing one. There are cartooned animals and soft spring colors in the scenes. In this version, the meadow looks like a flower garden. Unlike John Langstaff's version with the included music, Galdone's adaptation does not offer any musical support for the singing of this counting rhyme. The text in this Children's Choice book is appropriate for young readers who know the tune and can sing these words again and again as the animals increase (using cardinal numbers). Using test teams of students and teachers each year, the Children's Book Council and the International Reading Association record annually the votes for books published that represent the choices of children; Galdone's *Over in the Meadow* is one of these. Interested parents, librarians, and teachers may review the list of Children's Choices for each year that is published annually in *The Reading Teacher.* Recommended. K-2.

Features: numeric verses about meadow animals from one through ten.

Gerstein, Mordicai. *Roll Over!* Illustrated by the author. New York: Crown, 1984.

One little child says "R-O-L-L O-V-E-R!" to each one of ten humorous nighttime companions. A young viewer lifts a fold-out flap in this small book to see which companion rolls out of the big bed. There is Momma Mouse, Pappa Pig, Sister Seal, and several other animals. Can one name some of the animals' personal possessions? Has Brother Beaver been gnawing on that log he carries? What is the goose wearing? What does Sister Seal balance on her nose? As the pages of this small book are turned, a viewer should look carefully at the foot of the large bed and tell what is seen in the design (patterns). In addition, a girl or boy may look through the bedroom window shown in the illustrations. Do you see the way that the face in the moon changes as it rises higher and higher in each scene? An older child (ages 8–10), preparing to illustrate an original version of this counting song, may compare the bedroom window views and the headboard and footboard patterns with the views and patterns found in Merle Peek's version. Also, the viewer may notice the creative use of print that is shown in the text in the words the character says to the animals who are crowding the bed: the words get larger and bolder. Does anyone notice that the little character's words are shown with larger and darker print in the illustrations? (identifying, verbalizing, and extending a pattern in a sequence). Recommended. Pre-1.

Features: rhyming lines about personified animals and sequence of ten down to one.

Hartelius, Margaret A., reteller. *Over in the Meadow*. Illustrated by the reteller. New York: Bantam, 1987.

Hartelius's version presents counting from one up to ten as well as the day-into-night cycle (cardinal numbers). An audio cassette comes with the book and offers the song on side one and accompanying activities on side two. The learning activities reinforce counting and provide information about animals and their habitats. After learning this song, is anyone ready to contribute new words to the old familiar music? A title such as "Over in My Backyard," "Over in the Green Park," or "Over on the Next Street" may inspire an original composition (extending a pattern). Pre-1.

Features: rhyming lines from one through ten.

Hartelius, Margaret, reteller. *The Twelve Days of Christmas*. Illustrated by the reteller. New York: Bantam, 1988.

In this version, Hartelius uses collage to illustrate the traditional English counting song. The familiar objects are here: a partridge, swans swimming, lords leaping, and ladies dancing. An audio tape accompanies the book and enables an interested participant to sing along with the words or to join in with other selected songs of the season. Pre-2.

Features: objects and numeric verses to sing one through twelve.

Hawkinson, Lucy. *That New River Train*. Illustrated by the author. Chicago: Albert Whitman, 1970.

Jenny meets a tiny ladybug who follows along in every one of the illustrations as Jenny meets several animals, including a bird, squirrel, rabbit, and lamb. For numerals 6 through 10, other animals are identified: the fawn, horse, bear, giraffe, and elephant (cardinal numbers to compare quantities). The names of these animals are not given on the pages. Can someone find Jenny in every picture? Can a numeral and a number word be seen on each page? Can the animals in the field be counted? Does the number of animals in each group match the numeral that is shown (number-numeral correspondence)? Hawkinson, an author-artist, who has an appreciation for folk songs ends this number book with an accumulation of the animals and the final word "ALL" in the corner of the final illustration. To help one sing along with these rhymes (e.g. "Jenny, you can't love one, two, three . . . ten, all."), Hawkinson includes the music, a version adapted from *More Songs to Grow On* by Beatrice Landeck (Edward B. Marks Music Corporation). Pre-2. Features: numeric verses to sing and animals to count from one up to ten.

Hobzek, Mildred. *We Came a-Marching . . . 1 2 3*. Illustrated by William Pené du Bois. New York: Parents Magazine Press, 1978.

Hobzek, a librarian for the Cleveland Public Library, and du Bois, a Newbery Medal recipient, ask a beginning counter to march along and to count in this one. Stepping right along with Sacha and Stanislov, the young viewer follows one large bird to a hidden nest in a tall tree. With the help of a friendly woodsman, the children form an ascending body-ladder so they can see the baby birds. Marching along, a participant counts one, two, three, in twelve languages to the music of this Slavic folk song (using cardinal numbers). The illustrations are cheerful ones, the accompaniment to the song is included, and flags on the endpapers show the twelve different nations. Recommended. Pre-2.

Features: verses to sing and to count up to three in English, French, Spanish, German, and other languages.

Izawa, T. *Ten Little Indians*. Illustrated by T. Izawa and S. Hyikata. New York: Grosset and Dunlap, 1968.

In this version, the ten little people leave, one by one, (*one-less-than* sequence) until the group of ten decreases to zero or none (empty group or set). Izawa's text rhymes and the illustrations are on shiny, thick pages. The sturdiness of the book is appropriate for a preschool child. Pre.

Features: *one-less* sequence from ten down to zero.

Keats, Ezra Jack. *Over in the Meadow*. Illustrated by the author. New York: Four Winds Press, 1971/Scholastic, 1972.

Over in the Meadow is a title that some girls and boys will see again and again on the covers of other versions. Keats's version of this well-known counting song helps children count the number of animals living in a meadow, listen to repeating words and anticipate singing in a predictable pattern; it also assists in recognition of the meadow animals in the illustrations. After the song, is anyone ready to discuss some of the ways that these animals live together? Is any girl or boy ready to observe and count the number of living things seen in a backyard or on a neighborhood walk (cardinal numbers to compare quantities)? Recommended. K-2.

Features: numeric verses to sing about animals from one up to ten.

Knight, Hilary. *Hilary Knight's The Twelve Days of Christmas.* Illustrated by the author. New York: Macmillan, 1981.

Benjamin Bear wakes up in his hammock inside his log house. A holiday wreath hangs over the fireplace mantel. Benjamin's Christmas list shows the bright red heading, "1st Day" (ordinals to order quantities). One item is checked off the list: a partridge in a pear tree. This endpaper scene takes a viewer into the wordless story quickly and into the first of three parallel story lines. In the first story line, a viewer sees Benjamin, a bear in love, giving accumulating gifts to his sweetheart, Belinda Bear (*one-more* pattern). On succeeding days, the gifts are all delivered: two turtle doves, three French hens, and so on (correspondence of members of groups to cardinal numbers). Cats are dressed as the maids a-milking. Rabbits are the drummers drumming. Leaping frogs are the lords a-leaping.

In the second story line, Belinda continues the activities of her daily life as she receives gifts from Benjamin. She hangs a wreath on her front door, reads her holiday mail, and plays tunes on her piano. In the same order in which her gifts arrive, Belinda includes them in these daily activities. For instance, an addition to her two-story house suddenly appears to shelter the French hens, the geese, and the swans (cause and effect).

In the third story line, Reginald, a masked raccoon, quietly comes from the basement of Belinda's house. Dressed in a black shirt and beret, which give him the looks of a cat burglar, Reginald approaches a large steel can placed outside the house. Does the steel can contain trash or something valuable? Though Reginald tries to open the can, the lid won't come off: he ties the can to a tree for leverage and pulls on the lid; he uses a hacksaw on it; and he inserts a wedge under the ledge of the lid and hammers it. When Reginald finally succeeds and lifts the lid, he finds a package wrapped in red ribbon. Inside the package and dressed in pink-and-white is Rose, a seemingly friendly raccoon. Reginald and Rose go to Belinda's Christmas Fair where all of Belinda's gifts perform. The flap of the page is lifted to see such entertaining gifts as leaping frogs, swimming swans, and dancing pigs at this festive finale (more cardinal numbers to compare quantities). To sing this song, a singer needs to be familiar with the music and should be encouraged to make up original words from the wordless scenes on the pages. Neither text nor music is included in this version. K-up.

Features: parallel plots and visual accumulation of objects to count from one up to twelve.

Langstaff, John. *Over in the Meadow*. Illustrated by Feodor Rojankovsky. New York: Harcourt, 1957.

Langstaff and Rojankovsky offer another version of the old rhyme. From one turtle, two foxes, and three robins to eight owls, nine spiders, and ten bunnies, a beginning counter identifies the animals and counts the number in the groups. The names of the animals and the numbers are reviewed in a pleasant way as the lines are sung to the included music (using cardinal numbers to compare quantities). Recommended. Pre-1.

Features: numeric verses about meadow animals to sing and count from one through ten.

Leman, Jill and Martin Leman. *Twelve Cats for Christmas*. Illustrated by Martin Leman. New York: Pelham Books, 1982.

In this book, a viewer sees more of Leman's stylized cats, e.g., a striped ginger kitten, a smiling cat illuminated by moonlight, and a resting cat napping. Also, there is that familiar sentence with the beginning words, "On the first day of Christmas, my true love gave to me . . . ," as well as some unfamiliar gifts beginning with one black cat in a decorated pear tree (identifying, verbalizing, and extending a pattern in a sequence). When one uses this book as a number word recognition book, the user needs to understand accumulation, or may need to turn back the pages to count the cats in sequence from the first cat since Leman shows only one cat in each illustration. Pre-1.

Features: number words in lines of verses, one cat per page, no numerals.

MacDonald, Elizabeth, and Annie Owen. *My Aunt and the Animals*. Illustrated by Annie Owen. New York: Barrons, 1985.

My Aunt and the Animals serves as a counting book, as a review of the months of the year, and as a pattern of alliteration. In this variation of the carol entitled "The Twelve Days of Christmas," a young counter sees one enormous elephant eating an extra-large ice cream in January, brown bears blowing balloons in March, and a party for all of the animals in December. Animals are shown in colorful pastel drawings. Each drawing is filled with details about each humorous situation. With much to offer a young learner, this book can be followed by a variety of activities that focus on counting, the months of the year, and on alliteration (cardinal numbers to compare quantities; identifying and verbalizing pattern of alliteration and months of the year). Pre-K.

Features: variant with alliteration, sequence of months, and groups of animals from one up to twelve.

Mack, Stan. *10 Bears in My Bed: A Goodnight Countdown*. Illustrated by the author. New York: Pantheon, 1974.

Mack brings bears and toys to boys and girls in this 123 book. Browsing through the pages of this one, viewers see a young boy in yellow night-wear who tells each one of the ten bears to "Roll over!" The bears roll over and leave the cluttered bedroom in different ways with different toys: tricycle, toy horn, pogo stick, rocking horse, and so on (using cardinal numbers to compare quantities). Pre-K.

Features: *one-less* sequence from ten down to one.

Martin, Janet. *Ten Little Babies Count*. Illustrated by Michael Watson. New York: St. Martin's Press, 1986.

A toddler opens the covers of this board book to see color photographs of babies counting, dressing, and eating. The words are familiar ones and reflect the *one-less-than* sequence. The words are similar to the ones in the rhyme, "Ten Little Indians." However, several of the words have been changed from the original rhyme to describe the babies and older toddlers as they play (seeing visual characteristics to identify; cardinal numbers to compare quantities). Someone may be interested in singing the words in this rhyme to the familiar tune. Pre.

Features: variant of rhyme/song with objects from ten down to one in a *one-less* sequence.

Nipp, Susan, Kathy Bates, and others. *Over in the Meadow: A Musical Story Play*. Illustrated. Los Angeles: Price/Stern/Sloan, 1987.

After Billy asks why he has to brush his teeth, Mother expands on the idea of "sometimes we have to do things we don't want to do," and gives Billy a lesson about animals and the natural things they have to do each day. Billy finds that the bees buzz, the birds sing, and the spider spins. A viewer sees a rebus technique that offers objects on the pages at beginning of lines of text as well as full-color illustrations (cardinal numbers to compare quantities), while hearing the music on the accompanying audio cassette. A beginning reader will find words for performing this counting story as a short play. One fold-out script contains a lyric sheet. Pre-3.

Features: linking language in a musical story play to math.

Obligado, Lilian, reteller. *Over in the Meadow: A Nursery Counting Rhyme*. Illustrated by the reteller. New York: Golden/Western, 1983.

Obligado adapted this old nursery counting rhyme to include personified animals who wear clothes and carry objects. Mother Turtle shows her one turtle how to dig with a shovel, Mother Fish show her two fishes how to swim, and Mother Owl shows her three owlets how to sleep all day in the hole in the tree. Four mousies (reteller's word choice) squeak, five bees buzz, and six crows caw. Seven frogs jump in different ways: for instance, one has a jump rope, and another leaps a hurdle. Eight lizards, dressed in colorful tee-shirts, bask on a board fence while nine ducklings quack, and ten beavers gnaw (cardinal numbers to compare quantities). There is a review page given to answer the question, "Who lived in the meadow?" Recalling the number of animals takes place with a rhythmic chant of one little turtle, two little fishes, three little owls, and so on (possible early experience for reading information from a graph or table). After an adult models the telling of information gained from the final review page and describes the relationship shown by the sequence of objects, a listener may be encouraged to tell what information he or she gained. After the adult has a turn, then the boy or girl may have a turn to tell about the relationships shown by the sequence. In this review, the number words are capitalized. Obligado's version is small, approximately six inches square, and so is best suited for a youngster's home collection. Illustrations go clear to the edges of the pages and show blues, greens, yellows, and reds. Small details are added for additional counting: the little turtle has one shovel and pail to dig up sand while Mother Turtle wears a decorated hat. Other images of the personified mother animals are seen: in apron and hat, Mother Lizard knits while Mother Mouse, in her plaid dress, waits near the old barn door. Mother Duck ties a scarf on her white feathered head and Mother Beaver wears a red and white checked apron. Jewelery items may be noticed and counted: Mother Owl wears a necklace of green foliage; Mother Crow displays one ruby ring on her left leg, and Mother Frog puts on bracelets. Pre-2.

Features: number words in capitals and sequence of increasing animals in groups from one through ten.

Peek, Merle. *The Balancing Act: A Counting Book.* Illustrated by the author. New York: Clarion, 1987.

A youngster who enjoyed Peek's earlier book, *Roll Over: A Counting Song* (Houghton Mifflin, 1981), will also enjoy this rhythmic verse and its refrain (in yellow boxes inserted in the illustrations) about one little elephant who balances, step by step, on a piece of string (high wire), and calls to another little elephant to join him. Counting by ones begins as other elephants join the act (using cardinal numbers to compare quantities). All of the personified animal friends dressed in their best clothes arrive at the colorful amusement park as this balancing act accumulates. The young fan of Peek's may recognize the animal characters who watch this act as ones from another book by Peek, *Mary Wore Her Red Dress and Henry Wore His Green Sneakers* (Clarion, 1985). Park attractions such as the Bump-em Boats entertain Mary, Henry, and the other animals, as the elephants perform their stunts high in the background. Counting continues as two, three, then four elephants balance on the string. One sees the numerals in balloons floating on the pages (number-numeral correspondence). How many elephants will the string support? When a tenth elephant comes to join the others, what prediction will be made by the viewer? As the elephant act grows in number, so does the interest of the animals who arrive just in time to see the elephants, brightly colored in pink, lime green, orange, lavender, and blue, all tumble down to the net below. There is a second ending: a notice board announces, "Thank You for Visiting Elephant Land. Come Again." A musical score to help one sing the words is included in the author's notes. Recommended. Pre-3.

Features: numeral-number correspondence, numeric verses about elephants from one through ten to sing and to link language to math.

Peek, Merle. *Roll Over: A Counting Song.* Illustrated by the author. Boston, Mass.: Houghton Mifflin/Clarion, 1981.

Nine animals share a bed with a toddler, and one by one, they leave to tuck themselves away for the night. Singing along with the first "Roll Over!," a young viewer sees the monkey fall out of the big bed. After the monkey finds another place to sleep, a big bear falls out of the bed. Animal by animal, the other companions find unusual places to rest. One verse is found on each page for the different animals: snake, dog, deer, and others. With the last verse, the illustration shows the animals pictured in the border around the toddler's bedroom. Using the illustrations, there is counting back to one (*one-less-than* sequence) and the music is attached so a girl or boy can sing the counting song (rhythmic language link to math). An older child (ages 8–10) interested in illustrating a version of this counting rhyme, may appreciate some time to look at such details as the changing sky seen through the bedroom window and the changing expression on the bedposts and footboard of the toddler's bed. Recommended. Pre-2.

Features: *one-less* sequence from ten down to one in rhyme.

Random House Sing With Me; Play Along and Counting Songs. Illustrated. New York: Random House, 1987.

Playing outside on green grass, four children and a puppy get together to sing along in an illustration in this counting songbook. Approximately five inches square, the book is accompanied by a thirty-minute sing-along audio cassette. Following the words of the counting songs, a young listener counts the objects in the full-color illustrations (cardinal numbers). Pre-K.

Features: rhyming words in songs linking language to math.

Rees, Mary. *10 in a Bed.* Illustrated by the author. Boston: Little, Brown, 1988.

In this version, it is one little girl who pushes her nine friends (ethnic groups represented) out of bed so she can have the big bed all to herself. The first friend who rolls out of bed goes to the bathroom to brush her teeth. The second friend who rolls out of bed also walks to the bathroom to play with a toy sailboat. As the other friends roll over and out, they explore other rooms in the house (cardinal numbers). In humorous watercolor illustrations, one climbs on a bedroom dresser, others march down the stairs, and still others eat popcorn in the living room. In the kitchen they make tea and enjoy cereal and toast while one feeds the dog. Moving outside, the friends play, ride tricycles, and swing in a tire swing. Once all nine children are up and about, they return to the bedroom to have their revenge on the little girl (who does not want to leave the bed) and they playfully pull her (and her sheets and blankets) from the bed, leaving no one (empty group or set) in the bed to say, "Roll over!" A viewer may be encouraged to turn back through the pages again and discuss the antics of the dog and cat as the children wake up (parallel action). For older students (ages 8–10) preparing their own books, an adult may point out Rees's technique of increasing the space the characters need to correlate with the concept of waking up and moving about. Girls and boys interested in techniques of illustrating stories may discuss Rees's use of shadow in the illustrations, her attention to balance and symmetry with the lines of the walls, doors, and floors, and her insertion of amusing details in the illustrations. No music is included. K-2.

Features: *one-less* sequence from ten down to one.

Schneider, Erika, reteller. *The Twelve Days of Christmas.* Illustrated by the reteller. Natick, Mass.: Picture Book Studio, 1974.

In Schneider's version of this popular song, there are overlapping and stylized illustrations on the front sides of concertina-type folds (about six inches square). The music and words, without background, are on the reverse side. For the older child (ages 8–10) who is making original books, an adult may discuss the potato prints used in the illustrations (quantities), a natural lead-in to interest one in working with prints made by vegetables just as Schneider did. K up.

Pattern: alliterative verses to sing from one up to twelve.

Shuttleworth, Cathie. *One, Two.* Illustrated. San Diego: Corgh, 1987.

This book is a variation of the familiar verse "One, Two, Buckle My Shoe." Kittens mew (two), birds are found in a tree (three), and shells are counted on the shore (four). Rhyming lines continue along with full-color illustrations as a viewer sees bees in a hive, rooks (crows) in the heaven, sheep at a gate, clothes on a line, and a black hen. Pre-K.

Features: rhyming lines, number words from one through ten.

Swan, Susan Elizabeth, reteller. *The Twelve Days of Christmas.* Illustrated by reteller. Mahwah, N.J.: Troll, 1981.

On Swan's bright red cover, one sees a colorful partridge among the green leaves of the pear tree that bears one golden pear (quantities). For her version of this popular English folk song, Swan offers golden rings, dancers, and pipers as a few of the gifts that arrive on the twelve days of Christmas (ordinal numbers to order quantities). Some girls and boys also may enjoy the word-for-word cassette that goes along with the thirty-two pages of the paperback or the hardback edition. K-4.

Features: alliterative verses to sing and accumulating objects from one up to twelve.

Wadsworth, Olive A., reteller. *Over in the Meadow: A Counting-Out Rhyme*. Illustrated by Mary Maki Rae. New York: Viking, 1985.

Color and movement on endpapers introduce a young counter to the animals who live in the meadow. This is a bouncy, catchy counting-out rhyme in which baby animals travel home through their meadow in colorful double-page illustrations. First one, then two, and finally ten animals arrive (quantities). Young girls and boys will like reciting the familiar verses, identifying the large animals, and seeing the action words of animals in italics (e.g., we *dig*, we *swim*, and we *buzz*). Wadsworth and Rae have a final double-page spread that shows all the animals for a review (relationship shown by a sequence of objects). If music is needed, one may turn to the version by John Langstaff or another favorite. Pre-2.

Features: verses, accumulating meadow animals from one through ten.

Weiss, Nicki. *If You're Happy and You Know It: Eighteen Story Songs Set to Pictures*. Illustrated by the author. Music arranged by John Krumich. New York: Greenwillow, 1987.

Weiss offers songs about counting that include "This Old Man," "Five Little Ducks," and "Roll Over" (language about numbers). Each phrase of the song has a corresponding picture so the young singer has time to consider what comes next in the sequence (predicting outcomes). Chords for autoharp, guitar, and piano are given as letter names. Pre-3.

Features: rhyming words about numbers in songs, sequence of *one-more* and *one-less*.

Windham, Sophie, reteller. *The Twelve Days of Christmas: A Lift-the-Flap Book*. Illustrated by the reteller. New York: Putnam, 1986.

Windham's version offers girls and boys still another look at this celebration. The music on the endpapers gives a hint of the story-song to come. In this one, there are an increasing number of flaps to lift to see the gift or gifts for each day (quantities). On the fifth day, for example, an inquisitive viewer lifts five flaps and sees five wide-awake pigs who wear large gold rings in their noses. Best suited for home use because of the many flaps and their fragility, this book offers a model for paper-engineered pages for one's original version. Pre-2.

Features: one-to-one correspondence, accumulation of objects from one up to twelve.

Yolen, Jane. *An Invitation to the Butterfly Ball: A Counting Rhyme.* Illustrated by Jane Breskin Zalben. New York: Parents Magazine Press, 1976.

In this rhyme, the animals and objects accumulate, page by page. An elf offers invitations to ten different families of animals to attend the Butterfly Ball. Counting begins with one small mouse, dressed in a full-length dress for the ball, and continues up to ten porcupines who are arguing about a velvet evening jacket (cardinal numbers to compare quantities). The animals' preparations are varied: the mouse worries about her dress, two moles search for vests, and three rabbits sort out laces. With the introduction of each animal—whether it is a turtle, owl, or raccoon—the repetitive rhyme in this count-down sequence leads back to the one little mouse. At the end, there is time to count all the animal groups and their members. On a final page, all of the animals may be seen again as they appear in response to their invitations to the ball. This accumulation in Zalben's work adds emphasis to Yolen's story line for the number song. Since the verse is cumulative, girls and boys will remember the words and join in quickly to chant or sing the rhyme (identifying, verbalizing, and continuing a pattern in a sequence). Recommended. K-1.

Features: *one-more* sequence from one up to ten in accumulating verses.

Collections of Related Objects

Animals and Insects

Adler, David A. *Bunny Rabbit Rebus.* Illustrated by Madeline Gill Liden. New York: Puffin, 1987.

Using a mother rabbit's search for food to encourage counting, Adler invites a young viewer to join Mother Rabbit as Mother looks for lettuce and carrots to feed her little rabbit. Adler's 123 story is told with words, numbers, and a rebus (pictures instead of words) approach. Small watercolors hold tiny details reminiscent of the illustrations of Beatrix Potter. With the use of pictured objects in the story, a beginning reader finds it easy to comprehend. In a glossary, rebuses are shown in the order in which they appear in the story, and then, for the girl or boy who needs no pictures, a final version appears with words only. One activity is making original rebuses to count. 1–2.

Features: numeric narrative with rebuses.

Allbright, Viv. *Ten Go Hopping*. Illustrated by the author. New York: Faber, 1985.

Allbright tells and shows what happens as one little boy goes hopping in this patterned 123 book. Several animals, including a grasshopper and an elephant, accumulate on the pages and begin hopping along behind the boy (*one-more* pattern). Where are they all going in this follow-the-leader game? A final illustration shows them all playing at the beach. Playing follow-the-leader with friends and giving directions out loud gives a girl or boy an opportunity to count friends and to hear directions with spatial relations terms such as *over, under, around,* and others. Pre-1.

Features: *one-more* sequence up to ten, numeric narrative.

Ambler, C. Clifford. *Ten Little Foxhounds*. Illustrated by the author. Chicago: Children's Press, 1968.

Ambler's book offers a review of a *one-less* sequence of numbers. Flowers illustrate the endpapers and give a light touch to the opening where the foxhounds sing a favorite song about the hunt. One by one, the hounds are disturbed, disabled, or distracted in different ways during a fox hunt. For example, one hound gets stuck in the bars of a gate, another is nipped by a fox, and still another is stung by a bee. At last, only one foxhound is left to go home to the kennel while the old fox laughs nearby. Beginning with ten paper shapes of hounds, the young counter may remove them, one by one, as the hounds become unable to continue their hunt. Pre-K.

Features: *one-less* sequence from ten down to one, rhymes.

Annette. *La Ratita Mili y los Numeros* (Little Mouse Mili and Numbers). Illustrated by Annette. Barcelona, Spain: Editorial Molino, 1986.

A little mouse introduces children to numbers of objects in an attractive board book. There are cut-outs for windows. The cut-outs are placed carefully so one can see Mili la ratita, and her friends as counting moves from one to ten. This format provides a model for illustrations in an original number book. Pre-2.

Features: increasing numbers of objects from one through ten, die-cut openings, and object recognition.

Baby Bear Learns Numbers. Illustrated. New York: Derrydale/Crown, 1988.

On sturdy pages, one brown baby bear dressed in blue overalls asks a viewer to count objects by the blue pond. Objects pop up on the pages beginning with one green frog, two ducks swiming, and continuing with three brown rabbits jumping high, four baby birds, and five dancing butterflies. Numerals are in bold type near the objects and the object words are read in lowercase letters. Pre.

Features: numbers up to five, numerals in bold type, object words in lowercase letters, and pop-up objects.

Baby's First Counting Book. Illustrated. Bronx, N.Y.: Platt and Munk, n.d.

This teddy board book offers red, blue, and green numerals and words in capitals to support number and object identification. From one pony and two calves to nine little chicks who look for caterpillars and ten rabbits who eat carrots and cabbages, these illustrations are just the right size and weight for a "first" book for a young boy or girl. Some children may be familiar with other small books that offer object identification such as the *Animal Counting Book* (Japan: Froebel-Kan; distributed by Heian Intl., n.d.) or Scott Sullivan's *Hello Kitty Can Count* (New York: Random House, 1982). Both are animal counting books showing numerals. Pre.

Features: numerals, number words in capitals, and objects up to ten.

Baker, Jeannie. *One Hungry Spider*. Photography by Paul Melchert and David Blackwell. London: Andre Deutsch, 1982.

With research assistance by the Australian Museum in Sydney, Baker offers collage arrangements to show one hungry spider. Full-color illustrations on the recto pages are balanced with short phrases on verso pages. Large gray numerals are in the corners. Phrases offer the number words for the numerals, which reinforce the illustrations: one spider spins a web between two branches, three birds fly by, and four grasshoppers jump along. The numbers increase as five dragonflies appear, six spiderlings are carried on a breeze, and seven ladybirds (bugs) fly high. Along with the counting of eight butterflies who flutter, nine wasps who hum, and ten noisy flies who buzz, a reader discovers information about how a spider hides from birds and wasps and how insects break or tear a spider's web. Food for the hungry spider may be spiderlings and flies but not ladybird bugs (the spider dislikes their taste). From the two pages of information at the end of the book, a boy or girl learns the name of this particular spider, orbweb eriophora, reads of the spider's sense of touch, and hears about the spider's recycling ability (e.g., eating an old web before spinning a new one). For one activity, a web is drawn on gray felt. Puff balls or cotton (or pieces) may be placed on the web to show egg clusters of spiders and to be counted. For older girls and boys, one activity to consider is the "Number Sentence Mix-Up." Written separately on strips of paper, several sentences with number words from *One Hungry Spider* may be placed out of order on an expandable stretchy "web" (available in toy stores at Halloween) and a reader asked to read and rearrange the sentences so the number sequence is from one up to ten. A web mobile may be suspended above each table or desk area in a classroom and readers invited to stand to read the sentences on the mobile in sequence. K-2.

Features: numeric information, oversize numerals, number words in phrases from one up to ten.

Becker, John. *Seven Little Rabbits*. Illustrated by Barbara Cooney. New York: Walker, 1973.

Walking to visit their friend, Toad, seven little rabbits become weary and interrupt their walk along the road. The rabbits return, one by one, to rest at Mole's house and to demonstrate the *one-less* sequence. On their way, the traveling rabbits pick flowers, enjoy a picnic lunch of carrot sandwiches and carrot juice, and munch chocolate cookies. With Becker's words, the listener hears anaphoric beginnings for the repetitive lines. Seeing Cooney's illustrations of the seven little rabbits asleep in Mole's big bed may interest some girls and boys in telling a story about the picture. To help develop a short story about the picture, one kindergarten teacher distributes seven math counters to each girl and boy. Using one hand to represent Mole's house, each student puts the appropriate number of counters into Mole's house each time that a friend identifies a number from one up to seven and tells his or her own version of a short number story about the rabbits. For preschoolers, kindergarteners, and first graders, foods enjoyed by the seven little rabbits may be tasted and the results of the taste test recorded on a picture graph. One teacher serves tiny sandwiches of wheat bread and carrots, tiny cups of juice, and tiny bits of chocolate cookies to each student. Each one decides which of the foods he or she likes best, draws a small square picture of it, signs the picture, and attaches the small square in the proper column or row on a large graph, so that each individual decision is counted. Row or column headings are labeled: carrot sandwiches; juice; chocolate cookies. The students discuss what information the graph gives them. Each student, in turn, gives one fact (not previously mentioned by someone else) discovered from the graph. Recommended. 1–2.

Features: numeric narrative in rhyme, *one-less* sequence from seven down to one.

Berenstain, Stanley and Janice Berenstain. *Bears on Wheels*. Illustrated by the authors. New York: Random House, 1969.

How many bears are on wheels in this number book? First a viewer counts one bear on one wheel, a unicycle. As the pages are turned, one sees more bears to count on the unicycle. Then another variable is introduced as the number of wheels increase. There are two bears on two wheels, one bear on three wheels, and finally, ten bears on one wheel. Does anyone think that ten bears is too many bears on wheels (cause and effect)? What might happen? What prediction will be made? What has happened when the page is turned and the viewer sees four bears no longer riding on any wheels? Some boys and girls may want to count the bears and wheels again in projected pictures of this book from the filmstrip/cassette version from Random House School Division, Department 9260, 400 Hahn Road, Westminster, Md, 21157. Young children may enjoy drawing pictures of something with wheels and categorizing the pictures into a two-column graph: wheels for work (1) and wheels for play (2). Discussion is needed about what the graph tells about wheels. Pre-2.

Features: accumulation from one up to ten, cause/effect, prediction.

Berenstain, Stanley and Janice Berenstain. *The Berenstain Bears' Counting Book*. Illustrated by the authors. New York: Random House, 1976.

Fans of the Berenstain Bears will follow along and begin to count as one brown bear skates on the ice and two bears glide along. The counting continues up to ten with the ice skating antics of the bears. Each bear does something different. A young viewer may identify the bears by the numerals worn on their sweaters. Which bear is reading a *How-to-Skate* book while skating? Which bear is playing hockey? Playing leapfrog? Spinning? Cutting a figure eight in the ice? Falling down? Building a pyramid? Drinking hot cocoa? The illustrations show the bears colorfully dressed with hats, scarves, and, of course, large numerals are seen on their brightly colored, warm, winter pullovers (use of numerals). The distance skated by the bears may be measured with nonstandardized units, such as cut lengths of yarn, when the distance is represented by a bold curving line that turns (and turns again) on a chart. An interested girl or boy lays the yarn lengths along the line to see how many yarn lengths the bears skated (nonstandardized measurement). Different lines to represent different skating patterns of the bears may be presented on other large charts and measured. Sums of these measurements with the yarn lengths may be recorded on the back of the chart along with the names of the girls and boys who did the measuring. Pre-1.

Features: *one-more* sequence from one up to ten, uses of numerals.

Blum, Rochelle. *The Chipmunks' Counting Book*. Illustrated by Corny Cole and Jean Paynter. New York: Random House, 1984.

Alvin, Simon, and Theodore, the three well-known chipmunks, decide to clean up their messy room. During this clean-up, the chipmunks discover many lost items. First, they find one electric guitar and two drums and then stop counting after locating nine Christmas tree ornaments and ten marbles. All of the lost items are isolated at the heads of the pages in the order in which they were found. This arrangement makes the objects easy to identify and to count (one-to-one correspondence). Most young children will be attracted by the cover of this Cuddle-Shape Book which shows the chipmunks holding the *123* numerals along with a ball, bat, and block. At home, the beginning counter may identify numbers of objects picked up when keeping a room neat, when cleaning up, or looking for "lost" items. Pre-K.

Features: one-to-one correspondence, accumulation from one up to ten.

Boon, Emilie. *123 How Many Animals Can You See?* Illustrated by the author. New York: Watts/Orchard Books, 1987.

Animals go off to school across the countryside in this one. Rabbit, with his book bag, meets his friends (fox, duck, owl, deer, squirrel), and the counting begins. As each animal friend is met by Rabbit, the young listener may participate in chanting the predictable text. For instance, when Porcupine is met, the words are: "*Porcupine joins in. I see*——— (listener supplies the number word)." Oversize, colorful numerals from 1 up to 10 are found on each page. Each additional animal may encourage this chant: "Who joins in? I see two. Who joins in? I see three" (repetitive pattern). In the jacket illustration, a teaching bear is surrounded by the animal students. The bear is reading aloud a copy of *123 How Many Animals Can You See?* with its cover identical to the book the child is holding (replication). Teacher Bear counts the members of the class and uses vertical notation on the chalkboard as the animals sit on a log in front of the board. For a review, the final pages show each animal again standing near or behind one of the colorful numerals. Young girls and boys should like this one with its crayon and gouache illustrations of the accumulating animals in the forest: the bear, porcupine, and others (identifying objects). Is someone ready to distinguish between farmyard and forest animals (classifying)? What other animals could be named to go to animal school? Pre-1.

Features: *one-more* sequence from one through ten, predictable text, refrain, and oversize numerals.

Bridgman, Elizabeth. *All the Little Bunnies.* Illustrated by the author. New York: Atheneum, 1977.

All the Little Bunnies, a Margaret K. McElderry book, is a 123 account in rhyme. A boy or girl counts along as the little bunnies dress, scrub their dinner plates, and go out to play. From an early morning activity when one bunny blows her nose to a nighttime scene when another puts out the light and says goodnight, these illustrations help a young girl or boy recognize numbers in things around them, to count up to ten (*one-more* sequence), and then count back to one again in a descending order (*one-less* sequence). After reviewing the black and white illustrations with the touches of yellow which highlight the daily activities of the bunnies, one teacher in kindergarten places rabbit shapes, cut from felt, on a felt board in groups and then invites the children to count along. The counting is done solo, in groups of two, groups of three, and so on until all of the girls and boys are counting. For a future review, the teacher considers the big-book version available from Scholastic Book Services, 50 W. 44th St., New York, New York 10036. Pre-K.

Features: *one-more* and *one-less* sequence up to ten and back to one.

Bridwell, Norman. *Count on Clifford.* Illustrated by the author. New York: Scholastic, 1985.

With Clifford's help, a young listener counts up to ten in this book. In this presentation, Clifford is so big he is able to become an umbrella for his friends while he teaches them to count up to ten (accumulation). Which listener would like to talk about having a pet as special as Clifford, the enormous red dog? Big, warm, and lovable, Clifford always tries to do the right thing. The colors are bright, the drawings are realistic, big red Clifford is seen clearly, and the text is easy to read. Colorful oversize numerals (red like Clifford) may be selected and placed by identified numbers of things at home or in the classroom. K-3.

Features: *one-more* sequence up to ten, cardinal number identification.

Bruna, Dick. *Poppy Pig Goes to Market.* Illustrated by the author. Montclair, N.J.: International Playthings/Methuen,1981.

Poppy the pig gets up early so she can go to the market. At the market, Poppy buys cherries and then calls a friend to help eat them. Both enjoy the taste of the cherries and decide to save eight of them to wear as earrings. They use the stones for counting rhymes. Does anyone know the words to "Counting Cherries," a traditional counting rhyme? Number words are emphasized: "One, two, three, and four, /Mary's at the cottage door. / Five, six, seven, eight, /Eating cherries on a plate." Substituting Poppy's name (and then listener's name) for Mary's can be made. A natural extension for a girl or boy is tasting cherries, saving the stones, arranging them into groups, counting, and chanting the rhyme. Pre-1.

Features: numeric narrative and counting objects from one up to eight.

Bucknall, Caroline. *One Bear All Alone.* Illustrated by the author. New York: Dial, 1986.

Bucknall's teddy bear is home and alone. When two more bears come to play, some fun begins with increasing numbers of bears. Three bears take a train ride, four visit the zoo, and five climb a tree. Worn out from the hard work of playing all day, the bears return home where nine bears take a bath, and ten snuggle in their beds for the night (concept of *one-more-than*). The episodes are introduced with bright numerals, told in rhyme, and have attractive watercolor illustrations. Cut-out brown paper shapes of teddy bears pasted on tongue depressors and held by ten young volunteers may be used to portray this accumulation as the rhyme is repeated. Hidden behind each child's back, each bear makes an appearance at the appropriate place in the rhyme. Pre-2.

Features: original numeric rhymes for *one-more* sequence up to ten, cardinal number identification.

Burningham, John. *Pigs Plus: Learning Addition.* Illustrated by the author. New York: Viking, 1983.

A young boy or girl may need to be shown how to open and arrange the format of this book. The long unfolding frieze is to pulled from left to right in front of the viewer. Beginning on the left, the first illustration with *1* is read. Then, taking the foot of the page and lifting it up to look at the next illustration, one sees the action and accompanying math symbols. One pig in a red car is stuck, so another pig helps, pushes the car, and gets in to ride along. The symbols show + 1 and = 2. What prediction can be made about what might happen further? With two pigs in the car, the car gets a flat tire and a helpful mechanic pig comes along to repair it, making three pigs in the car. Young pig meets a succession of difficulties but in every situation, another pig helps him out of the difficulty (cause and effect) and joins in to make it fun. When steam boils out of the hood, they stop, and a friendly farmer pig pours in water from his watering can. Now, with four pigs in the car, the car tips over and all tumble out onto the neaby grass. One big, strong pig lifts the car, rights it, and gets in to ride, too, but as they continue the ride, their weight causes the car to fall apart! All walk away in a single line having shown the simple relationships of numbers (addition) in this humorous story. With cut-shapes of cars from art paper, a young counter may use a paper punch to show Burningham's relationships of numbers. To represent two pigs getting into the car, a volunteer punches one hole for one pig and a second hole for the second pig. If ready developmentally, the volunteer may write the number sentence under the punches: 1 + 1 = 2. To show commutativity, the volunteer turns the shape over, sees the punches again, and writes the second sentence for the punches. After writing the second sentence for 2 pigs + 1 pig = 3 pigs, and turning the shape over, one can will see that the punches are arranged in the order of 1 + 2 (commutativity). There are more books to consider in this Number Play series published by Viking (1983): *Five Down: Numbers as Sizes; Count Up: Learning Sets* (various animals are counted as one lifts flaps on pages); *Just Cats: Learning Groups;* and *Read One: Numbers as Words.* In all of these, Burningham's people and animals are colorful and found in attractive illustrations on heavy cardboard pages that fold out from side to side as well as up and down. Recommended. Pre-K.

Features: wordless, *one-more* sequence from one up to five, symbols for addition, and fold-out pages.

Butler, M. Christina. *Too Many Eggs: A Counting Book.* Illustrated by Meg Rutherford. Boston: David R. Godine, 1988.

Upon opening the book, a viewer finds two pages of die-cut eggs and directions to place all the eggs from one sheet into the basket inside the cupboard at the back of the book before reading the story. The viewer turns to the back and places the eggs inside a large basket behind the paper-flap doors of a large cupboard. Beginning the story, Mrs. Bear is making a cake for Mr. Bear's birthday. She collects all the ingredients except the eggs and she mixes together sugar, butter, honey, and flour. Is it too much or too little? Mrs. Bear does not know the answer because she cannot count. She takes six eggs out of the cupboard (a reader may go to the back of the book and get six eggs from the basket inside the cupboard and put them into a bowl on the page). Numerals 1 through 6 are shown. Next, Mrs. Bear puts five eggs into the mixing bowl (a young counter may get five eggs to place in the bowl and see numerals 1 through 5). Then, thinking she has forgotten the eggs, Mrs. Bear puts nine eggs into the mixing bowl (the eggs may be counted into the bowl as the numerals 1 through 9 are seen). Rabbit stops by and asks Mrs. Bear, "What are you doing today?" When Mrs. Bear replies that she is baking a cake, Rabbit runs away to spread the word to badger, owl, squirrel, fox, and the ducks. While the cake is baking, Mrs. Bear falls asleep and the cake begins rising. It rises up through the kitchen door, out of the house and down the hill. The animals follow the cake and find Mr. Bear, who is surprised when he sees his birthday cake flowing downhill. With plenty of cake for everyone, all the animals join in Mr. Bear's birthday celebration on the hillside. Mr. Bear thanks Mrs. Bear, mentions she must have used a lot of eggs for such a big cake, and hears Mrs. Bear say she used *only six*. A young counter is asked to collect all of the paper eggs from the bowls on the pages and to count them again to find out how many eggs Mrs. Bear *really* used. K-1.

Features: number narrative, numerals 1 through 9, die-cut eggs to move, place, and count.

Calmenson, Stephanie. *One Little Monkey.* Illustrated by Ellen Appleby. New York: Parents Magazine Press, 1982.

In rhyming lines, a listener hears Calmenson's story of one little monkey who is stung by a bee and then is followed by increasing numbers of animals who all think that hunters are after them. Seeing the monkey run by, two hippos sense there is trouble and start to run. The zebras follow, then the antelopes, and then the lions (accumulation). When the ten tigers stop playing leapfrog to run along, all follow the monkey to the water's edge where he sits down and puts his tail into the cooling water to soothe the burn of the sting. Standing up to talk to the animals, the monkey begins to explain what happened to him when the second ending in the story takes place: another bee (or is it the same one?) stings the monkey again—the beginning for a second counting adventure for the viewer to continue in this jungle setting. K-2.

Features: numeric narrative with rhymes about accumulating animals from one through ten.

Carle, Eric. *The Rooster Who Set Out to See the World.* Illustrated by the author. New York: Collins, 1968.

A child's first glimpse at Carle's endpapers will introduce the shapes of the animal characters who appear in the story. One rooster gathers together groups of animals (accumulation) to explore the world. After exploring for one long day through the large, colorful illustrations, the animals are hungry and cold by nightfall. The animals want food and shelter, and each group of animals decides to return home. Five fish swim and four turtles crawl down the road; three frogs jump away and two cats leave for an unfinished meal. The homesick rooster is left all alone to return home to eat, to sleep, and to dream of another trip—a trip around the world. Silhouettes of the animals are isolated in the corners. As the animals first join the rooster, group by group (*one-more-than* pattern), to begin their adventures, a young viewer can match the animals to their silhouettes and add the number of shapes that are shown in the upper right-hand corner of each page (one-to-one correspondence). Recognizing the animal shapes and counting the shapes will answer the question, "How many?" Then as the animals leave the rooster to return home, a girl or boy may count the shapes again to see how many are leaving and how many are left (*one-less-than* sequence). Carle's artistic techniques and the way he composed his illustrations may be discussed if anyone is interested. If a budding young illustrator appreciates Carle's illustrations, the girl or boy may want to work on original illustrations just as Carle worked. Tissue paper, tracing paper, or onionskin paper may be painted and then glued or pasted into arrangements of numbers of things. The beginning artist may explore the use of other textured papers: aluminum foil, clear plastic wrap, corrugated cardboard, paper toweling, pieces from paper cups or plates, and table napkins. Then, using colored crayons, colored pencils, markers, or watercolors with brushes, the artist may add additional details to the pasted arrangements just as Carle did to make his illustrations. Recommended. K-2.

Features: *one-more* and *one-less* sequences up to five and back to one, accumulation, and one-to-one correspondence.

Carle, Eric. *The Very Hungry Caterpillar*. Illustrated by the author. New York: Thomas Y. Crowell, 1970.

Some young girls and boys may enjoy this story whether or not they are interested in math as Carle's metamorphic insect helps youngsters recognize several concepts. There is counting in sequence, recalling the names of the days of the week, reviewing the life cycle of a butterfly, and recognizing repetitive sentence patterns. First, a youngster counts along as the caterpillar eats one apple, two pears, and more, and then reviews the days of the week as these meals take place on Monday, Tuesday, and so on. Third, a boy and girl sees an insect's life cycle beginning with a small egg and continuing through the caterpillar's shape to the final gorgeous butterfly. Next, the listener hears similar sentence patterns that identify each day of the week and a number of fruits (concept of groups or sets) that are eaten. If interested, a boy or girl may be introduced to the composition of the illustrations. Cut-out openings in the fruit, showing fruit eaten by the caterpillar, help emphasize the meaning of *hungry*. If interested, a girl or boy may draw large pictures of fruit, cut out the shapes, and use a paper punch to punch one bite (hole) out of the first fruit drawn, punch two bites out of the second fruit drawn, and so on. Fruits may be glued in order from one bite to ten bites to show sequence on a paper strip. Recommended. K-2.

Features: sequences of days of week, *one-more* pattern, identification of fruit, and cycle of catepillar to butterfly.

Carter, David A. *How Many Bugs in a Box? A Pop-Up Counting Book*. Illustrated by the author. Design by Intervisual Communications. New York: Simon and Schuster, 1988.

On the verso pages are the questions (e.g., "How many bugs in a red box?") and on the recto pages are flaps where one finds the answers along with boxes of bugs to count, one up to ten. The pattern of numeral-adjective-name of bug is behind each flap. Numerals are in the left corners of pages to show the number of comical bugs as they run, eat, and swim. To begin, one reads about one tough bug in a red box who lifts weights, two purple dot lady bugs in a polka dot box, and three pretty bugs in a tall box. Other bugs to discuss are the fast fleas in a small yellow box (they are so fast that they move out of sight when the flap is pulled). Mellow yellow fish bugs swim, a red monster bug lurks, and hungry frog bugs snap their tongues at the same fly. Recognizing the sequence, does anyone want to predict how many bugs can be found in a floating box? Or how many bugs in the square orange box? In one box are eight twisted noodle bugs: however, the twisted arrangement may make counting difficult for some children. Carter's collection concludes with ten sawbugs who have sawblades extending out of the board sides of a wooden box. On this box is a warning: "Open if you dare and don't let them out!" To review with an overhead projector, an outline of a large box may be drawn on a transparency. A single die (or dice), when rolled, may determine the number of bugs to collect together and show on the overhead. Dry beans of different shapes (large lima, small navy, pinto) may represent groups of bugs, be placed in the outlined box on the transparency, and counted. If interested, a young reader may replicate the number in each group for a page in an individual miniature book about bugs or continue the pattern of numeral-adjective-name of comical bugs beyond ten for original number book pages. Pre-2.

Features: *one-more* pattern with numeral-adjective-nonsense name of fanciful bugs from one up to ten.

Charles, Donald. *Count on Calico Cat*. Illustrated by the author. Chicago: Children's Press, 1974.

Wearing a bright red polka-dot neckerchief, an orange cat displays a numeral chart that shows 1 to 10 in this book and in the Spanish version, *Cuenta con Gato Galano*. Calico Cat and his friends show boys and girls some of the humorous activities that they like. The animals present the number-numeral relationships as familiar objects to be counted. For example, young viewers enjoy seeing Calico Cat try on six shoes. The shoes are discrete objects to recognize, count, and describe: one blue tennis shoe; a purple high-heel shoe; brown walking shoes; and one red boot. What other shoes can be named? If children are willing to take off one shoe each, the shoes may be placed in the center of a circle of students. Using a large plastic sheet as a graph, the teacher may elicit discussion of the shoes and headings to be used for classifying them. After writing the agreed upon headings for categorizing the shoes, the teacher invites each student, in turn, to place a shoe in the proper place on the floor graph. Later, each listener may draw a favorite pair of shoes on a small square of paper and sign the drawing. Squares may be classified on a classroom wall graph and pasted under headings that identify shoes classified as to color, function of work or play, laced or unlaced, and so on. Further discussion may center on the information gained from the graph. Pre-K.

Features: number-numeral relationships and familiar objects to count and categorize from one through ten.

Cheney, Janet. *1 Nose, 10 Toes.* Illustrated by Art Seiden. New York: Grosset and Dunlap, 1981.

A boy or girl opens this small accordion-stretch book to read that everyone has a nose. The words are from a small brown mouse and are found in a word balloon. The mouse can be seen on every page as the animals are counted and the corresponding numerals are seen. The mouse's final comment about seeing ten toes ends the counting activity. If there is interest, a child's original accordion book is easily made. With a strip of paper, approximately three inches by eighteen inches, a youngster creates back-and-forth folds along the strip to make pages to show the writing of numerals and the drawings of numbers of objects from one up to ten. Pre-K.

Features: dialogue in word balloons, numerals, numbers of familiar objects to be counted from one through ten.

Cleveland, David. *The April Rabbits.* Illustrated by Nurit Karlin. New York: Coward, McCann and Geoghegan, 1978.

In this joint effort by Cleveland and Karlin, the days of April are presented as ordinals. The first day, April Fool's Day, begins Robert's fantasy. Each subsequent day, Robert sees an increasing number of rabbits in Karlin's black and white illustrations (use of ordinals). From the first day of the month and his first sighting of one rabbit to the twenty-ninth day when twenty-nine rabbits depart with their suitcases, Robert notices rabbits everywhere. The rabbits tap dance, paddle a canoe, and race by on skateboards. On the last day of April, Robert notices that the rabbits are all gone. Is it possible that his fantasy has ended now that April is over? Does someone notice that in a final illustration one hippopotamus has followed Robert home? What prediction will be made about what happens to Robert and the hippopotamus in May? Which girl or boy is ready to use this event as a beginning for an original story of ordinals for another month? Who is ready to count the days of the current month with ordinal numbers? To review, each student may be given an ordinal card with both the ordinal word and ordinal number on it. Each may draw one rabbit on the card. If desired, cotton puff balls may be added to give texture and three dimensions to the drawing. As the ordinals are chanted aloud together, the student with the appropriate card takes his or her proper place in a position sequence in front of the room. Ordinal cards may be kept to order sequence during other times, e.g., taking proper places for going outside for recess, for lining up as teams, for dismissal for physical education activities, lunch, and departure for home. Recommended. Pre-2.

Features: numeric narrative and ordinal number identification.

Cole, Joanna. *Animal Sleepyheads: 1 to 10.* Illustrated by Jeni Bassett. New York: Scholastic, 1988.

Cole, author of several children's books, and Bassett, artist of another 123 book mentioned in this bibliography, *Bunches and Bunches of Bunnies*, offer the answer to the question, "Who is sleepy?" Just about every animal in this book is sleepy as Mama Koala reads to her baby koala and says the nighttime rhyme about the animals going to bed. Mama Koala begins with the words about one sleepy bunny who is curled up, warm and snug. The oversize numeral is on one page and the sleeping animal on the facing page. Next, a young listener, and baby koala, see two sleepy puppies dreaming on a rug. Mama continues through the number words as the full-color illustrations show increasing numbers of animals (including six mother kangaroos—some wearing hats and others wearing scarves—all hopping with sleepy joeys in their pouches). Seeing ten sleepy mice all squeezed into one bed, the young viewer finds baby koala fast asleep, too. Baby koala is snuggled under a blanket with his head on a pillow and holds a toy stuffed koala bear. Cole's ending tells the viewer to "Count them all, now close your eyes. Sweet dreams, you sleepyhead!" The similar beginnings provide a predictable chant with the words, "one sleepy bunny, two sleepy puppies," and so on. When the last word in each rhyme is covered, one may predict the needed word, remove the cover, and be assured of the word Cole used. Borders have patterns of numbers. Does any young viewer have difficulty counting for the number six? Adult guidance may be needed to point out the two groups of six: six mother kangaroos as well as the six sleeping joeys. Pre-1.

Features: number words in rhyming lines about accumulating sleepy animals from one up to ten.

Corey, Dorothy. *Will It Ever Be My Birthday?* Illustrated by Eileen Christelow. Chicago: Albert Whitman, 1986.

So anxious for his birthday to arrive that he does not enjoy the parties of others, Rabbit counts the months until his birthday arrives. Not originally designed as a counting book, this one shows number use in the story line. While he waits, Rabbit reluctantly attends birthday parties of friends through the year, including the bears' party with ice skating and honey cake to eat. In October, Rabbit finally has his own party with the words, "Everybody else can have a party now, I had mine." Looking at a calendar with an adult, a youngster may recognize the use of numbers in counting days left in the month before a birthday (or another special day) or in counting the months left until a birthday month. Pre-1.

Features: use of numbers in narrative, counting days, and months of year.

Crowther, Robert. *The Most Amazing Hide-and-Seek Counting Book*. Illustrated by the author. Paper engineering by Kestrel Books. New York: Viking, 1981.

Crowther introduces children to a hide-and-seek approach to numbers and numerals. From one to twenty, some objects cover (or hide) the next sequential number of objects that the boys and girls will want to find. For example, an interested viewer lifts one mushroom to see two black spiders. Three stones are moved to find four snails—big ones and little ones. Another viewer peeks under five lily pads and sees six goldfish. At twenty, counting by tens begins with groups of ants, beetles, caterpillars, and grasshoppers to count. On the last large page, one hundred creatures are found in a final pop-up culmination. A chanting game may take place as the number of hidden animals and insects are recognized. As the paper-engineered object is moved, a boy or girl says the words, "I'll move one mushroom and then I'll see . . . two black spiders hiding from me" or "I'll move three stones and then I'll see . . . four slow snails hiding from me." 1–2.

Features: accumulating objects, *one-more* sequence up to twenty, and *ten-more* sequence to one hundred.

Cushman, Doug. *The Pudgy Fingers Counting Book*. Illustrated by the author. New York: Random House, 1981.

Shaped like a small hand, these seventeen thick pages invite a young viewer to get ready for a party. Pudgy dogs wrap presents, tie ribbons on the packages, and paint a "Happy Birthday" sign. Wearing sweaters with the numerals 1 through 10, these pudgies accumulate with each page. On the last double-page spread, a young counter sees and counts ten fingers. Each finger holds a finger puppet that represents one of the colorful pudgie dogs (one-to-one correspondence). In a playful game, the child's fingers may be called pudgy dogs and counted several times as a different number of fingers are shown. If interested, one may sing Cushman's words of "One little, two little, three little pudgy dogs . . ." to the tune of "Ten Little Indians." Pre.

Features: *one-more* sequence up to ten, numeral recognition, one-to-one correspondence, and use of numerals.

Cutler, Ebbitt. *If I Were a Cat I Would Sit in a Tree.* Illustrated by Rist Arnold. Montreal: Tundra Books, 1987.

If the young reader pretended to be one cat, or two cats, or three cats, and so on, what would happen? Would an imaginative reader pretend to be one of several lions playing in a cave, cougars tobogganing, or Siamese cats exploring a temple? A girl or boy can count along with the silliness of these colorful, detailed cats as the illustrations show the cats romping in the snow, playing hide-and-seek, and staying up late. These rhythmic verses may be read aloud and the pattern of numerals observed around each of the illustrations. Someone may be interested in dictating an original situation about being a cat or seeing a number of cats doing something silly. Pre-1.

Features: original, humorous, numeric verses about accumulating cats from one through ten, and illustration frames made of numerals.

Davis, Barbara Steincrohn. *Forest Hotel: A Counting Story.* Illustrated by Benvenuti. Racine, Wis.: Golden/Western, 1972.

Into the office of the Forest Hotel clumps a huge hippopotamus who wants a place for ONE (number words in capitals) where he can roll around, and the rabbit clerk takes the hippopotamus to a muddy river in the Forest Hotel. Two brown bears lumber in and request a dark cave for the winter and three woolly lambs bounce in to take a rolling green meadow. In full-color illustrations, the objects are easy to count as four spotted frogs enjoy a peaceful pond with lily pads, five bearded mountain goats roam a high cliff, six penguins find a large chunk of ice on the north side of the forest, and seven chirping birds choose a leafy elm tree. Number words continue in the text as eight furry otters climb a slippery hill, nine busy bees find a beehive in a tree, and ten little rabbits hop home to meet their father, the hotel clerk, and go home to dinner. Repetitive phrases offer the opportunity to join in during the telling of this story. As each animal asks for a place in the Forest Hotel, the rabbit clerk says, "I know just the place." After each group of animals is settled in the hotel, one can repeat the words telling the clerk's return to his office with, "The rabbit hippety-hopped back to his office." A final review page is offered with pictures of the arriving animals in a sequence of groups from one up to ten along with numerals (early experience in reading tables). Girls and boys may think of things that could be found in a forest. They each draw a picture of one of the things they thought about in a forest. One by one, the teacher invites them to come to the front of the class and tell about their picture. The teacher then directs the child to the right side of the room or the left side to stand. Students are invited to identify the two groups the teacher is forming (examples are plants/animals; animals/not animals; alive/not alive). If a student thinks he or she knows the names of the groups, the student gives the teacher a signal (finger on nose, on ear, thumb up, hand on head, etc.) and the teacher chooses that student to tell which group the next child should join. If correct, the teacher knows the student understands the particular classification in use and invites the student to return to the group to allow another one who thinks he or she knows the classification to participate in guessing which group the next child should join. Pre-K.

Features: numeric narrative with accumulating animals one up to ten, repetitive refrain, and a review.

Davis, Jim. *Garfield Counts to 10*. Illustrated by the author. New York: Random House, n.d.

Most children have heard of Garfield, the tubby orange tabby, and his love for lasagne. In this Garfield-shape book, girls and boys follow the cat's activities. For the numbers one through ten, each activity may bring a smile: one rain cloud disturbs Garfield's nap on Monday; Odie chases four sleeping mice; and Garfield counts six pooky bears in his sleep. For the number ten, Garfield eats ten pans of his favorite food—lasagne. Comic strips of Garfield may be distributed and objects found in the illustrations counted and discussed to answer the question, "How does Garfied use numbers?" Pre-K.

Features: accumulating numbers of objects from one through ten.

De Brunhoff, Laurent. *Babar's 123*. Illustrated by the author. New York: Random House, 1986.

De Brunhoff's endpapers show elephants wearing numerals 1 to 10 and Babar sends Alexander and Flora out to "count everything" they see to ten. In this oversize book, the elephant children count one bird, two balloons, and three race cars with three sounds of *whoosh* in the text. Numerals are found in page corners along with number words in cursive (script) writing. Counting accumulates in the text with 1, 2 . . . 1, 2, 3 . . .

up to 10. De Brunhoff's book is one of the few that shows what counting out loud looks like in print since the sequence of numbers are written with numerals in the narrative of a text. After ten, the book shows a second ending: twenty elephants. Focusing on this, a review page shows how to count up to twenty. Always showing a group of ten that is recognized easily, the review emphasizes the adding of *one-more* object in this sequence of groups from eleven to twenty elephants. After the review, Babar awards a royal decree to the young viewer who can count to twenty and includes an award on the last page of the book. In groups of two or three, some students may be interested in playing a number game called "Babar's Twenty-One." In this game, twenty-one markers are spilled on the desk top or floor. The object is to collect one, two, or three of the markers during each turn (player's choice), and with individual strategy, to avoid being the player who must pick up the last marker. For fans of Babar, Portal Publishing Company (Corte Madeira, California, 1986) offers a large poster of Babar's numbers that shows the *one-more* sequence from one up to ten. Recommended. K-1.

Features: numerals, number words in cursive, counting in print up to ten, *one-more* sequence from ten up to twenty, and a review.

de Regniers, Beatrice Schenk. *So Many Cats!* Illustrated by Ellen Weiss. New York: Clarion, 1985.

Amusing rhymes, counting, and an accumulating refrain that names the cats as they arrive are found in this book. A young viewer sees objects from a cat's eye view with the help of Weiss's pen-and-ink illustrations. Seeing only the legs and shoes of the members in this family, a young viewer finds out why so many cats live in this house. First, one counts the family's only cat who is sad and lonely. Then other cats arrive. There is a one-eyed fighting cat, two stray cats, a cat who becomes a mother with three kittens, and more, up to the twelve cats the viewer can count on the railing of the staircase (accumulation). Is any girl or boy interested in making the appropriate number of meow sounds (correspondence) for each number of cats as the pages are turned? During a second reading, who is ready to help predict the words in the rhymes (patterns) and chime in during the refrain? *So Many Cats* has been chosen as a Notable Children's Trade Book in the Language Arts. Each year the Notable Trade Books in the Language Arts Committee of the Children's Literature Assembly of the National Council of Teachers of English select books which are outstanding for use in the language arts, K-8. These books are unique in their language style, deal explicitly with language, and invite a listener's participation or response. Recommended. Pre-K.

Features: numeric rhymes about accumulating cats from one through twelve and a predictable refrain.

Dobbs, Siobhan. *Elizabeth Hen.* Illustrated by the author. New York: Joy Street/Little, 1988.

Elizabeth the hen is proud of the egg she has laid and spreads the news to the animals on the farm. First, Elizabeth tells the cow and her two calves, then the sheep and her three lambs and, finally, the rabbit and her ten bunnies. Every animal mother Elizabeth meets has an increasing number of animal babies. When Elizabeth returns to her nest, she finds her egg cracking and rocking, and when her one little chick pops out, she is quite proud. If a young counter wants to see all the baby animals again, one may ask each group to be identified by number (e.g., the ten bunnies, the three lambs, and on down to one). Pre-K.

Features: *one-more* sequence with increasing numbers of baby animals in narrative from one up to ten.

Duvoisin, Roger. *Two Lonely Ducks: A Counting Book.* Illustrated by the author. New York: Knopf, 1955.

In this number book, Duvoisin's ducklings are found on the endpapers and introduce the reader to the duck family. Line drawings have touches of green and yellow and alternate with black and white sketches to show the drake and the duck who want a family of ducklings. Little Mother Duck prepares her nest with twigs, haysticks, and some soft white down. Her eggs accumulate, one by one, until there are ten. Which boy or girl is ready to count the eggs? Duvoisin provides the number words for the numerals. For several days, Mother Duck sits on the eggs. Is one ready to count the number of days Mother Duck protects the eggs? Finally, the ducklings break out of their shells and may be counted. A reader may help Father Drake with the counting to get the number-after sequence of the ducklings (*one-more* sequence), or if interested, may review the ordinals with first, second, third, and on to the tenth, as the ducklings hatch. Recommended. Pre-K.

Features: numerals, *one-more* sequence, number words from one to ten.

Flemming, Denise. *Count in the Dark Glo Worm*. Illustrated by the author. New York: Random House, 1985.

When the light goes off in the child's room, selected items on the pages of this counting book will glow. Treated with nontoxic ink, such things in the illustrations as the full moon, the eyes of an owl, and three lanterns will glow in the dark after the pages have been exposed to light. One may count five candles, seven street lamps, nine shooting stars, and go up to ten glow bugs. Pre-K.

Features: numeric narrative of increasing numbers of glow-in-the-dark objects from one up to ten.

Flynne, Jill O. *Hooray for Counting*. Illustrated by the author. Mahwah, N.J.: Watermill Press, 1987.

Tiny Bear collects things and fills his room. When his sister, Sara Bear, decides to make Tiny Bear's birthday present, she borrows three crayons. Together, Tiny Bear and Sara Bear count the items in the room. A boy or girl reads, counts, and writes numerals in response boxes. If desired, the reader colors the appropriate object e.g., airplane, beach balls, and dogs. In addition, one is asked to locate a numeral, circle it, or find a missing numeral in a row of numerals from 1 to 10. This counting story is one to read and color and ends with a birthday surprise. The surprise is discovered when the reader connects the dots in their order of numerals from 1 to 10 (numeral usage). Anyone who likes Tiny Bear will find him in another book to read and color, *Hooray for Numbers!* Pre.

Features: numerals and numbers of familiar objects from one up to ten with child participating in page activities.

Flynne, Jill O. *Hooray for Numbers*. Illustrated by the author. Mahwah, N.J.: Watermill Press, 1987.

On a stormy day, Tiny Bear cannot play outside with his friends, so he takes a nap, and dreams of numbers of friends: one pink bunny, two orange and brown giraffes, and three blue bears. For each number, the reader is asked to color the numeral, write it, and then trace and copy the written word for the number of objects (written language link to math). From one through ten, the numerals are personified with happy faces. Pre.

Features: numerals-numbers of animals from one up to ten with viewer participating in page activities.

Forte, Imogene. *Beginning Math*. Illustrated by Susan Eaddy. Nashville, Tenn.: Incentive Publishers, 1986.

With this paperback book, a girl or boy looks at personified frogs, colors the numeral shapes, counts frogs, adds spots to frogs to designate numbers, and matches numerals with numbers of objects. Permission is given by the publisher to reproduce these pages for children in a classroom or in a household. K-1.

Features: numerals-numbers relationships, one-to-one correspondence, with child participating in page activities.

Freeman, Don. *Corduroy's Day*. Illustrated by Lisa McCue. Old Greenwich, Conn.: Listening Library, 1986.

Based on Don Freeman's teddy bear character, a bear always dressed in green corduroy overalls fastened with two buttons, this book is entitled *Corduroy's Day*, and is a counting lesson. In each sentence about Corduroy, one sees a numeral from 1 to 10 that represents a number of things Corduroy sees or uses during the day. Corduroy fastens two buttons, eats three things for breakfast (milk, bread, and honey), and finally, counts ten bubbles in the bathtub (*one- more-than* sequence). Corduroy's counting story is available in a sturdy board book format or as a read-along book accompanied by an audio cassette. Large discarded buttons may be grouped and counted by a young girl or boy to review the numbers in Corduroy's day. For instance, during a second reading when the listener hears the words about Corduroy eating three things for breakfast, three buttons may be selected to identify the number three. Buttons may be used in another way—to classify. A young counter is asked to select a favorite button from the collection, count the number of holes in the button, and then find the heading under which to place the button on the sorting board. Pre-K.

Features: numerals-numbers of objects from one up to ten in narrative.

Freschet, Bernice. *The Ants Go Marching*. Illustrated by Stefan Martin. New York: Charles Scribner's Sons, 1973.

Climbing up from a deep, brown underground tunnel, the ants march over sticks, leaves, and someone's foot as the ants head for a nearby picnic. In the text and in the woodcut illustrations, the ants increase the number of their marching formation one by one, two by two, and so on up to ten. Then, in a decreasing sequence, ten by ten and nine by nine, the ants return to their quiet, warm nest in the earth (groups or sets). Figures of these ants in groups are best shown on a felt board and displayed as the rhyme is repeated. One kindergarten teacher sings the words to the tune of "When Johnny Comes Marching Home Again" during a review of the numbers of ants and the kindergarten children quickly join in and sing along. K-1.

Features: accumulating numbers of groups of ants from one up to ten and back to one.

Fujikawa, Gyo. *Can You Count?* Illustrated by the author. New York: Grosset and Dunlap, 1977.

Fujikawa's 123 animal collection is on sturdy, tough pages. Some of the animals are dressed in people's clothing and some are not. Members in each group may be identified. From the monkey in a pink tutu to a bright feathered rooster, a young viewer sees the members in groups of animals from one to ten. To establish one-to-one correspondence, cards with corresponding dots with numbers from one to ten can be selected as each number of animals is seen again on the pages. Pre.

Features: numbers of animals one through ten.

Gai Quiqin. *Little Mole Goes Out for a Walk.* Illustrated by Zhou Xianche. Beijing, People's Republic of China: Zhaohua Publishing House, 1985.

One happy little personified mole wears a dress and carries a basket for a walk in the woods. She sees three little mushrooms, finds four apples, and picks five pretty flowers. Objects are shown out of the usual number sequence from one to ten when, first, two eggs are found in a bird's nest and then six large bunches of ripe grapes are picked. At home, the mole arranges the collected flowers and fruits on a table in groups, while the viewer count everythings the little mole has found. A final review page shows the sequence and enables a counter to recognize numbers of objects in groups. Pre-K.

Features: sequence from one up to six, flowers and fruits in groups to recognize.

Ginsberg, Mirra. *Kitten from 1 to 10*. Illustrated by Giulio Maestro. New York: Crown, 1980.

One white kitten leaves home and meets different groups of animals and objects. After the number in each group is counted (cardinal number identification), perhaps some girls and boys will enjoy miming the actions of the animals they see on the page. Appropriate numeral cards could be displayed before each action: the numeral 3 for chasing three squirrels up a tree; 4 for hissing at four puppies on the floor; 5 for watching five ducklings; and 10 for stalking ten small chicks. All of the listeners may join in with clucking and clacking sounds as Mother Hen gives a warning to the kitten to protect her small chicks. Does anyone predict what the little kitten will do when it hears Mother Hen's warning? For another activity, an adult may draw a long line to show the distance the kitten traveled on one day and then draw a shorter line to show the distance the kitten traveled on a second day. With a cut length of yarn, the girl or boy may measure the length of the lines and announce which line represents the longer walk and the shorter walk. Pre-K.

Features: oversize numerals, number words for increasing numbers of animals from one up to ten.

Gray, Catherine. *One, Two, Three, and Four. No More?* Illustrated by Marissa Moss. Boston: Houghton Mifflin, 1988.

Personified animals introduce the numbers from one up to four and their addition and subtraction combinations. With number words only in the text, one little cat looks for his hat, two bears sit on chairs, and three baby bumblebees are tumbled by a clown's sneeze. For another example, one sees Mr. Frederick J. Fox hanging out his laundry items. Among the items are four tiger-striped socks. In a following illustration, a tiger-striped cat walks on tiptoes away from the laundry line and carries away two of the socks. An accompanying verse tells the young listener that two socks disappeared without a clue. Then, in a combination of words and numerals, the horizontal number sentence is shown: 4 - 2 leaves two. The other numbers to four are introduced in a similar way. Adding begins with rhymes about one clam plus one sister Sue. Subtraction begins with four frogs minus one frog and ends with a goose's two teeth minus one tooth that is loose. Objects to count are easy to see in the full-color illustrations. Pre-2.

Features: rhyming lines, sequence one up to four, addition and subtraction combinations.

Gregorich, Barbara. *Nine Men Chase a Hen.* Illustrated by John Sandford. Grand Haven, Mich.: School Zone, 1984.

In this Start-to-Read book, Gregorich deals episodically with the counting of hens from one up to ten. One hen wants a hat, four get wet, and five write a letter. After nine men chase a hen, the chase reverses, and ten hens chase the men, then they all regroup as friends to pose for a final photograph. Who can count the number of hens in each illustration? Is someone ready to draw pictures of the arrangement of different numbers of hens (matching and comparing groups)? Pre-1.

Features: groups of hens, *one-more* sequence from one through ten.

Gretz, Susanna. *Teddy Bears 1 to 10.* Illustrated by the author. New York: Follett, 1969.

Ten teddy bears are engaged in unusual antics as they move through the numbers from one to ten in Gretz's bright, colorful illustrations. From one brown bear all alone on a white background and two old teddy bears patched with cloth patches and bandages to eight bears at the dyers who want new colors and nine bears who ride the bus, a young viewer sees groups of bears in unusual settings (*one-more-than* pattern). To get ready for a tea party, some bears go in the wash to be cleaned, hang on a clothesline or rest on a warm radiator to dry. Others visit the dry cleaners and ride the moving clothesline in clear, plastic bags. At last, the bears all arrive home in time for tea. With each numeral and number word, the number of bears in a group are seen. One pattern of a teddy bear may be enlarged and then reduced on a copy machine so different sizes of bears are available to be colored. Buttons of different colors and in varying numbers may be placed on some of the bears. Interested girls and boys are asked to first place all the large bears in a set, all bears of the same color in another set (brown bears, red bears), and finally, identify all bears with the same color buttons in still another set. Cards showing one numeral on each card and a second set of cards showing one number word on each card may be matched. Recommended. Pre-1.

Features: numerals, number words, and *one-more* sequence from one up to ten teddy bears.

Gundersheimer, Karen. *123 Play With Me.* Illustrated by the author. New York: Harper and Row, 1984.

Two mice, Minna and Memo, are playing with toys. On one page, Minna holds a card with a numeral on it, and on the facing page Memo plays with the appropriate number of toys beginning with one birthday hat, two puppets, and so on. As the number of toys increase, the previous toys are thrown to one side, giving the viewer an opportunity to review them and to see the accumulation in the illustrations. Pre-K.

Features: numeral-number relationships from one up to ten.

Gustafson, Scott. *Animal Orchestra*. Illustrated by the author. Chicago: Contemporary Books/Calico, 1988.

What would one see in an orchestra made up of ten animal musicians? In this counting book, accumulating animals gather to form this unusual group. Dressed in a tuxedo with a white vest and white bow tie, a long-billed toucan waves a baton and conducts. There are lions, flamingos, and kangaroos; a turtle beats the timpani, while a koala and a peacock play in the horn section. Full-color illustrations make the animals easy to see and count. In a related activity, girls and boys may think about things that make music or musical sounds, and each draw a picture of one of the things. They can take turns showing the drawing, and telling about what was drawn. The teacher thinks of two mystery categories (percussion and wind instruments), and without announcing them, directs each child to stand in one of the teacher's mystery groups with an appropriate drawing. All the girls and boys are invited to guess the teacher's categories. Drawings are added to a bulletin board. Pre-1.

Features: Sequence from one up to ten.

Hague, Kathleen. *Numbears: A Counting Book*. Illustrated by Michael Hague. New York: Holt, Rinehart and Winston, 1986.

For each number, one through twelve, Kathleen Hague writes the rhymes and Michael Hague illustrates the bears and their objects to count. Meghan the bear has just one bear friend—herself. Sam runs into difficulty tying his shoes so he's glad he has only two. At the number ten, Mary sees shapes of ten lambs in the white fluffy clouds overhead. Then, Kevin has eleven wind-up toy bunnies that hop and Heath has twelve balls to hit, to throw, and to kick. One bear pattern may become the shape of numeral-number cards for a matching activity. On one side of the card is the numeral, and on the other side, the appropriate number of dots appear as buttons on the bear's coat. 1–2.

Features: personified bears in rhymes introduce the numbers from one up to twelve.

Hall, Nancy. *Snoopy's 123*. Characters created by Charles Schulz. Background illustrations by Art Ellis and Kim Ellis. Racine, Wis.: Golden/ Western, 1987.

Snoopy puts on his brown scout leader's hat and takes Woodstock and his feathered friends for a hike. One is represented by one small yellow bird, two is for two small yellow birds, and so on up to ten. Woodstock and his friends camp out, build a fire, and rest in their tiny sleeping bags. At the number ten, the birds decrease, one by one, until Snoopy is left alone on the hike. Colorful pages from the comics section may be used to cut out favorite characters from Schulz's comic strip. The characters may be pasted side-by-side to form review charts to show the *one-more* sequence up to ten or the *one-less* sequence with numbers from ten down to one.

Features: numbers from one up to ten and back, numeric narrative about Charles Schulz's characters.

Hargreaves, Roger. *Count Worm*. Illustrated by the author. New York: Grosset and Dunlap, 1982.

Hargreaves, author of *Mr. Bounce's Numbers* (Price/Stern/Sloan, 1981), introduces Count Worm who wears a black top hat in this 123 book. Out for a crawl, Count Worm sees a crying boy who wants to learn to count. Beginning with one nose as the first object to count and the numeral shape of 1, Count Worm bends, twists, and stretches to form the numerals 1 through 9. As the numerals are formed, the boy counts other objects seen on the walk: five fence rails; six clouds; and nine apples (groups or sets). To form the shape of the numeral 10, Count Worm needs some help from a friend, Percy Worm: one forms the shape of the numeral 1 and the other forms the shape of 0. An adult might question: When the numerals 1 and 0 stand together in the illustration, what might be a child's mental construction about the number ten? Is it possible that when seeing the numeral 1 in this situation, a viewer is getting a mental picture of one group of one (instead of one group of ten) and of another group called the empty group? This may be discussed with the beginning counter. For review, one can count numbers of rails, clouds, apples, and other objects. Is someone ready to draw numbers of objects in rows? To compare the rows? Which number in which row is greatest? Adult guidance may be needed. Pipe cleaners representing Count Worm can be twisted and bent into numeral shapes and pasted to charts in the *one-more* sequence (or *one-less* sequence) along with the appropriate number of sketched objects one would see during a walk. Pre-1.

Features: numeric narrative, numerals, recognition of numeral shapes, numbers of objects in environment found from one up to ten.

Hawkins, Colin. *Adding Animals*. Illustrated by the author. New York: Putnam, 1983.

Hawkins, a British illustrator-author, activates animals in number sentences up to five, with objects that move with four-color illustrations, Hawkins aska questions about various humorous animals and situations, such as "How many crows have far to go in a motorcycle?" A tab is pulled and three crows appear in the motorcycle's sidecar to join the one crow riding the motorcycle. The number sentence shows 1 + 3 = 4. For following number sentences, a responding viewer pulls an appropriate tab, is introduced to a visual addition combination, and enjoys an illustrated joke. For a review, girls and boys may use paper strips and paper punches to see commutativity of numbers may be used. As an example, when the first-grade teacher reintroduces the page showing the crows in the sidecar and the 1 + 3 = 4, the students may punch the corresponding holes in paper strips. Seeing one punch on the left side of the strip and three punches on the right side, each may write the appropriate number sentence below the openings: 1 + 3 = 4. Then, turning the strip over, each will see the openings in a different sequence and may write the number sentence for this arrangement of punches: 3 + 1 = 4. 1–2.

Features: paper engineering, humorous math sentences summing to five.

Hawkins, Colin and Jacqui Hawkins. *How Many Are in This Old Car? A Counting Book*. Illustrated by Colin Hawkins. New York: Putnam/Grosset and Dunlap, 1988.

Wearing his driving goggles, one bear begins a drive in his rickety old car. Bear is joined by other animals to count: a hippo, an elephant, and a rhino, which add to four, then other animals: a pelican, an alligator, a dog, and so on through ten. One horse, standing nearby, leads the counting as the animals get into the crowded car. Dialogue in word balloons above the animals leads the story. For example, after seven animals in the car have been identified, the young viewer sees Mrs. Ostrich, all dressed in her finery, run after Bear's car calling," Wait, wait. Let's make it eight." The horse in the background counts aloud and the numeral 8 is seen in the word balloon above the horse's head. The other animals in the car reply to Mrs. Ostrich with rhyming lines. The alligator delivers the opinion, "She's very loud and we're enough of a crowd." Concerned about his overloaded car, the bear cries, "I'll be late and my car's in a state." This is one of the few books that shows the process of counting in the text. Pre-K.

Features: accumulation from one up to ten, rhyming lines, word balloons, humor.

Hefter, Richard. *One Bear, Two Bears: The Strawberry Number Book.* Illustrated by the author. New York: McGraw-Hill, 1980.

Hefter, author-artist of *Lots of Little Bears* (Optimum Res. Inc., 1983) also presents numbers and numerals and bears to young children. Opening the covers to find yellow endpages with colorful red strawberries, a counter may see groups of five on each of six rows. The counting continues as the action begins with one waiter-bear carrying one bowl of soup, two cups of coffee, and other increasing numbers of food items. Outside, the bears walk, skate, ride a unicycle, balance, and fall down. Wearing shirts that display the numerals 1 to 10, the bears jog, charge up a hill, and wait for an arriving bus. In a decreasing sequence from ten down to one, the bears leave the pages. The last bear goes jogging home alone, leaving no bears. Pre-K.

Features: numeral-number relationships, cardinal number identification of bears up to ten, and *one-less* sequence back to zero.

Heuck, Sigrid. *Who Stole the Apples?* Illustrated by the author. New York: Knopf, 1986.

When the apples on a nearby tree disappear, the horse decides to find the thief. Accompanied by a small bear, the horse travels to a seaport where they both board a ship. On the way, increasing numbers of travelers are met by the bear and the horse as they see one chimney sweep, two cows, three dogs, and others. By ship, they travel to a distant sunny land where they meet an elephant and a parrot who tell them the crows stole the apples. Not originally designed as a counting book, Heuck's pages show uses of numbers and rebuses in the story line. Each rebus is different and adds variety and interest to the page. K-2.

Features: rebuses; number use in narrative.

Higgins, Stephanie. *One, Two, Three: A Counting Book.* Illustrated by the author. La Jolla, Cal.: Green Tiger Press, 1983.

These block prints in black and white by Higgins introduce the numerals 1 through 10. Framed in a black border, each print shows the numbers of animals in groups. How many geese are seen? Rabbits? Piglets? There may be a subtle difference in one or more of the animals in some of the groups. For instance, noticing the ears on each one of the four rabbits, isthere something different about the ears on one them? How about the bills on the three ducks? Is one duck's bill different from the other two? What other differences can be found? There is a small version of this counting book to send to a friend, perhaps, in its accompanying red envelope. Bordered in red, the pages show groups of animal from one elephant up to ten piglets. Pre-K.

Features: numerals and numbers of animals one through ten.

Hill, Eric. *Spot Learns to Count.* Illustrated by the author. New York: Putnam Publishing Group, 1983.

Endpapers introduce the numerals; black and white illustrations alternate through the book with full-color pages, as Spot, the friendly puppy, meets a variety of animals to count. This story and others about Spot are seen in a variety of formats. There are lift-the-flap books, color-a-story books, and soft vinyl books that children can put into water (e.g., the water table in preschool, the backyard wading pool, the water sprinkler, the kitchen sink, the bathtub). Pre.

Features: numerals and numbers of animals one up to ten with child participation in page activities.

Hindley, Judy, and Colin King. *The Counting Book.* Illustrated by the authors London: Usborne/Hayes, 1979.

There are lots of details in the illustrations for a young boy or girl to laugh at about the adventures of a cake. Two monkeys steal the cake, three elephants toss it around in the air, and it has many other adventures before twenty children eat it and only crumbs are left. Page corners hold red numerals with corresponding stars to count while humorous sentences are at the foot of pages. There is a final page to review numbers from one up to twenty with objects, red numerals, number words in bold type, and a corresponding number of stars (one-to-one correspondence, place value reinforcement). K-1.

Features: narrative, numerals in red, number words in bold, one-to-one correspondence, and place value reinforcement from one up to twenty.

Holabird, Katharine. *The Little Mouse House 123*. Illustrated by Helen Craig. New York: Little Simon/Simon and Schuster, 1983.

Along with Holabird's telling, Craig presents a detailed picture for each of the numerals, 0 to 12. A few sentences describe something about each numeral and the number it represents. For instance, zero is referred to as *nothing*, the number one as *something single,* and two as *a pair of subjects*. Craig's illustrations are small and some children may find that there is too much to see and count in the pictures. Other girls and boys may have difficulty understanding the concepts of *single* and *pair* as these words ask more than what usually is required of a youngster when counting to twelve (e.g., identify objects, count the number of members in a group, and recognize a corresponding numeral). Familiar objects in the house may be collected and identified as single or as a pair. Adult guidance needed. K-2.

Features: numeric narrative from zero up to twelve, concept words.

Hooks, William, JoAnne Oppenheim, and Betty D. Boegehold. *Read-A-Rebus: Tales and Rhymes in Words and Pictures*. Illustrated by Lynn Munsinger. New York: Random House, 1986.

Pictures appear in place of words to help a young viewer "read." In "The Picnic," a boy or girl sees the animals who gather together for a picnic in the rebuses: a sheep in a jeep; two cows with plows; and three dragons pulling wagons. The rebus phrases are arranged in horizontal fashion from left to right. For instance, to read "one sheep in a jeep," one sees the red oversize numeral 1, a picture of a black and white sheep, the words "in a," and then the picture of the sheep driving the jeep. The rhyming number lines end with eight kangaroos paddling canoes, nine frogs riding on logs, and ten giraffes floating on rafts. In another selection, "Good Night, Me." the reader says goodnight to two ears, two hands, and two feet (use of numbers) and other body parts (nose, mouth, toes) until the words, "Good night, all of me." Pre-K.

Features: numerals from 1 to 10, rebuses, and rhyming lines.

Hopper, Meredith. *Seven Eggs.* Illustrated by Terry McKenna. New York: Harper and Row, 1985.

Certain preschool youngsters and kindergarten children will enjoy seeing one egg after another hatching on successive days of the week. What hatches on Monday? A baby penguin. On Tuesday? A baby crocodile. As each egg hatches, the animals who preceded play together on the pages (accumulation). The animals watch the next egg hatch to see what animal will appear (prediction). When Sunday arrives, the last egg, the seventh, cracks. Will someone make a prediction about what animal might appear? Is anyone surprised when seven chocolate eggs are seen? Is that one chocolate egg for each of the hatched animals? Is there *one more* for the girl or boy who is listening to this story? Who notices that the pages of the book and the flaps become larger and larger with each day of the week (patterns)? Some young artists may want to return to these pastel watercolors for a second time and just enjoy the pictures of the animals in this springtime story. Others may be interested in counting the numbers, in reviewing the ordinals, and in saying the names of the days. Still others will recognize the repeated pattern in the limited words on each page. Ranking this book as "very predictable," Heald-Taylor discusses it in her *Reading Teacher* article about predictable literature selections and activities for language arts Instruction and suggests an accompanying research activity of finding out all one can about one animal which hatches from an egg and making a picture or story chart to show the findings. Pre-1.

Features: numeric narrative, sequence of days of the week, ordinals, and cardinals from one up to seven.

Irons, D. *The Bears' Berries.* Illustrated. Crystal Lake, Ill.: Rigby, 1987.

The Bears' Berries is available in a big-book format, approximately thirteen by seventeen inches, and has double-page spreads. Two panda bears face the problem of dividing up some berries so each will have the same number. Bingo, wearing a hairbow, and Bongo, wearing a bow tie, sit at a table covered with a white tablecloth and divide the juicy red raspberries, so there are two on each plate. The number word, *two*, is shown in bold type, and the words, "Two berries for Bingo Bear. Two berries for Bingo Bear. " A question is asked, "How many are left for each hungry bear?" The illustrations provide the information, for in the grassy background, three red berries are shown on each side of the double-page spread: three on Bingo's side of the table and three on Bongo's. This title is available only in a set with three other titles (all 1987) by Irons that provide early experience in division. *The Pixies' Toyshop* and *Even Steven* are in the section about Monsters and Other Creatures while information about *The Nice Mice* is included in this section. The set contains four copies of each of the titles, teachers' notes, black-line masters, audio tape, and suggested hands-on activities.

Irons, D. *Birds, Birds, Everywhere.* Illustrated. Crystal Lake, Ill.: Rigby, 1987.

In this book, odd and even numbers are found. On the recto pages are odd numbers of animals and on the verso pages are even numbers of animals, all in humorous situations. For example, birds with either bright red feathers or royal blue feathers are having a picnic as the rhyme tells about two birds in the tree and four drinking tea. On the facing page the birds are chasing cats and some are wearing hats. Offering a young reader an opportunity to predict words and to chime in on the reading, one repetitive refrain is seen on every page: "Birds, birds, everywhere." This title is available in a set about addition with three other titles, *What's in the Cupboard?*, *Penny Penquin's Party*, and *Fish for Supper*. In *Penny Penguin's Party*, a young viewer sees objects to count and colors of objects to recognize. A beginning counter may count the red (or green) paper streamers Penny hangs to decorate the room for the party, or identify the penguin-guests who wear purple ties with red and yellow dots or the ones who wear large bright blue bows around their necks. In *Fish for Supper*, two brown bears sit by a stream and fish. Emphasis is on counting by twos and color recognition as Bossy catches two green fish and Bashful catches four red ones. *What's in the Cupboard?* has pages of graduated widths that, when turned, simulate opening the door of the cupboard. Concepts of big and little, along with recognizing colors, and cardinal number identification are presented. For one example, when a girl or boy opens the door, size relationships and color identification are emphasized: two big bones, three little bones, four pink ice cream cones and three yellow cones are seen. 1–3.

Features: rhyming lines, odd and even numbers, counting by twos, color recognition, and concepts of big and little.

Irons, D. *Frog on a Log*. Illustrated. Crystal Lake, Ill.: Rigby, 1987.

In this big-book format, approximately fourteen by seventeen inches, one large green frog tells what he sees around him. To see that multiplication is addition, a young mathematician counts two groups of living things. The number of snails in two groups of four (one group of four on each of two silver pails) are counted for a total of eight snails. Two groups of five brown speckled moths are counted. With one of the groups on each of two speckled cloths hanging on a clothesline, the number of moths sum to ten. Other examples are given (early experience with addition and multiplication). This title is available only in a set with three other titles—*Zany Zoo, Mirror, Mirror,* and *Shoes in Twos* (all 1987). *Zany Zoo* is discussed in a following annotation but the other two titles are described: *Mirror Mirror,* characters hold up objects (one hat, two hands) in front of a mirror and count all the objects (two hats, four hands) they see; in *Shoes in Twos,* there are many pairs of shoes to see and count, informative lines to read about shoes with straps, flaps, or ties, and one repetitive line to chant, "but all shoes come in twos." The pairs of shoes are seen clearly on each page so a viewer easily may count them by twos. The multiplication set contains one big-book copy of *Frog on a Log,* four small copies of each of the other titles, audio tape, black-line masters, suggested hands-on activities, and teachers' notes. 1–3.

Features: counting one up to ten and seeing addition and multiplication.

Irons, D. *The Nice Mice*. Illustrated. Crystal Lake, Ill.: Rigby, 1987

Tossing a red ball over their mouse clothesline to play a game, three mice children wait for Mother to bake cookies. At the front door of the large shoe that serves as their house, Mother Mouse, dressed in a white apron, puts twelve tiny cookies out to cool on the stairs The mice children, now jumping rope with the clothesline, wait while Mother counts the children so all can have a fair share. Pre-1.

Features: numeric narrative, equivalency in groups, and early experience in division.

Irons, D. *Zany Zoo*. Illustrated. Crystal Lake, Ill.: Rigby, 1987.

To emphasize looking at members in two groups, a viewer sees two groups of animals to count on each page. For examples, there are two litters of kittens in two separate groups in a yard and two herds of goats in two boats to count. In *Zany Zoo,* the word zany is repeated, and a viewer sees a close-up of such animals as two herds (four in each herd) of zany goats sail in their purple boats and two litters (three in each litter) of zany kittens look for their woolly mittens. 1–3.

Features: numeric narrative, adding groups for early experience for multiplication.

Johnston, Tony. *Whale Song*. Illustrated by Ed Young. New York: Putnam Publishing Group, 1987.

Johnston's book offers no numerals—only the number words written out in italics. Words mention the behaviors of the whales and discuss numbers from one up to ten. To complement this, Young's illustrations of the large whales in their undersea home are shown in strong blues and greens. However, there is no one-to-one correspondence between Johnston's given numbers and Young's whales on the pages. For example, the page for the number one shows two whales; for the number three, there is only a whale's tail, and on the page for the number seven, there is a mother whale and her calf. Girls and boys may be confused by the inappropriate number of whales to match with a number word. An adult may want to talk about the number of whales that should be shown on the pages and sketch the correct number as each page is turned. How many are needed? For the child who is interested in whales, there is *Whalewatcher*, a quarterly journal of the American Cetacean Society. For more information, write to P.O. Box 2639, San Pedro, California 90731–0943. K-1.

Features: information, number words from one up to ten in italics.

Johnstone, Janet, and Anne Grahame Johnstone. *Ten Little Teddy Bears*. Illustrated by the authors. Newmarket, Eng.: Brimax Books, 1982.

Ten teddy bears fish, then one finds another pond, goes away, and leaves nine in the group. In this *one-less-than* sequence, one bear leaves at the end of each short episode in which the bears wait at the airport, have a party, and camp out. At last, one bear is left behind to play alone on a sandy beach. For Brimax Books with sequences of *one-less- than* and additional illustrations by the Johnstones, see *Ten Little Chicks in the Farmyard* (1976) where the chicks meet a rooster, duck, rabbit and kitten; and *Ten Little Ponies* (n.d.) where pony behaviors are shown: patient, skittish, helpful, and lonely. For the sequence of *one-more-than* from the Johnstones, *Ten Little Rabbits* (n.d.) has numbers that move from one up to ten as one little rabbit is all alone and sad until nine others return. In *Ten Little Dogs* (1979) and *Ten Little Kittens* (1971), as well as in other Brimax titles, the top margins of the pages are cut with index tabs. These tabs show illustrations of the animals in the books and make it easy for one to find a favorite animal, locate a special page, or turn to a selected counting rhyme. Pre-K.

Features: rhyming lines, *one-less* sequence from ten down to one with illustrated index tabs on pages.

Kahn, Peggy. *10 Little Care Bears Counting Book*. Illustrated by Barbi Barto. New York: Random House, 1983.

Barto's small illustrations may encourage a boy or girl to begin a count-down from ten to one. The bears sit down to dine and decrease their group down to one grumpy bear. Kahn's accompanying rhymes may be read aloud. Will someone predict the rhyming words that are needed? After guessing, a young listener may discover the object and its word that completes the rhyme. For example, Birthday Bear plans a treat to bake. What word rhymes with bake? When the cardboard flap is lifted on the picture of the oven, one sees the cake inside. Pre-K.

Features: with page flaps, *one-less* sequence in rhymes about personi-fied bears from ten down to one.

Kapral, Joan. *The Little Lost Bee*. Illustrated by the author. Chicago: Children's Press, 1972.

One lost bee introduces this number story. Bee meets two spiders, three flowers, and so on up through ten. These things all give the little bee directions about how to find the right way back home. Kapral's double-page spreads include the numerals, colorful drawings, and words for the numbers in her story-rhymes. Kapral provides a summary on the last four pages (early experience for reading tables or graphs) with the number of objects beside each number word and its numeral symbol (cardinal number identification) and talks about the relationships of num-bers shown by the sequence of objects (*one-more* pattern). Pre-K.

Features: rhyming narrative with *one-more* sequence of objects found in environment and numerals from 1 up to 10.

Killingback Julia. *One, Two, Three, Go!* Illustrated by the author. New York: Morrow, 1985.

Another book about a busy little bear. A young listener might talk about the objects counted and discuss, "How does counting along with the numbers help this busy bear?" Pre.

Features: increasing numbers from one through ten.

Kitamura, Satoshi. *When Sheep Cannot Sleep: The Counting Book*. Illustrated by the author. New York: Farrar, Straus and Giroux, 1986.

Woolly, a white sheep, goes for a walk when he cannot sleep. He chases one butterfly, finds two sleeping ladybugs, and hears the *Hoo-Hoo* of three owls. Story sentences are found under each full-color illustration of Woolly and the objects he counts. There are no numerals to see in the text, only number words within the story (language link to math). Sometimes the objects may be difficult to identify (e.g., the rungs of the ladder for the number seven and the grasshoppers in the green grass for the number nine may be difficult to see). Outside, Woolly counts the windows of a house, and inside the house, counts the closed doors. The doors lead to rooms where Woolly counts other objects: colored pencils, pictures on a wall, and green peas in a kitchen skillet. On the page showing a large dining table set with plates and surrounded by chairs, Woolly sits alone and eats the peas. Up to this point, each illustration holds a single thing or set to count. Beginning with this illustration of the dining table, there are two groups of objects to count on each page: seventeen chairs and eighteen plates. Later that evening Woolly counts nineteen bubbles in his bathtub and twenty stars from his bedroom window. In bed, in his blue and white striped pajamas, Woolly thinks about twenty-one family members and friends with his eyes closed. Finally, his insomnia is cured and Woolly is asleep, snoring, with 22 Zs in the illustration. A final index offers a chart that shows the colorful numerals to 22 (early experience for reading tables and graphs, recognition of place value), number words, and increasing sequence of objects in groups (relationships between groups or sets). For an older child (age 8–9), this book has some complex pictures that ask boys and girls to visually discriminate, a task that is more difficult than using rote counting skills. 2 up.

Features: number words and objects from one up to twenty-two, with numerals only in review chart.

Kitchen, Bert. *Animal Numbers*. Illustrated by the author. New York: Dial, 1987.

Each animal mother has a numeral, a large black oversize one (seven inches high) which shows the number of babies in her family. Counting begins with one baby kangaroo in the mother's pouch and continues to ten cocker spaniel puppies, and beyond. The numbers increase to seventy-five baby turtles and one hundred tadpoles swimming in the water. All animals are intertwined with the large numerals, and Kitchen asks a viewer to count the babies in each brood. There are clear, warm colors in the illustrations of the animal mothers and babies on these pages including birds, fish, mammals, and reptiles. All, familiar and unfamiliar, are identified with brief and clear informative annotations for each in the back of the book. Included are such facts as: the joey stays in the pouch of a mother kangaroo for 190 days; the female frog lays up to 30,000 eggs in clusters; and the eggs of swans hatch into cygnets. This is a companion book to the author's *Animal Alphabet*. Recommended. Pre-2.

Features: annotated names of animals, oversize numerals from 1 up to 15, then groups of animals to twenty-five, fifty, and one hundred.

Koelling, Caryl. *Cory's Counting Game: Learning Numbers with a Finger Puppet Friend*. Illustrations by Carol Wynne. Los Angeles: Intervisual Communications, 1979.

A girl or boy finds a die-cut hole on the first page and puts a finger through to bring Cory Bird to life as a finger puppet. Using the puppet, a counter touches one nest, two raccoons eating berries, three porcupines, and other animals up to ten. At ten, one may count everything again by using the numeral sequence and the object chart on the final pages. Another friendly bird to help one count, there is *One Happy Little Songbird* (Standard Publishers, 1979) by Neil Rabens. Both of these books are small and are best suited for individual use at home. Pre.

Features: numbers of animals from one through ten, numeral recognition, *one-more* sequence of objects in groups, die-cut openings, and a review.

Kohn, Connie. *An Animal Counting Book*. Illustrated by Nora Sheehan. New York: Dandelion, 1979.

Viewers come along with Michael, Barbara, and David as they count animals in different settings. Michael counts his pets: one dog, two turtles, three cats. Barbara travels to a farm and counts the animals in groups: five sheep, six cows, and twelve frogs. David visits the zoo where the sequence continues with thirteen lions and up to twenty birds. In the text, large black numerals are seen as well as the words for the pets, farm animals, and zoo animals while in Sheehan's clear illustrations, all of the animals are shown in full color. Original drawings of favorite animals may be discussed and classified on a picture graph. K-1.

Features: oversize numerals in black, number words in text, groups of animals to twenty, classification of animals as pets, as farm animals, and as zoo animals.

Kulas, Jim E. *Let's Count All the Animals*. Illustrated by Terry Wickart. Racine, Wis.: Golden/Western, 1979.

If a boy or girl wants more animals to count, there is additional variety on the pages of *Let's Count All the Animals*. This small, easy-to-read volume from the Tell-a-Tale series, has many full-color illustrations, and with similar ones, offers background information to a learner who is interested in classifying animals for picture graphs. K-1.

Features: increasing numbers of animals from one through ten.

Kunnas, Mauri, and Tarja Kunnas. *Ricky, Rocky, and Ringo Count on Pizza*. Illustrated by the authors. Translated from Finnish by Tim Steffa. New York: Crown, 1986.

Ricky the rhino, Rocky the raccoon, and Ringo a magpie, are the heroes of this book with its bright and detailed illustrations. The personi-fied animals make a pizza and use such nonsense ingredients as four buckets of carrots and seven hats with strawberries. Numerals in the scenes reinforce counting skills, while each illustration adds to the non-sense. In one scene Ricky pushes Rocky in a wheelbarrow. Numerals are seen on the objects scattered about in the illustration. The numeral 1 is on a bag of flour, 2 is found on the side of the wheelbarrow, and 8 is on the basket of eggs balanced on Rocky's head. Pre-3.

Features: humorous episodes with numerals in illustrations and num-ber words in text from one through ten.

Leman, Martin. *Ten Cats and Their Tales*. Illustrated by the author. New York: Holt, Rinehart and Winston, 1982.

This book should attract the viewer who likes dark formal backgrounds, distinctive colors, and round quiet cats with striking eyes shown in a variety of poses. Each cat does something different in the scenes: sits on a mat, has a taste for milk, or a taste for the sea, paws at a bee, or jumps on a wall. Some of the cats walk in the park, stalk in the dark, befriend a mouse, and sleep in someone's house. Since there are no numerals or accumulating objects, a counter should know the sequence of the numer-als from 1 to 10 and be ready to turn back to the first illustration of one orange cat sitting on a mat to initiate the counting and to turn other pages to see all the cats as a group of ten in this 1982 Children's Choice book. Pre-1.

Features: single cat per page, number words in rhymes from one up to ten.

LeSieg, Theo. *Ten Apples Up on Top*. Illustrated by Roy McKie. New York: Random House, 1961.

With this counting book, Theo LeSieg gives readers a humorous story in rhyme. A reader looks to find the answer to the question, "How many animals can carry ten apples on their heads?" A tiger, a lion, and a spotted dog try to outdo each other by balancing numbers of apples on their heads, while they skate, climb trees, and play ball. Entering a bear's house, they are chased out by the angry bear waving a broom. Running away, they bump into a large wagon filled with apples and send apples flying everywhere. The scene shows all of them—bear, birds, tiger, lion, and dog—landing in a tangled heap after the crash, and on each animal's head are stacked ten apples. Using a transparency (divided into three columns) on an overhead projector, one teacher begins a pattern of stacking a number of paper shapes of apples on an outline of the tiger's head in one column labeled *Tiger*. Two other columns are labeled *Lion* and *Dog*. Working with sheets divided into columns at their tables, girls and boys match the number of apple shapes on the tiger's head with an equivalent number on the outlined heads of the lion and the dog in the other two columns. Girls and boys may see this entertaining story again with the filmstrip/cassette that is available from Random House or hear the words a second time with the audio cassette that comes with the read-along version. Recommended. Pre-1.

Features: humorous numeric narrative in rhyme from one up to ten.

Lewin, Betsy. *Cat Count*. Illustrated by the author. New York: Dodd, Mead, 1981.

Here are many cats to count—some friends' cats, some relatives' cats, and some cats who are new arrivals. They all find their way to Lewin's crowded double-page spread of fifty-five cats. A viewer may enjoy the cat who plays with a wind-up mouse, one who rides a unicycle, or one who walks a tightrope. Each cat is a lively individual; some are humorous. All are lively. An older girl or boy interested in illustrating an original book might review Lewin's black line drawings. Pre-2.

Features: black and white line drawings, numbers from one up through fifty-five.

Lewin, Betsy. *Hip, Hippo, Hooray!* Illustrated by the author. New York: Dodd, Mead, 1982.

On a hot day in July, one hundred hippos get ready to march, wearing their colorful red uniforms and their high military style hats with plumes (shakos). During this long annual march, the temperature goes higher and higher, and hippos wilt and drop out of the parade. When one hippo on the tuba tuckers out, a viewer sees the math sentence at the foot of the page:100 - 1 = 99 (subtracting relationship). When the twenty hippos who play the spoons leave the parade, a math sentence states: 99 - 20 = 79. Next, the hippo majorettes and the honor guards leave, represented as: 79 -15 = 64. However, the big bass drum is played to the last and that drum-beating hippo receives a hero's cheer! In a first-grade classroom, students may each draw versions of three (or more) different hippos, paste the drawings in the cells of a "One to One Hundred Chart," and take turns recording one numeral on each hippo shape in the sequence from one up to one hundred. Recommended. 1–2.

Features: numeric narrative beginning with one hundred and ending with one, subtraction with two-digit numbers, number sentences.

Leydenfrost, Robert. *Ten Little Elephants: A First Counting Book.* Illustrated by the author. New York: Doubleday, 1975.

The elephants demonstrate the meaning of *one-less-than* as one counts in a sequence from ten down to one. One of ten elephants sees a mouse, the elephant disappears, and this story in rhyme begins with only nine. One by one, the other large elephants disappear from Leydenfrost's cleverly illustrated pages, leaving with numeral 1, a last little elephant with a lonely look. The other elephants return when the little elephant draws nine more elephants to make a sum of ten. Can anyone draw a favorite animal enough times to make a sum of ten? Strips on a duplicated sheet with each one containing ten squares gives a listener an opportunity to recreate this *one-less* sequence, using an inked stamp to make an elephant outline in each of ten squares on the first strip. On the second strip, nine squares are stamped, then eight, and on down to one. 1–2.

Features: rhyming lines, *one-less* sequence from ten down to one, and *one-more* sequence up to ten.

Lloyd, David. *Hello, Goodby.* Illustrated by Louise Voce. New York: Lothrop, Lee and Shepard, 1988.

A preschool boy or girl may enjoy the humorous illustrations in this book while saying hello and goodby to the different animals. One bear begins the number pattern and says hello to a tree. Two bees then say hello to the bear. How many animals will say hello next? There are birds and bugs to count. Will the young viewer be able to predict the next number of animals in this *one-more* sequence? When the rain comes, the animals say goodby. Is there another number pattern to find as they do this? Pre-K.

Features: repetitive words, *one-more* sequence begins with one bear.

Lynn, Sara, and Rosalinda Kightley. *1–2–3*. Illustrated by the author. Boston: Little, Brown, 1986.

On verso pages, a preschooler sees the selected numeral and the appropriate number of dots in the same insert. On recto pages, numbers of farm animals are seen with the number word in bold type below. The numerals and numbers increase from one up to ten. At ten, numbers are seen in descending order with the sequences of numbers in groups (early experience for reading tables and graphs). For a second ending, a final double-page spread shows a barnyard scene and the question, "How many of each sort of animal can you find?" Pre-1.

Features: numerals, number words in bold, classifying, animals in *one-more* sequence up to ten and in *one-less* sequence back to one, and a second ending.

McCue, Dick. *Bunny's Numbers*. Illustrated by Lisa McCue. New York: Simon and Schuster, 1984.

Rhyming lines accompany a bunny's investigation of objects from one watermelon to ten other food items that are good for a bunny to sniff and chew, including two tomatoes, three pumpkins, and four ears of corn. Illustrations of other foods a bunny might like may be found in discarded magazines, newspapers, and grocery market advertisements, and cut out, pasted on art paper, and the rhyming count continued. Pre-K.

Features: food items from one up to ten with rhymes.

McCue, Lisa. *10 Small Puppy Dogs*. Illustrated by the author. New York: Random House, 1987.

Rhymes about numbers of puppies are found in full-color illustrations on board pages in this small book. Beginning with one puppy all alone, two hiding a bone, and up to nine rushing for a meal and ten in their beds, this book shows the numerals, and a *one-more-than* sequence in the activities. Final pages offer a review with phrases and rebuses. The rebuses show additional objects to count—fleas, a dinner bowl, a leash, and flowers dug up by the puppies. Pre-K.

Features: numerals, rhymes from one up to ten, objects associated with puppies in *one-more-than* sequence, and a review with rebuses.

McCully, Emily Arnold. *Picnic*. Illustrated by the author. New York: Harper and Row, 1985.

While not designed as a counting book, McCully's wordless *Picnic* shows the use of numbers to a beginning counter. One bright sunny day, the mouse family gets into a red pickup truck and goes for a ride in the country. How many members are in the family? Who will describe the ride? What happens to one little mouse riding in the back of the truck? Now, how many members are in the mouse family? How many are missing? How was the small mouse found? Is everyone happy when the small mouse is found? How do you know this from the book? A young listener may be invited to tell this story in original words. To visit another mouse family on an outing, see *Ten in a Family* (Knopf, 1960) by Charlotte Steiner. Pre-K.

Features: number use in a wordless book.

Maestro, Betsy, and Giulio Maestro. *Around the Clock with Harriet: A Book about Telling Time*. Illustrated by Giulio Maestro. New York: Crown, 1984.

In bright pictures, Harriet gives a practical lesson in telling time. Harriet the elephant wakes up at eight, breakfasts at nine, plays outside at ten, and goes to the library at eleven. With four-color illustrations, this book helps make sense of the numerals as shown on a clock. Using a wind-up clock with a traditional face, a boy or girl may point to times shown by hands as the adult turns the hands from the back of the clock. Using a simulated clock face made from a paper plate with cut-paper hands, one may move the hands to show the times seen on the face of Harriet's clock. Pre-1.

Features: numeral use with clock face and time-telling.

Maestro, Betsy, and Giulio Maestro. *Dollars and Cents for Harriet*. Illustrated by Giulio Maestro. New York: Crown, 1988.

Harriet shows how coins make up a dollar and how dollars add up, too. One day Harriet sees something in a toy store that she wants to buy. The toy costs five dollars. Running home, she empties her piggy bank and finds one hundred pennies. The narrative continues on the verso pages while the recto pages show the illustrations. A viewer sees one hundred full-size pennies on sky-blue pages, a representation useful for a one-to-one correspondence activity if a counter wishes to place one actual penny on top of each of the illustrated ones to count to one hundred. Harriet thinks of a way to earn four more dollars. First, Harriet earns twenty nickels by doing yard work for Snake (count by fives to one hundred as a page of nickels is seen). Next, she earns ten dimes weeding Cat's garden (count by tens to one hundred and verify the correct number of dimes). How does she earn the rest of the money (pages show four quarters, two half-dollars, and five one dollar bills)? What toy does Harriet buy to fly in the park? As a language link about measurement with money, an adult might introduce the newspaper, advertisements of items for imaginary purchase, and discuss some of the prices: "What could be purchased with our pennies?" "Which costs more?" Pre-1.

Features: counting by fives and tens to one hundred, concept of coins adding up to dollars, and use of money.

Maestro, Betsy. *Harriet Goes to the Circus: A Number Concept Book.* Illustrated by Giulio Maestro. New York: Crown, 1977.

Harriet, the elephant on roller skates, arrives first at the circus tent. The other animals line up behind her: a duck who carries a cane; a snake who wears a purple and white hat; and a lizard with a striped shirt. Numbers are used in the ordinal sense for classifying as the order of animals (according to position) is established. Who is first in line? Second? It turns out that a door to the tent opens next to owl, the tenth and last animal in the line. Now, every animal in line turns around to face the entrance. Owl is now first in line. Who is second? Last? Harriet is relieved when she gets inside and finds that everyone sits in a circle. They all have front row seats and easily can see the performing acts against the full-color backgrounds with bright colors of purple, orange, and yellow. An adult and listener may count together with the ordinals from first through tenth. Recommended. Pre-1.

Features: ordinal number recognition, first through tenth, change of starting point.

Maestro, Giulio. *One More and One Less: A Number Concept Book.* Illustrated by the author. New York: Crown, 1974.

Maestro uses the introductory pages to show the numerals. From 1 up to 10, large white numerals in a row are found on a purple background. In a second row, the numerals are from 10 down to 1. Bright, colorful backgrounds of blue, green, and orange attract a young viewer's eyes. On a background of yellow, a sketched outline of a chicken leads to the words, "This is one," and the numeral 1 is seen. When the page is turned, one more is added to the group and Maestro writes, "One and one more is two." A mathematical sentence is seen: $1 + 1 = 2$. Each time a page is turned, a counter may anticipate that one more of something is added to the group. First, a cat arrives, then a bird joins the cat and the chicken. Is there a pattern in cat-bird-chicken? Or another pattern? With other animals, they all line up in rows. Characters are identifiable, and easy to count. The viewer is asked to subtract, so, page by page, and one by one, an animal leaves the total group. The animals leave in the same sequence in which they arrived. Clear, simple, colorful representation of the addition and subtraction operations shows how one operation is related to the other. Someone might be interested in comparing Maestro's book with Margery M. Fisher's *One and One* (Dial, 1963). The interested reader might explain what happens on the pages of both books to other friends in the classroom. Which presentation is preferred? In the illustrations, what surprises one the most? Recommended. K-2.

Features: oversize numerals, *one-more* sequence, *one-less* sequence, addition and subtraction symbols in sentences.

Manley, Deborah. *Animals One to Ten*. Illustrated by Michele Noble. Milwaukee, Wis.: Raintree Children's Books, 1971.

For each numeral from 1 to 10, Manley asks if a viewer has seen an animal that looks like the one shown on the page. At the numeral 10, the question is how many birds are in the illustration. Bright numerals in blue, green, orange, and purple show in the corners of the pages. The animals and their shapes are shown in full color a second time in different group arrangements. Manley's list of key words and the guide to sound pronunciation may help a boy or girl with a word review. From *ant* to *stripe*, the key words are presented in alphabetical order (language link to math). 1–2.

Features: increasing numbers from one through ten, members rearranged in groups, name identification, and pronunciation guide.

Margolin, Harriet. *Busy Bear's Closet: A Book about Counting*. Illustrated by Carol Nicklaus. New York: Grosset and Dunlap, 1985.

Busy Bear invites a young viewer to see all of the objects in his closet. Margolin, a former teacher, and Nicklaus, the illustrator, provide bright and appealing objects to count on the heavy coated pages. What items may be found in the child's closet that can be counted? Pre.

Features: board book, numbers of objects from one up to ten.

Margolin, Harriet. *Busy Bear's Cupboard: A Book about More Than One*. Illustrated by Carol Nicklaus. New York: Grosset and Dunlap, 1985.

Busy Bear's cupboard needs to be filled. He selects a couple of vases, a stack of plates, a row of cups, and other objects, until the cupboard is filled to the top with groups of things that are more than one. What objects would a beginning counter select to fill an empty cupboard? What items are in a cupboard at home that can be counted? Pre.

Features: board pages with *one-more* sequence showing numbers of household objects that are more than one.

Martin, Jr., Bill. *Ten Little Caterpillars*. Illustrated by Gilbert Riswald. New York: Holt, Rinehart and Winston, 1967.

Inspired by George Mendoza's "The Caterpillar Man," Bill Martin, Jr. wrote this account of ten crawling, wriggling, climbing caterpillars, while the illustrations in soft watercolors help a boy or girl explore the sequence of numbers from one up to ten. One caterpillar crawls into a bower—a shelter of tree branches and vines. Another wriggles up a flower. Still another climbs a cabbage head. A young listener watching closely can count and repeat the words about scaling an apple tree, hanging there patiently, and then, becoming a butterfly. For a bulletin board display, egg cartons can be cut apart and turned into caterpillar forms for painting, grouping, and counting. Pipe cleaners make the antennae. For a further activity, a shape of a large leaf may be cut out of on green felt, and one for each child is is stapled to cardboard so that small caterpillar shapes (dry lima beans) can be added to the leaf and counted as *Ten Little Caterpillars* is reread. Volunteers may walk their fingers as imaginary caterpillars to various locations (mentioned in the book or original). "Where is your caterpillar hiding in the bower? Climbing on the flower? Climbing on the cabbage head?" For further variation in the classroom, the teacher may identify a convergence of two points and ask the listeners to move their caterpillars to that location. K-1.

Features: number words in rhyming lines from one up to ten.

Mathews, Louise. *Bunches and Bunches of Bunnies*. Illustrated by Jeni Bassett. New York: Dodd, Mead, 1978.

Count the bunnies! With this book, a child's knowledge of addition may introduce multiplication as another way of adding groups when each group has the same number of members. It is noticed that the bunches of bunnies represent the numerals from 1 up through 12 and one bunny flips over once in the clover. Two bunnies beam and smile while two more dream. Seeing these two groups of bunnies, each of which has two bunnies, children can first arrive at the answer by adding 2 + 2. They can then be shown that 2 X 2 arrives at the same answer (multiplication is repeated addition). They should be aware that 2 bunnies (in first group) + 2 bunnies (in second group) are two groups of two bunnies or 2 X 2. They should realize the math sentence for addition (2 + 2 = 4) is equivalent to the multiplication sentence of 2 X 2 = 4. To show that 3 x 3 = 9, three groups, each of which has three bunnies, plant seeds, pull weeds, and spray the garden rows with a green water hose. Using these activities for reinforcing the concept of multiplication as repeated addition, an adult may discuss the math symbols and the problem situations. Some of the actions in the problems may be sketched on paper as one's ideas about the groups are discussed. 2 up.

Features: equivalent numbers of objects in each of two groups show multiplication as repeated addition.

Mathews, Louise. *Cluck One*. Illustrated by Jeni Bassett. New York: Dodd, Mead, 1982.

Awakened from sleep in a tree, a weasel sees a cuckoo roll her egg into Mrs. Cluck's nest. Being mischievous, the weasel collects other eggs to place in the nest, too. First, a girl or boy may focus on number-numeral relationships as the weasel collects a green egg, a shiny egg, an egg from a long-legged bird, and a round egg from the sandy beach. Next, focus in upon ordinals as each egg is pictured in light colors and shown in a bordered illustration at the foot of each page. Which egg is shown first? Second? Third? Can someone predict the inhabitant of each egg? The eggs accumulate, are labeled, and hatch in the order in which they were added to Mrs. Cluck's nest. There is a chicken, a cuckoo, a duck, and other animals. There is a final touch of humor in a cause-effect situation. Now, because of his actions, Weasel, who likes to sleep, is kept awake from sunup to sundown by the noisy racket of all the babies in the nest. K-2.

Features: numeric narrative with numerals-cardinal numbers relationships, ordinals, one-to-one correspondence, and cause and effect.

Mayer, Marianna. *Alley Oop!* Illustrated by Gerald McDermott. New York: Holt, Rinehart and Winston, 1985.

McDermott's illustrations show balancing animals who wear numerals. Beginning with a mouse and an alligator, a pyramid of animals builds and builds in the manner of a circus balancing act until one butterfly lands on the elephant's trunk and causes the pyramid to collapse. Does a viewer discover that the numerals they wear are hidden by the positions of the animals? If it seems difficult for a boy or girl to count the animals because of their mixed arrangement in the illustration, adult guidance will be needed. Pre-K.

Features: numeral recognition and use.

Mayer, Marianna. *The Brambleberry Animal Book of Counting.* Illustrated by Gerald McDermott. Stanford, Conn.: Riverbank Press/Long Meadow Press, 1987.

Mayer's counting book is a numeral-word-object book begins with one red balloon that flies off through the pages to lead the viewer's eye. As the mouse chases it, he sees increasing numbers of things to count: three birds in a nest; four sailboats in a pond. Objects accumulate in groups with six elephants, seven swans, and eight giraffes (comparing quantities). Past nine monkeys and ten bananas, the counting ends as the mouse captures the balloon. An adult may ask a young viewer: "If you could follow a flying red balloon, what numbers of things would be seen?" Pre-K.

Features: numeral-object-number word arrangement from one up to ten.

Mermaid, Vanessa. *Little Simon One Two Three.* Illustrated by Mik Brown. New York: Simon and Schuster, 1982.

Brown's framed illustrations in bright colors show pinks, purples, and blues. Selected objects to count include one mouse in the rain, two elephants having a bath, and others, up to ten orange monkeys swinging. A game of grouping may be played by recognizing and then counting all of the animals who sit, stand, box, and eat. Some animals have spots, wear glasses, or have curly tails and wait to be recognized and counted. Later, can a viewer find all of the animals who hide in Brown's jungle? Will someone recognize the number of animals in certain groups and identify the snakes, giraffes, and birds? K-1.

Features: increasing numbers of animals in groups from one up to ten.

Michelini, Carlo. *One Green Frog*. Illustrated by the author. New York: Grosset and Dunlap, 1982.

With an English text by Yvonne Hooker, the rhyming lines on the verso pages tell of two toucans and three floating jellyfish and continue up to twenty bees gathering nectar. Full-color illustrations show: parrots who squawk, snails who won't unpack, and fish with flicking tails. The viewer is challenged to find two ladybugs that are different from others (ones referred to as the *odd-men-out* in a crowd of ladybugs). The eyes of every creature are die-cut holes rimmed in bright yellow. Pre-K.

Features: visual discrimination, rhyming lines about animals and insects from one through twenty.

Miller, Elizabeth. *Cat and Dog Give a Party*. Illustrated by Victoria Chess. New York: Franklin Watts, 1980.

Dog suggests that Cat have a party, and readers have the opportunity to count the items that the animals bring, and to create original problems. How many cupcakes does Raccoon bring to the party and what do Rabbit, Squirrel, and Chipmunk contribute? How many animals were there? Later, what events happen to cause the animals to leave the party? When the first animal leaves, how many are left? When all of the guests have gone, Cat becomes angry with Dog. How do they share their feelings? Do Cat and Dog become friends again? 1–2.

Features: narrative with numbers of party objects from one up to ten.

Miller, J. P. *Learn to Count with Little Rabbit*. Illustrated by the author. New York: Random House, 1984.

Introduced in a foot-tall book format, Little Rabbit counts the objects he meets on his way to the farm, while the listener counts along, too. These include five baby chipmunks, six lambs, seven squealing piglets, and on up to ten (cardinal number identification). The dragonflies, the clouds, and the flowers may be recognized as objects to be counted, too. When Little Rabbit takes honey home to Mother, she bakes something special. What is Mother's baking surprise and can it be counted? Pre-K.

Features: cardinal number identification of objects one through ten.

Milne, Alan Alexander. *Pooh's Counting Book*. Illustrated by Ernest Howard Shepard. New York: E. P. Dutton, 1982.

Writing activities are shown in Shepard's drawings on the endpages, which show Pooh, Piglet, and Eeyore writing. Rabbit uses Eeyore's side for a desk; Tigger makes an ink splot; and Owl concentrates on his letters. Additional pages include Milne's poetry and prose about Christopher Robin and his friends as they introduce the numerals in bright blue, 1 to 10. Blue highlights the capitalized number words in the text as well as at the foot of each page. There is a creative use of print with the words shown in capitals with ONE, TWO. Best suited for individual use because of its small size, this book shows Pooh giving ONE balloon to Eeyore, there are TWO friends, and THREE cheers for a favorite bear character, Pooh. Interesting mental images may be discussed after hearing the words about five big men after a little black hen, about singing a song six times in seven verses, and after reading that nine pots of honey are needed for Pooh. Notice the accumulation of honey pots for Pooh in the corners of pages. Recommended. Pre-1.

Features: numerals in blue from one through ten, number words in capitals, and accumulation of objects from Pooh stories.

Moore, Lilian. *My Big Golden Counting Book*. Illustrated by Garth Williams. Racine, Wis.: Golden/Western/Simon and Schuster, 1957.

Bunnies use colored string and bright beads for an abacus on Williams' colorful endpages. The large double-page spreads show the numbers of animals, the number words, and the numerals. The listener hears about one little puppy who is alone, counts two lambs, three horses, and four furry paws on the kitten. Hatching chicks, marching ducklings, and flying geese are represented by increasing numbers, and there is a squirrely touch of fun as ten acorns wait to be discovered by the squirrels. On the final endpapers, the animals are lined up in rows so one may point to them, touch them, and count them all again (sequence of numbers in groups). Pre-K.

Features: cardinal number identification of groups, one through ten.

Nedobeck, Don. *Nedobeck's Numbers Book*. Illustrated by the author. Milwaukee, Wis.: Ideals Publishing, 1981.

One shaggy dog, two colorful cats, and three-toed tree toads encourage a boy or girl to count. Other animals include a flying fish, sleepy seagulls, and egg-laying hens, who take the counting on up to twelve. Nedobeck's large, attractive watercolors brighten each double-page spread and decorate the endpages with the numerals to recognize and to name. On a final page, the shaggy dog waits to lead a young counter back to the first page to begin a number-numeral review. K-1.

Features: cardinal number identification of animals from one up to twelve.

Noll, Sally. *Off and Counting*. Illustrated by the author. New York: Greenwillow, 1984.

There is a lot to be counted while following a windup frog through a toy shop. On the double-page spreads, the frog leaps over two spotted rocking horses, three train cars, and other toys, reaching ten outlined blocks with numerals. The frog's moving action is seen in overlapping frog shapes as he leaps over the toys, and a shattered blue line shows his hopping path and leads the viewer's eyes to a frieze at the foot of the page with a repeated number word. The word is reinforced with the appropriate numeral showing in an upper corner. The number of pictured frog-hops do not always correspond to the numeral being represented on the page. To recreate the number of hops the frog makes, one kindergarten teacher moves a paper frog-shape across a chalkboard number line to review the sequence of numbers that is shown in the book. Pre-K.

Features: with verses at beginning and ending, numerals, repetitive number words, and corresponding number of toys from one up to ten.

Obligado, Lilian. *Little Wolf and the Upstairs Bear*. Illustrated by the author. New York: Viking, 1979.

Little Wolf rides the elevator up from floor one to ten to find his playmate, Buster Bear. On each floor, Little Wolf meets a different animal, and on the top floor, he finds the Friendly Health Club (leads to ordinal use of numbers). Seeing all of the animals again at the swimming pool of the club, a girl or boy counts the animals in their different groups (comparing groups or sets, accumulation, cardinal number identification). Recommended. Pre-K.

Features: numeric narrative, *one-more* sequence from one up to ten, members rearranged in groups.

123 Numbers. Illustrated. New York: Modern Publishers/Unisystems, 1982.

A beginning counter sees the yellow cat on each page of this Honey Bear shape book. Objects beginning with one ball and two skeins of yarn and continuing to nine frogs and ten fish can be counted from page to page (sequence of numbers in groups). Pre.

Features: cardinal number identification of objects associated with cats from one through ten.

Perry, Katherine. *The Elephant Counting Book.* Illustrated by Tony Forde. New York: Mulberry Press, n.d.

Wearing numerals 1 to 10, elephants visit Grandma. In these illustrations with shades of brown, orange, and tan, the visits continue until Pop Elephant, who wears the numeral 10 (numeral use), appears and takes all of the elephants home again. More elephants may be counted with Manny Campana's illustrations in *The Shaggy Baggy Elephant's Great Big Counting Book* (Goldencraft/Children's Press, 1983). After seeing this book, some of the numerals in it may be written by an adult and a viewer asked to identify them. Is a girl or boy ready to find the numerals again on the blankets of the elephants in Forde's illustrations? Pre-1.

Features: numeric narrative, numeral use, and *one-more* sequence from one up to ten.

Petré, Harris. *Billions of Bugs.* Illustrated by the author. Englewood Cliffs, N.J.: Prentice-Hall, 1975.

Billions of Bugs may stimulate interest in insects in realistic settings, and also numbers. Small and rectangular in size, this book is about all kinds of bugs in words and pictures. Large number concepts are taught through the illustrations and the counter moves by tens to 100 and then to 1000. There is one praying mantis who eats a grub and ten walking sticks who hide in shrubs. At the numeral 10, the insect groups increase by tens: dragonflies (sun-loving); grasshoppers (carry sound-producing organs on their wings); and earwigs (found near fruits, flowers, and vegetables). Then sixty mosquitoes, seventy baby spiders, and ninety ants lead up to one hundred yellow jackets. At this point, Petré's groups increase by hundreds. There are fireflies (whose light flashes attract one another), fleas (who leap as high as seven inches) and flies (who can have ten generations a year). Finally, there is a cluster of one thousand butterflies. On the way to one thousand, though "one can't count them all." Some bugs, such as vine chafers and no-see-ums, may have to be explained. 2-up.

Features: cardinal number identification of familiar and unfamiliar bugs from one up to ten, *ten-more* sequence to one hundred, *one hundred-more* sequence to one thousand.

Phillips, Mildred. *Cats to Count.* Illustrated by Sal Murdocca. New York: Random House, 1984.

Here rhyming lines accompany full-color personified cats. For the numeral 1, Murdocca's cat rests in the shade of an umbrella attached to a wooden lounge chair, wears sunglasses and shorts, reads a magazine in one hand, and holds a refreshing cool drink in the other. For 2, two cats are in a shoe, and others are counted in humorous situations on up to twelve. Is someone ready to extend this idea beyond twelve and draw an illustration or dictate a story about an increasing number of cats? Pre.

Features: humor, rhyming lines with number words, and numerals from one up to twelve.

Pomerantz, Charlotte. *One Duck, Another Duck.* Illustrated by Jose Aruego and Ariane Dewey. New York: Greenwillow, 1984.

In this, girls and boys see things from a high tree branch and look down on a pond below (perspective). They notice Grandmother Owl and her grandson, Danny, and several ducklings with Mother Duck. How many ducklings can be seen? Danny begins to count the ducks with the word, *one,* then instead of using number words, Danny continues with the words, *another* and *another,* and so on. Grandmother Owl reminds him that he can begin to count with the words, *one,* then *two,* then *three* (relationships among numbers). Danny counts again, and feeling pleased when he reaches the end of his ducks, Danny wants to count more objects: the stars in the sky. In this Caldecott Honor book, the large clear illustrations make it easy for a young viewer to see and count the ducks. Further discussion can begin with, "If you were sitting high on a branch in a tree and could see for a long distance, what could be some of the things you could count?" Recommended. Pre-K.

Features: Numeric narrative with the counting process, one through ten.

Potter, Beatrix. *Peter Rabbit's 123*. Illustrations by the author. New York: Warne, 1988.

Peter Rabbit and some other friends are in this approximately seven inches square book. There are illustrations for each number from one up through twelve, each with excerpts from Beatrix Potter's tales. Best suited for individual use because of its small size, the book contains numerals are set in the colorful boxes inserted into the corners of the illustrations. Place value is reinforced with the numbers of ten, eleven, and twelve. The story of *Peter Rabbit* may be requested as a rereading experience and lends itself to organizing one's thoughts about the order of the vegetables in rows in Mr. McGregor's garden and in presenting them in a drawing of the garden (logic). Also available is *Peter Rabbit's 123 Frieze* (Warne, 1988). Peter Rabbit, Tom Kitten (Does anyone recognize his sisters?), and Squirrel Nutkin are just a few of the characters that help a beginning counter learn numbers with this full-size frieze that folds out to 108 inches. An adult may read and discuss the frieze or the counting book about Peter Rabbit while the stuffed character of Peter is incorporated into the listener's reactions and comments. If a girl or boy is interested in the character of Peter Rabbit, a soft replica of Peter is available for school and home use. The doll character, wearing a brass-buttoned blue jacket, is one for a boy or girl to hold while counting the numbers of things found in Potter's illustrations and may be found in selected nearby children's book stores or ordered from Listening Library, 1 Park Avenue, Old Greenwich, CT, 06870–9990. Soft stuffed characters of other animals seen in these counting books are available, too. Recommended. Pre-K.

Features: *one-more* sequence from one up to twelve, place value reinforcement, and characters from Beatrix Potter's stories.

Punnett, Richard D. *Count the Possums*. Illustrated by Tom Dunnington. Chicago: The Child's World, 1982.

More unusual personified animals to count appear in *Count the Possums*. Mama Possum looks upward to the limb of a tall brown tree to find one of her babies hanging by his tail. Where are the other possums? The rhyming text makes this number book good for reading aloud. The reading aloud includes child participation when a girl or boy is asked to supply the final rhyming word on each page. Did Mama Possum find all of her babies? The listener counts to find out the answer. The animal characters are shown in full-color illustrations. Pre-2.

Features: numeric narrative in rhyming lines with participation on each page.

Rice, Paul. *The Garden of One.* Illustrated by Shawn Rice. New York: Oxford University Press, 1987.

In a beautiful garden, one rabbit who lives alone meets a second rabbit. The two rabbits have a family, which increases quickly, with numbers used as names. The young rabbits bite, hit, and kick one another. With all of this action, the garden is destroyed: the trees become barren; the flowers and grass refuse to grow. When springtime comes again, only two rabbits are left. These rabbits, in turn, decide to have a family of rabbits (prediction about condition of garden). There are small stylized illustrations in colored pencil and watercolors. The effects of large numbers of animals in a small area can be discussed (cause and effect). For young children, the decreasing number of rabbits in the garden may be shown in a rhyme with a countdown by twos. Using hand-held paper-bag puppets of rabbits the children have made, girls and boys may join in saying the words for "Twelve Little Rabbits." 2–3.

Features: numeric narrative, number usage, prediction, and cause and effect.

Richards, Dorothy Fay. *Wise Owl's Counting Book.* Illustrated by Helen Endres. Chicago: Children's Press, 1981.

On Endres's cover illustration, Wise Owl points to the numerals scattered around him to introduce the concept of groups represented by symbols. Numeral use also is presented. On subsequent pages, Mr. Owl plans to take a trip alone. Being alone means o-n-e, just 1, to Mr. Owl (spelling of number words shown). However, some other family members are interested in taking the trip . Mrs. Owl wants to go and that makes 2. Baby Owl makes 3. Three more brothers help add up the family members to a total of 6 who want to go on the trip. Do Grandpa and Grandma Owl want to go? Do Uncle Posie and Aunt Josie seem interested? They all pack their luggage, get in Mr. Owl's bright red car, and start off. The counting isn't over yet for twenty joggers appear. Thirty firefighters follow the joggers and forty children fall in behind. There is counting by tens with these groups up to one hundred. 1–2.

Features: numeric narrative, sequence of *one-more* from one up to ten and *ten-more* to one hundred.

Robison, Nancy L. *Where Did My Little Fox Go?* Illustrated by Tom Eaton. Champaign, Ill.: Garrard, 1977.

Nine little foxes play hide-and-seek in Eaton's colorful illustrations, chase a chicken, search for one another, and finally, count off from one to nine. At the page for the number nine, Mother Fox focuses her camera and captures all of the little foxes in a photograph. The foxes all pose to show off the large numerals on their shirts (numeral use). Sheets of paper with duplicated outlines of tee-shirts may be presented so interested boys and girls in kindergarten or first grade may write the large numerals the foxes wore on their shirts. Additional shirt outlines encourage writing other numerals. Pre-1.

Features: numeral recognition, *one-more* sequence from one up to nine, and numeral use.

Rosenblatt, Arthur S. *The Baby Hugs and Baby Tugs Bear Counting Book*. Illustrated by Joe Evers. New York: Random House, 1984.

Some preschool girls and boys may enjoy *The Baby Hugs and Baby Tugs Bear Counting Book*, in the Young World of Care Bear series. In the bright pictures, a preschooler counts objects in the land of Care-a-lot, sees the active little bears, Baby Hugs and Baby Tugs, and discovers where the bears live, and how they play. Pre.

Features: numeral-number relationships from one up to ten.

Rosenburg, Amye. *Pup's Numbers*. Illustrated by the author. Racine, Wis.: Western, 1986.

On a rainy day, one pup gets one scissors, two paint brushes, three jars of paint, four balls of yarn and five crayons, and gets busy making six paper birds that fly, seven masks, and other colorful items. To end the afternoon activity, Mother makes ten cookies. Numerals are shown in sentences. For review, an adult may ask a child to find selected numerals with, "Where is numeral 4?" Pre-K.

Features: numeral recognition, cardinal number identification, household objects from one through ten.

Ross, Katharine. *Nighty-Night, Little One*. Illustrated by Lisa McCue. New York: Random House, 1988.

Nighty-Night, Little One has rhyming lines about one puppy, one squirrel, and other animals. Mother and baby animals may be identified. Some, such as the owls, may be familiar, while others, such as the possums, may be unfamiliar. Since there are no numerals showing on the pages, counting is done without any guiding symbols. If guiding numerals are needed, they may be written on index cards and displayed as the number words are read. Pre-K.

Features: rhyming lines, cardinal number identification of animals from one up to ten with no numerals for guidance.

Scarry, Richard. *Learn to Count*. Illustrated by the author. Racine, Wis.: Golden/Western, 1976.

Scarry's animal characters introduce the number-numeral relationships from one through twelve. They help to identify objects such as one banana and two pears, tell what object is *little,* and which one is *a lot of something.* In the full-color illustrations in the last part of the book, one sees numbers and numerals that are out of sequence (numeral recognition) and counting begins again. Who notices Scarry's humor and counts all of the birds in the nest that rests on Bramble Warthog's head? Pre-K.

Features: humorous characters, numeral recognition, and cardinal number identification from one up to twelve.

Scarry, Richard. *Richard Scarry's Best Counting Book Ever*. Illustrated by the author. New York: Random House, 1975.

Scarry invites a young reader to count along with Willy Bunny and determine the number of objects such as boats, bunnies, fireflies, and pies, up to one hundred. A boy or girl may count by tens, see the meaning of *more than* (or *greater than*), and recognize numerals and number sentences such as 1 + 2 = 3 and 5 + 5 = 10. For a review of Willy Bunny and his day-long counting adventure, one first-grade teacher shows this book again with the available filmstrip/record set. The set is accompanied by duplicating masters. Recommended. K-1.

Features: numeric narrative, numeral recognition, *ten-more* sequence, and symbols in addition sentences.

Scarry, Richard. *Richard Scarry's Lowly Learns to Count*. Illustrated by the author. New York: Random House, 1987.

Beginning with January, the first month of the year (ordinals), and the number one (cardinals), Scarry asks questions in the text. In January, for the number one, Scarry asks if one tree, one sled, and one apple tractor can be found in the illustration. Lowly Worm is seen on each page as he gives away valentines in February, loses his hat in March, and finds shelter in a basket of Easter eggs in April. Names of the months are in capitals, numerals are oversize and colorful, ordinal words are spelled out, and cardinal number words are found in corners of pages. Text is beneath illustrations that show Lowly, Huckle, and other Scarry characters. In November, the eleventh month, Lowly has his birthday party and blows the cake right off the table, while in December, Lowly helps Santa Claus bring presents to twelve good little bugs. The review page offers numerals by the names of the months and the sequence on colored circles. Pre-K.

Features: cardinals from one up to twelve, ordinals to the twelfth position, numeral-number words in corners, names of months in capitals, and text with illustrations.

Schulz, Charles M. *Snoopy and the Twelve Days of Christmas: A Pop-Up Book*. Illustrated. New York: Holt, Rinehart and Winston, 1984.

Fans of Snoopy and the other characters by Schulz will emjoy celebrating the holidays on these pop-up pages. On the first day, one sees Woodstock in a fir tree. Lucy is one of the two ladies dancing; when the page tab is pulled, the dancing action begins. At nine, there are nine players playing softball (Charlie Brown, Lucy, and others are in the game). Schulz's characters also are the eleven eaters eating (pizza) and twelve skaters skating (playing on ice). Pre-1.

Features: board pages with numerals and objects from one up to twelve.

Szekeres, Cyndy. *Cyndy Szekeres' Counting Book 1 to 10*. Illustrated by the author. Racine, Wis.: Western, 1986.

Decorated endpapers introduce mice to count, and on the sturdy pages, boys and girls find the number words and numerals and phrases with the pattern of number word-noun-verb about mice. Within full-color illustrations, one mouse works, two mice run, and three mice dance (verbalizing, extending patterns). After closing the counting at the number ten, the viewer finds the sleeping mice with a final message, "Happy Counting." Is someone ready to wake up the ten sleeping mice and extend the number word-noun-verb pattern with increasing numbers of mice? Eleven mice stretching? Twelve mice washing? Thirteen mice eating? Pre-K.

Features: numerals, number words, phrases with pattern of number word-noun-verb about mice from one through ten.

Szekeres, Cyndy. *Little Bear Counts His Favorite Things*. Illustrated by the author. Racine, Wis.: Western, 1986.

Szekeres presents the numerals and the number words in the corners of the pages of this square book. The young viewer finds one chair, two wagons, three jars for insects, four spoons, and on up through nine cars and trucks, and ten blocks (quantity, cardinal numbers, comparing groups). At ten, there is a close-up of the wooden blocks which provide a review of counting in the *one-more* pattern from one to ten again. What are some favorite things to identify and count? Things that are not favorites? Drawings of favorite and nonfavorite objects may be categorized on a picture graph and discussed. Pre-K.

Features: numerals, number words, and a review page from one up to ten.

Tafuri, Nancy. *Who's Counting?* Illustrated by the author. New York: Greenwillow, 1986.

A golden retriever puppy leads the way through the counting and is always to be found somewhere in every double-page spread. This Caldecott honor book begins as the puppy heads home for supper. The counting moves from one squirrel (group or set with one element) to seven tadpoles to ten sleeping puppies watched over by their parents (group or set with ten elements). In addition, a viewer sees birds, geese, moles, pigs, and other numbers of objects. Children should enjoy the endpapers decorated with the puppy's paw prints, illustrations with the partly visible puppy on each page (just a paw or a nose), and the scene of ten puppies romping about. There is a changing point of view in some of the scenes (perspective), in which one may look across the meadow, find rabbits in a gray and green scene, notice daisies in an orange and pink display, or experience the perspective of looking up through a bed of flowers. There are other views with different perspectives from under the water and from overhead in the trees. Young viewers should be attracted to the bold black lines and the bright watercolors in these illustrations. For a review, turn back through the pages with questions about the numbers of objects. Recommended. Pre-K.

Features: numeric narrative, points of view, and increasing numbers in groups of animals from one through ten.

Thomson, Ruth. *All about 123*. Illustrated by Martin Ursell. Milwaukee, Wis.: Gareth Stevens Children's Books, 1987.

The full-color illustrations are double-page spreads showing selected flora and fauna in bright watercolors. Children are asked to help Sam, a jungle explorer, count animals, as well as the more difficult task of counting the animals that have specific physical traits or actions. Is it difficult to determine an animal's physical traits or actions from the illustrations? Adult guidance may be needed. Pre-1.

Features: cardinal number identification and classification by traits or actions.

Trinca, Rod, and Kerry Argent. *One Woolly Wombat*. Illustrated by Kerry Argent. New York: Kane/Miller Book Publishers, 1987.

Useful as a focus on rhymes for listening, reading, and writing, Argent's full-color illustrations on the recto pages introduce one large woolly wombat resting in a lounge chair at the beach, with words the verso pages. Rhyming lines tell of two cuddly koalas, three warbling magpies, and four thumping kangaroos. An appropriate number of objects (from one to fourteen), different from those featured in the words but accompanying the illustrations (lounge chair), appear at the foot of each page. The chair is shown in a position different from its position in the facing illustration (location in a group does not affect number). For another example, when two cuddly koalas have gumnut tea, the smaller pictures feature two teapots. For a prediction activity, one first-grade teacher reads the text, shows the large illustration, covers the corresponding picture at the foot of the page with a paper mask, and asks the viewers to predict which object or objects might be shown, reminding them that the object shown in the smaller picture at the foot of the page is always something that the animal is using in the larger illustration. The number words are spelled out—a challenge to a beginning reader to recognize the number words (language linked to math). There are no numerals shown, so a young counter needs to be able to recall numbers without the guidance of numerals in sequence. 1–2.

Features: no numerals to guide the sequence, number words in lower-case letters, *one-more* sequence, associations, and information that position in a group does not affect number.

Twinn, Colin. *Counting*. Illustrated by the author. London: Warne, 1988.

In illustrations reminiscent of Beatrix Potter's, small bunnies at home get ready to go to the fair. There are Ma and Pa, Susan, Victoria, and Harry. Number words begin with capitals: One is for Susan who was selected to be the Maid of the Fair and the numbers continue up to ten with eight ribbons, nine balloons, and ten pottery teacups to hit and break at a game booth. With its small pages (approximately four by five inches), this book is best suited for individual and home use. Pre-K.

Features: narrative, objects at the fair, and sequence from one up to ten.

Vogle, Ilse-Margaret. *1 Is No Fun But 20 Is Plenty*. Illustrated by the author. New York: Atheneum, 1967.

Rhyming lines accompany Hippo's adventures with a friend, Lion. While pirates visit, Hippo prepares 18 meatballs and they dance to a 19-piece band. The pirates stay for 20 days until they sail off in a lavender haze, leaving Hippo to comment that twenty is "an enormous amount." Illustrations are black and white outlines with highlights of yellow and light green. Pre-1.

Features: Numerals from 1 up to 20 within text of rhyming lines.

Warren, Cathy. *The Ten Alarm Camp Out*. Illustrated by Steven Kellogg. New York: Lothrop, Lee and Shepard, 1983.

Mother Armadillo and the little armadillos line up to get ready for a camp out. Attired in tennis shoes and tee shirts, the armadillos wear numeric information, 1 through 9, with Mother Armadillo number 10 (numeral use). When the armadillos curl into balls and fall asleep, they are mistaken by the people in the town for loaves of bread, balls, bombs, dinosaur eggs, and melons. Kellogg's humorous illustrations show all of the action and the large type makes reading the story easy. Children may enjoy hearing the words, music, and sound effects on a read-along cassette that is available from Random House. K-2.

Features: humorous numeric narrative with personified armadillos, *one-more* sequence from one up to ten, shows use of numerals.

Weihs, Erika. *Count the Cats*. Illustrated by the author. New York: Doubleday, 1976.

Weihs's book gives young children who like cats (very energetic ones) an opportunity to follow a simple text that includes the numbers from one to ten, with crayon drawings of cats and their adventures. Is someone ready to make crayon drawings of original cats for counting? Pre-K.

Features: numeric narrative, *one-more* sequence of cats, one up to ten.

Wild, Robin, and Jocelyn Wild. *The Bears' Counting Book*. Illustrated by the authors. New York: Lippincott, 1978.

In the Wilds' variation of *The Three Bears*, numbers and numerals are introduced through a familiar storyline. As the disruptive bears explore a house they move from room to room, finding objects to count. When the bears find three beds, they start a pillow fight. They find four pans and cook something to eat, try on six shoes, eat seven pastry tarts, and sample eight bottles of liquids (mustard and milk). Can someone count along with all of the objects that the bears find? At the number ten, the bears go outside the house and count by tens up to fifty apples, then, disturbed by the returning family, run home and back to the woods. The bears show good manners when they present their apologies by returning and leaving gifts for the family: a pile of mushrooms, a bouquet of flowers, and one sticky honeycomb at the front door. Is anyone ready to dictate some additional numbers of things the bears could count? Recommended. K-1.

Features: numeric variant of folktale from one up to ten, then the *ten-more* sequence up to fifty.

Williams, Garth. *The Chicken Book*. Illustrated by the author. New York: Delacorte, 1970.

On the double-page spreads one squirming chick who looks for a worm, a second looks for a little green slug, and a third wants some yellow meal. Mother Hen, in a green garden patch, advises them to scratch and scratch. Finger movements (one-to-one correspondence) may match the words and turn the rhyming lines into a finger play. Flash cards may present the numerals and number words below the appropriate numbers of outlines of chicks. Once a boy or girl can identify the number of chicks on each card from one to five and "read" the numerals and number words, the outlines of chicks may be cut apart in zig-zag fashion from the numerals and words, which are then taped to the back of the outlines. The outlines of the chicks serve as self-checks as numerals and words are reviewed. Recommended. K-1.

Features: *one-more* sequence about little chicks from one up to five, number words in rhyming lines.

Wong, Herbert H., and Matthew F. Vessel. *My Ladybug*. Illustrated by Marie Nonnast Bohlen. Reading, Mass.: Addisonian Press, 1969.

Though not intended as a counting book, this title from the Science Series for the Young offers opportunities to see number use in an informational book. Looking at a ladybug through a magnifying glass in the illustrations, a boy or girl reads the text about two legs, four legs, and six legs, two hard wings, and two soft wings. Six insects are put into a jar. After three weeks, eggs are laid, and other ladybugs are hatched. On a final double-page spread, there are thirteen different kinds of ladybugs to count. Classifying may begin as one counts the ladybugs that do not have spots but black bands instead or are not red or are the largest. Among the largest are the yellow fifteen-spotted ladybug, the orange sixteen-spotted ladybug, and the red convergent ladybug. 1 up.

Features: number use in informative text and up to thirteen kinds of ladybugs to count.

Wood, A. J. *Animal Counting*. Illustrated by Helen Ward. Los Angeles: Price/Stern/Sloan, 1987.

To count the animals, one looks through the colorful jungle foliage made from cut-paper shapes and opens flaps to find animals in groups.

From one tired toucan to ten ladybugs, there is a link of language to math and some alliterative patterns as a viewer finds four big baboons, five cheeky chipmunks, and nine merry mice. Directional phrases lead to the flaps with "Can you see . . . ," "Have you found . . . ," and "Can you count . . . ?" With number words to read and numerals to recognize, the repetitive phrases are found again under each fold-over page, and the listener can chant along. K-2.

Features: numerals and number words from one up to ten in bold type, alliteration, repetitive phrases, fold-over pages.

Wylie, Joanne. *A More or Less Fish Story*. Illustrated by David Wylie. Chicago: Children's Press, 1984.

In this one, bright red and blue fish show the number-numeral relationships. Though labeled as a story, the format emphasizes counting to ten to determine how many fish are caught in groups. Boys and girls enjoy the contrasting colors of blue, orange, red, and yellow, and some children especially like the sight of the fish blowing bubbles and the fish faces with their varied fishy expressions. Can someone count the fish in groups and identify the corresponding numeral for each group? Crackers shaped as goldfish are eagerly received markers to push into different group arrangements for counting purposes because when the activity is over, one may eat them! Pre-K.

Features: numeric narrative, cardinal number identification of groups of fish from one through ten.

Youldon, Gillian. *Counting*. Illustrated by James Hodgson. New York: Franklin Watts, 1980.

Anyone who enjoys the outdoor scenes and the split pages in Youldon's *Numbers* (Franklin Watts, 1979) should like *Counting*, too. In this All

a-Board story book's bright and colorful illustrations, the chase begins
when three happy cats take four fish from five cooks. Two, six, and finally,
eight dogs pursue the cats. How will the cats get rid of the fishy evi-
dence? What prediction might be made? A reader who likes cats might
turn to another counting book title such as Patricia Miles Martin's *That
Cat! 123* (Putnam, 1969) to see number use. Pre-K.

Features: cardinal number identification in narrative, *one-more* sequence from one through ten.

Ziefert, Harriet. *A Dozen Dogs: A Read-and-Count Story.* Illustrated by
Carol Nicklaus. New York: Random House, 1985.

A note to parents explains the grade levels assigned to this Step-into-
Reading Book and the others in the series: (Step 1: Pre-1; Step 2: 1–3;
and Step 3: 2–3). This group of twelve dogs of different colors, shapes,
and sizes is playing at the beach. In the cartoon-style illustrations, it is
easy to see what the dogs are doing. How many are swimming? Fishing?
Full-colored illustrations are taken right to the page edges, and in large
type, the words describe the dogs; two are dressed in swim suits. A total
is given with the sequence of counting with the numerals on the pages.
One sees the dogs playing in the sand with shovel, pail, boats, sitting on
their towels, and building sand piles. This book also introduces the feature of chapter headings in bold oversize type. Chapter 2 offers examples
of problems. For instance, a dozen dogs are on a raft; five dive into the
water and how many are left? Then two more dogs jump in, and now how
many are left on the raft? The words answer the questions. In Chapter
3, the dogs go fishing and other addition and subtraction situations occur
(relationships of numbers in groups or sets). Two dogs catch four fish (one
dotted, one spotted, one big, and one little), then another four fish, until
they catch . . . (prediction). One large whale, filling the illustration, is
caught on the end of the line and is the surprise ending for a young
reader. As an activity for the number twelve, each may receive a cup of
20 beans with some colored red, blue, yellow, and green. Selecting
twelve beans from the larger group, a counter places the beans in a paper
cup, and rolls the beans out on the table top. Four red beans means to
color four shapes of dogs red on a corresponding activity paper showing
outlines of dogs in rows. Beans of other colors guide the young counter
to coloring appropriate numbers of shapes. Once this one-to-one correspondence is completed, the counter writes the appropriate math sentence. For example, beans dictating that the outlines of the dogs be
colored with four red, four blue, and four green would make the math
sentence: $4 + 4 + 4 = 12$. 1–2.

Features: recognizing attributes, process of counting seen in text, symbols in addition and subtraction sentences, numeric narrative from one up to twelve.

Carnival and Circus

Corbett, Grahame. *What Number Now?* Illustrated by the author. New York: Dial, 1982.

A clown juggles items to show a *one-more-than* sequence in the numbers of objects. As different numbers of items are juggled, the clown balances on one foot and drops different numerals at his feet. The viewer may recognize the numerals but not fully understand what numbers the numerals represent unless they are correlated with objects to count. K-1.

Features: numeral recognition from one up to ten.

Dayton, Laura. *LeRoy's Birthday Circus.* Illustrated by Susan Huggins. New York: Elsevier/Nelson, 1981.

Double-page spreads with oversize numerals in red, yellow, and black introduce the guests beginning with one birthday boy and two girls and ending with dozens of cousins. From one cat acrobat to a dozen dressed-up hounds, a beginning counter also meets the performers in the circus. Internal rhymes feature five bears juggling chairs and six bears eating pears. With a second reading. listeners may show the correct number of markers when the corresponding number is heard in the story (five of something) and then place a pre-cut numeral or numeral on a card (5) beside the objects. Pre-K.

Features: *one-more* sequence from one up to twelve, internal rhymes, numerical narrative.

Dreamer, Sue. *Circus 123.* Illustrated by the author. Boston: Little, Brown, 1985.

Published by arrangement with Ringling Brothers and Barnum and Bailey Combined Shows, the sturdy board pages offer full-color illustrations of objects to count at the circus. There are numbers of acrobats, bears, and performing dogs to recognize and unusual acts to see. The drawings are clear and uncluttered. The circus performers may be reviewed with matching numeral cards in sequence from one up to ten. Pre-K.

Features: *one-more* sequence of circus objects from one up to ten.

Kramer, Anthony Penta. *Numbers on Parade, O to 10*. Illustrated by the author. New York: Lothrop, Lee and Shepard/William Morrow, 1987.

One monkey forms the shape of zero (0) with his hands. There are framed illustrations and colorful red numerals are in blue boxes in the corners of the pages. Number one begins the count with the alliterative words of a ready ringmaster. There are giraffes, side by side, with the ringmaster on the next page and the words, *two gentle giraffes*. Young viewers may anticipate an accumulation of parade characters but the pattern changes and only the alliteration continues with three extraordinary elephants but no giraffes. There are four outlandish orangutans, five lively lions, and six streamlined seals. A listener may repeat the alliterative words with seven able acrobats, eight prancing ponies, and nine performing poodles. These performers are shown again from ten to zero in a *one-less- than* order in the parade to be counted down to the one monkey, who again forms the shape of the zero with his hands. This final scene unfolds to forty-five inches long and shows the number words across the top (numbers as words). The sentences describing the animals in the parade may be presented as tongue twisters or as examples of alliteration with a focus for listening, reading, or writing. Pre-1.

Features: alliteration, accumulation, numeral recognition, number words, *one-more* sequence from zero up to ten and *one- less* sequence from ten to zero, unfolding page.

Peppé, Rodney. *Circus Numbers: A Counting Book*. Illustrated by the author. New York: Delacorte, 1969.

The ringmaster leads the way to the circus acts and the humor in the bright illustrations. Three elephants stand on their back legs but only two of them seem to be able to balance striped balls on their trunks. Four jugglers juggle objects but only three are successful. One of ten clowns stands on a black numeral10 and and other performers group together for the answer to the question, "How many?" At twenty, who is ready to identify two groups of ten? One hundred elephants, in groups of ten, seem to have bodies made with fingerprints, and end the counting. Can anyone count the elephants by tens? By ones? Recommended. Pre-1.

Features: numerals, *one-more* sequence of circus performers from one up to ten, and the *ten-more* sequence up to one hundred.

Sendak, Maurice. *Ten Little Rabbits: A Counting Book with Mino the Magician.* Illustrated by the author. Philadelphia: Rosenbach Museum and Library, 1970.

Published during an exhibition of original drawings and other materials by Maurice Sendak at the Rosenbach Museum and Library, this tiny paperback (approximately three by two inches) is best for individual and home use and invites the viewer to see the magic show of Mino the magician. Mino bows to his audience, taps his wand on a black top hat, and calls forth one yellow rabbit. With each succeeding numeral (*one-more-than* pattern), a rabbit appears in a color sequence: yellow, blue, gray, and white. After five rabbits accumulate, the color sequence begins again (patterning with color). The rabbits cluster around Mino. One sits on Mino's head, some hop around his feet. When ten rabbits on stage, Mino is completely covered and crowned by rabbits—so he makes them vanish again (meaning of *one-less-than*). Alone, Mino takes his final bow in a final black and white drawing. Pre up.

Features: colors in a pattern, *one-more* sequence of rabbits from one up to ten and *one-less* sequence from ten to one.

Ziner, Feenie. *Counting Carnival.* Illustrated by Paul Galdone. New York: Coward, McCann, 1862.

Just one child playing alone is no fun. In Galdone's illustrations of black and white with their touches of gray and red, one boy wears a headband with feathers. With the numeral 2, the first boy is joined by another who wears a paper tricorner hat and carries a bugle. Other children arrive and march together in a parade to celebrate a unique carnival day. With balloons, costumes, and drums, all twelve boys and girls participate in some way. balloons. Can someone identify and classify some of the common geometric figures (triangle, circle, sphere) in the illustrations and use correct vocabulary about these shapes? Recommended. Pre-K.

Features: numerals in bright red, number words in rhyming lines, cardinal number identification from one up to twelve, geometric figure recognition.

Countries

Cretan, Gladys Y. *Ten Brothers with Camels*. Illustrated by Pietro Ventura. Racine, Wis.: Western, 1975.

Colorful endpapers set the scene as ten men on camels travel over brown sand dunes. A young boy waits for his nine uncles, and as each one arrives, the boy, accompanied by his small dog, counts his uncles and their camels. The names of the uncles and some place names (Beirut) may be unfamiliar to some children: Kosgrove, the oldest; Levon, the quietest; Sarkis, the juggler; Bedros, the singer; Aram, the almond seller; Nazaret, the wrestler, and so on. In full-color double-page spreads, people prepare for the feast, as one carries loaves of bread over a shoulder, another carries a tall jug, and still another balances pottery on his head while walking upstairs. Woman with veils and men with turbans prepare different dishes of food while meat roasts over an open fire. With the exception of the last three illustrations, the camels and the men are counted easily on most of the pages. In the last three double-page spreads, only parts of the camels can be counted. In the second spread of the three, the text says "Here are ten camels . . . " but there may be some difficulty counting all ten camels because one is distorted by being hidden again in the center binding. To extend mathematics with a personal collection of animal pictures—including camels to classify—a child may sort pictures into two or more containers, to count, and to discuss, "Why did you put these animals together?" Pre-2.

Features: numeric narrative from one up to ten.

Dee, Ruby, reteller. *Two Ways to Count to Ten*. Illustrated by Susan Meddaugh. New York: Henry Holt, 1988.

In this African tale, the animals of the jungle need a new king, and all of the biggest and strongest animals compete for the job. They take turns throwing a spear into the air for a count of ten to see who will marry the Leopard King's daughter and become the next ruler of the animals. As Elephant, Chimp, and Lion throw the spear, the repetitive confident words of the animals, "I can do this thing," allow a young listener to join in with the story. Though not planned as a counting book, this story shows the use of numbers in a folktale as each animal in turn counts after throwing the spear into the air and Lion gets up to a count of nine. Then, Antelope tosses the spear and calls out, "Two, four, six, eight, ten." King

Leopard laughs and says, "Sometimes the cleverest wins the prize," and a young counter is introduced to counting by twos with Antelope's clever shortcut. K-2.

Features: number use, the process of counting in the text, refrain, introduction to counting by twos.

Dunham, Meredith. *Numbers: How Do You Say It?* Illustrated by the author. New York: Lothrop, Lee and Shepard, 1987.

A viewer is to look at the central illustration from all four sides of the page, and each quarter-turn of the page shows different words in English, French, Spanish, and Italian that name one object. On the facing page, a blank square is surrounded by the words in phonetic transcription to help with the pronunciation. Each image of the selected objects is interesting as it is seen from different angles as the book is turned. Useful as a first reference book, this book helps a girl or boy learn different ways to use language with numbers. Pre-up.

Features: number words in four languages and pronunciation guide.

Feelings, Muriel. *Moja Means One: Swahili Counting Book*. Illustrated by Tom Feelings. New York: Dial, 1971.

Muriel and Tom Feelings capture East African village life and culture in the text and in the soft brown and white paintings. Each double-page spread shows a numeral, a Swahili word for the numeral, a pronunciation guide, and an informative sentence. If the number of objects related to each number is not clear, an adult may discuss the page with a young viewer. For older children, there is added information; for instance, a map of Africa showing where the Swahili language is spoken. Many details are shown in the village scenes in this Caldecott Medal Honor Book. Most valuable, the pronunciation guides provide assistance for a pre-reading review before one reads these African words aloud to others. Recommended. 2-up.

Features: numeral, Swahili word for the number word, pronunciation guide, illustrated objects, and an informative sentence for each number, one up to ten.

Haskins, Jim. *Count Your Way through the Arab World* Illustrated by Dana Gustafson. Minneapolis, Minn.: Carolrhoda Books, 1987.

Each double-page spread shows the number, the characters of the words for it, the pronunciation, and a full-color illustration. Each page offers the numerals in both Roman and Arabic styles. The text offers brief facts about life in the Arab world. Numeral 1 (WAH-hid) stands for one language for many people, Arabic. The number five tells about the importance of prayer fives times a day for a Muslim. Numeral 10 (AH-shahrah) is for sand dunes as long as ten miles. A map shows information about Arab countries and culture. This book, and the others in this series, may find a place as introductory materials for activities in social studies. 1–4.

Features: numeral in Roman and Arabic styles, Arabic characters of the number word, pronunciation guide, and full-color illustration of objects, one up to ten.

Haskins, Jim. *Count Your Way through China*. Illustrated by Dennis Hockerman. Minneapolis, Minn.: Carolrhoda, 1987.

This series for children from kindergarten through grade three has several books that introduce a foreign country with counting from one to ten. All have double-page spreads that show the number, the characters of the words for it, the pronunciation, and full-color illustrations, and in this one, brief paragraphs give facts about life in China. For counting, numbers used are from Mandarin. Ten (SHUR) stands for the ten major dynasties in China beginning with the Shang dynasty (1766–1122 B.C.) and ending with the Ch'ing dynasty (1644–1912). Illustrations show, for example, the two pandas donated to the United States in 1972 and the seven zones of vegetation in China. Pronunciation guides after the number words help the reader study unfamiliar words and practice the accents on syllables. 1–4.

Features: numerals, Chinese characters for the number words (Mandarin), pronunciation guide, illustrations of objects, and informative paragraphs.

Haskins, Jim. *Count Your Way Through Japan*. Illustrated by Martin Skoro. Minneapolis, Minn.: Carolrhoda Books, 1987.

Full-color pictures accompanying counting experiences from one up to ten are associated with the Japanese way of life. Double-page spreads show the numbers, the characters of the words for each, and pronunciations, and is information about aspects of life in Japan. The Japanese language has two sets of numbers one through ten. One set is based on Chinese numbers and the second set on a Japanese counting system; however, the characters which represent the numbers are basically the same for both systems. This book uses the numbers of Chinese derivation. One is pronounced (EE-chee) and stands for Fujiyama, the volcanic mountain; two (NEE) is for two chopsticks, the eating utensils; three (SAHN) stands for three elements some people fear in nature: earthquakes, fire, and typhoons; and ten (JOO) is the age when children start practicing to be adults. Some of the topics in this counting book will lead to discussion and an adult's further explanation. As an example for such a discussion, there is the number seven, the Japanese characters for the words, "How many?," characters that require seven strokes. Isolated on white backgrounds, the objects are easy to see and to count. 1–4.

Features: numerals, numbers from Chinese derivation, Japanese characters of the number word, pronunciation guide, informational paragraphs, and illustrated objects of Japan to count.

Haskins, Jim. *Count Your Way through Russia.* Illustrated by Vera Polovka-Mednikov. Minneapolis, Minn.: Carolrhoda, 1987.

This book could find a place as introductory material about Russia in social studies. One Russian juggler shows the numerals on the cover to introduce the numbers from one (ah DEEN) to ten (DYEH-SEHT). The number word, one, stands for the Kremlin, a group of buildings for the government, and ten indicates the age at which boys and girls may join the youth group called Young Pioneers. The importance of seven (SEEYAM) is seen in this culture.

Seven domes are found on churches, seven bells seen in bell towers, and seven dolls nest inside one another from the largest doll down to the smallest, the famous Matryoshka dolls. The pronuciation guide ends the book. 1–4.

Features: numerals, number words in Russian, pronunciation guide, illustrated objects, and explanatory words.

Nic Leodhas, Sorche. *All in the Morning Early.* Illustrated by Evaline Ness. New York: Holt, Rinehart and Winston, 1963.

In this accumulating Scottish tale, a Caldecott Honor book, a listener counts along as Sandy, walking down the road that leads to the mill, meets increasing numbers of people and animals. After each group (whether it is one huntsman, three gypsies, or ten bonny lasses) is met, a girl or boy may be invited to repeat the rhythmic refrain about the "clicketty-clicketty-clicketty-clack" of the old mill wheel that never stays still. Recommended. K-2.

Features: *one-more* sequence in story-song to ten, repetitive refrain.

Nic Leodhas, Sorche. *Always Room for One More*. Illustrated by Nonny Hogrogian. New York: Holt, Rinehart and Winston, 1966.

During stormy weather, every traveler who passes by MacLachlan's house is invited by Lachie MacLachlan to come into his wee house, which has a large room and a small room. Boys and girls can count the travelers as they arrive: the tinker, tailor, sailor, and many, many others (using cardinal numbers to compare quantities). Most children like to chime in on the refrain that tells about the events of traveling and repeat the words, "there is always room for one more, one more" (identifying and verbalizing a pattern in a sequence). Safe from the storm, the travelers sing and dance until the house falls down. When this happens, the helpful visitors build a new house for Lachie MacLachlan, one twice as wide and twice as high as the original house. The music for this story-in-song is included and certain Scottish words are defined in a glossary. Definitions in a short, helpful list give some explanatory words to review either before or after the reading. This list is a self-checking device and enables a reader to practice reading the story aloud before one reads this story-song in rhyme to others. Recommended. 2 up.

Features: numeric story-song in rhyme from one to ten, *one-more* sequence.

Zaslavsky, Claudia. *Count on Your Fingers African Style*. Illustrated by Jerry Pinkney. New York: Thomas Y. Crowell, 1980.

A reader who liked *Moja Means One: Swahili Counting Book* should like this one with full-page pencil drawings in black and white. These illustrations bring more information about the East African marketplace into a young child's life. Zaslavsky tells how the price of objects and the quantity of objects are told to buyers with the finger counting used by the merchants. This book may interest some girls and boys in organizing a special place as a market of their own where finger counting is used to exchange objects temporarily with "buyers." 1-up.

Features: number use, numeric narrative.

Family, Friends, School, and Community Life

Alain. *1, 2, 3, Going to the Sea: An Adding and Subtracting Book*. Illustrated by the author. New York: Scholastic, 1969.

This book is a resource about the ocean and the beach, and for reviewingthe shapes of certain seaside animals and other objects. Will one find a crab on the pages? A gull? A buoy? Some will discover that this book has predictable words. Reading this text aloud may help readers develop math language cues, ones they can use in future oral language activities. Interacting with shapes of objects seen on the pages may help others develop the concept of numeration. For instance, using an inside clothesline and clothespins, a youngster may clip cut-out figures of objects in number groups on the line (numeration). *1, 2, 3, Going to the Sea* may be compared (discuss what is similar) and contrasted (discuss what is different) with another counting book, Samuel Morse's *Sea Sums*. The discussion can lead to naming objects and places found above and below sea level and the use of positive or negative numbers to indicate a location above or below sea level. 1–2.

Features: predictable text from one up to ten.

Anastasio, Dina. *The Romper Room Book of 123*. Illustrated by Nancy Stevenson. New York: Doubleday, 1985.

UpUp has ten pennies to spend, and the numbers of objects from one through ten are shown. What would a boy or girl buy with ten pennies today? To extend interest in addition using money, a young counter may be asked to arrange UpUp's ten pennies into stacks so that the same number of pennies are in each stack (Hyde and Bizar, 1989). The child who has discovered one arrangement, can then discover another. A written record of the arrangements may engage a learner's attention in discovering the place in the record where the arrangement, or pattern of numbers, reverses its sequence. This is discovered by comparing the numbers on the left side of the written record with the right side (introduction to multiplication). If a record of the penny stacks and the number of pennies in each stack are kept, the counter will be able to see a visual pattern—a similarity of numbers between the left-hand column and the right-hand column. Here is the pattern for ten pennies:

Number of Penny Stacks	Pennies in Each Stack
1	10
2	5
5	2
10	1

Different sums of pennies (even numbers) will result in different written records of the arrangements; however, there will be a similarity of p patterns with the numbers reversing the sequence at some point. This activity may be repeated with other even numbers or odd numbers of pennies (possible readiness for prime numbers and factors). What pattern is discovered when using an odd number of pennies to stack? Pre-K.

Features: numerals and numbers from one up to ten.

Anglund, Joan Walsh. *How Many Days Has Baby to Play?* Illustrated by the author. New York: Harcourt Brace Jovanovich/Gulliver, 1988.

Bear, dressed in his jacket, and Baby begin a week of days visiting relatives and friends. As each page is turned, the names of the days are revealed and Baby learns about time to play, time for friends, and time for learning activities. There is time to play with pets, build with blocks, and go on a picnic. Though not designed as a counting book, this asks for an answer to the title question and shows number use and measurement of time by days. Pre-K.

Features: bold type, simple text, and sequence of days.

Anno, Mitsumasa. *Anno's Counting Book: An Adventure in Imagination.* Illustrated by the author. New York: Thomas Y. Crowell, 1977.

Mitsumasa Anno, a Hans Christian Andersen Award recipient, shows an imaginative and wordless math adventure. Anno's adventure leads a viewer from sunrise to sunset, from January through December, and from one to many mathematical relationships. Counting begins, along with recognition of various groups, and with the creation of short number stories or original rhymes to accompany the illustrations. One sees changes over time in people, their shelter, and the nearby animals on numerical double-page landscapes in soft watercolors. A careful observer finds one-to-one relationships, groups to count, and a scale. For instance, at the numeral 4, four pigs gather to eat, four pumpkins rest in a cart, and four fish swim upstream. A group of three white geese with black-tipped wings flies through a gray-blue sky. Following behind and alone is one goose to show that a group of three and one form a group of four. The sketched scale of ten cubes is matched by a colorful tabulation of four cubes on the page that shows the number four. In the margin, these cube colors are repeated in groups of five beginning with brown, then orange, yellow, blue, and gray. Along with this tabulation, a corresponding numeral from *1* through *12* is seen on every page of this fine introduction to our number system. Encourage the young participant to use such words as *under, over, above, below, beneath,* and *between.* All of the aesthetic and mathematical pleasures are perhaps too complicated for the very young boy or girl. For instance, the watercolor landscapes show seasonal and regional changes that offer still more kinds of counting and grouping possibilities.

One spin-off activity begins with the adult placing alternating red and blue squares up on a flannel board. The activity is introduced with, "Tell me fast or tell me slow, what comes next in this row?" The observing boy or girl places the next square that belongs in the pattern. Additional numbers of patterns in sequences may be shown, and the difficulty increased in different ways: 1) by only giving two clues (e.g., yellow circle, red circle); 2) by using shapes of different sizes (small, large); 3) by increasing the number of colors used; or 4) by increasing the number of shapes used. One or more patterns may be left on the felt board each day for a young participant to complete. A youngster may set up a pattern, challenge another to continue it, and take turns with others in extending one another's patterns. Recommended. 1-up.

Features: patterns, scales, changes over time, cardinal identification of numbers from one up to twelve.

Anno, Mitsumasa. *Anno's Counting House.* Illustrated by the author. New York: Philomel, 1982.

Ten little people are ready to move from a furnished house to an empty one. Notes are included to help adults talk to children about addition, subtraction, groups and subgroups, matching, and conservation of number. The young viewer may take time to look through the cut-out windows to see Anno's people and perhaps give names to them. What is seen in the cut-out windows of the second house? Can all of the people who wear hats be found? One by one, all of the little people move until the new house is occupied and furnished. Recommended. 1–2.

Features: *one-less* sequence from ten down to one and *one- more* sequence from one up to ten, odd and even numbers.

Baird, Ann. *No Sheep.* Illustrated by the author. New York: William Morrow, 1984.

A nighttime reading book for younger children who can count the sheep as they enjoy turning the pages to see the colorful, humorous illustrations. For a following activity, a numeral-number match may be considered. On one side of a table (or chair, bed, or floor), paper strips that display groups of cotton balls may be arranged from one to nine in sequence. On the other side, a set of cards with numerals may be mixed up. Selecting a card from the stack of cards showing numerals, a boy or girl identifies the numeral, and matches it with the corresponding strip of cotton balls. Pre-K.

Features: numerals and cardinal number identification from one up to ten.

Bang, Molly. *Ten, Nine, Eight*. Illustrated by the author. New York: Greenwillow, 1983.

A Caldecott Honor book artist writes the words and draws the illustrations in this father and daughter bedtime countdown. Many objects to count in bright colors are found in the little girl's bedroom, including ten warm toes, nine soft stuffed animal friends, eight window panes, and so on down to one sleepy girl (one-to-one correspondence). Some children may enjoy seeing this book in one of its other versions, and it is available in a video cassette with Alaina Reed singing the countdown lullaby; in a filmstrip/cassette set; and in a hardcover edition accompanied by a read-along tape. All are available from Random House School Division. Recommended. Pre-1.

Features: cardinal number identification of objects in bedroom, *one-less* sequence from ten down to one.

Baum, Arline and Joseph Baum. *One Bright Monday Morning*. Illustrated by the authors. New York: Random House, 1962.

Familiar sequences in this accumulating number book form a pattern of math language. The words are easy to predict. From Monday through Saturday, different numbers of objects are seen: one blade of grass, two flowers, and so on. Page by page, the flowers increase; trees also increase in number; raindrops fall; clouds hover; the wind blows; more plants grow; and trees bloom. With the blooming trees, bees buzz, worms wiggle, and ants crawl. Everything accumulates or shows life in warm, bright illustrations with colors of blue, brown, green, and pink. Objects and illustrations build toward a colorful double-page spread announcing the arrival of spring. Pre-1.

Features: accumulation, predictable text, days of week, and number use.

Blegvad, Lenore. *One Is for the Sun*. Illustrated by Erik Blegvad. New York: Harcourt, Brace and World, 1968.

Number words in poetic phrases begin with number one for the sun, and continue with eight for ponds, nine for meadows, and end with the number ten for the houses. Full-color illustrations alternate with black and white ones and the *one-more* sequence up to ten begins again with millions. A listener hears words about one million raindrops, two million insects, and up to nine million flowers and ten million stars. It is not until a final illustration that the viewer realizes that one small child in bed sees these things from a bedroom window. Since no numerals guide the sequence, a girl or boy should be familiar with the number sequence from one up to ten. What sequence of numbers of things could an observing reader see from the kitchen window, the car window, or the bus window, and then talk about? 1–2.

Features: with no numerals to guide the sequence, numeric narrative from one up to ten by ones and in millions.

Bradman, Tony. *The Bad Babies' Counting Book.* Illustrated by Debbie Van der Beek. New York: Knopf, 1986.

On each double-page spread, a viewer sees an oversize numeral and the corresponding number of babies to count with a rhyme to read as the numbers increase from one up to ten. Some words reflect the action while others reflect just the opposite of the action shown. For example, for the words, "cleaning up the bath room," the illustration shows a busy disarray of babies, toys, and bathroom paper. After reaching the number ten, the ideas of "some," "two," and "one" are addressed. Ethnic representation is found in the illustrations. Through the day, babies overturn breakfast plates on their heads and bounce up and down on the bed mattress, enjoy bathtime—behaviors to talk about at home if appropriate for one's age. For an activity after the book, numerals on colored index cards are arranged in order one to ten. On the other side of the table are index cards with pictures of numbers of children in groups (cut from discarded magazines or catalogs) from one up to ten. Selecting a card showing a group of children, a child matches the number in the group with the corresponding numeral card. Pre-K.

Features: rhymes, oversize numerals, and cardinal number identification from one up to ten.

Brenner, Barbara. *The Snow Parade.* Illustrated by Mary Tara O'Keefe. New York: Crown, 1984.

When no one in his house is interested in marching in the snow, Andrew goes off alone and begins his own parade. Walking through a nineteenth-century village, he is joined by a spotted dog, a waddling duck, and a friendly rabbit (accumulation), as more and more marchers fall into line. Finally, everyone in the village—including a girl on a sled—has joined to march along in Andrew's wintry day parade. After reading this numeric story aloud, an adult may ask a young listener to review the illustrations and count the groups of snowflakes found in the margins of the pages. Children who have seen snowflakes, may want to make snowflakes cut from paper, sign them, and discuss ways of categorizing the snowflakes on a large graph, displaying the children's names down the left-hand margin and Yes and No columns across the top to answer the question, "Who has seen a snowflake?" Discussion may include responses to such questions as, "What are the names of our friends who have seen snowflakes?" Pre-1.

Features: numeric narrative, accumulation, *one-more* sequence from one up to ten.

Bright, Robert. *My Red Umbrella*. illustrated by the author. New York: William Morrow, 1959.

The red umbrella is very colorful and easy to see as the rain comes down. Joining the little girl under her umbrella, the arriving animals increase in size from small animals (dog, kitten, chickens, and rabbits) to those in a group of larger animals (lamb, goats, pigs, and foxes). The last animal who seeks shelter from the rain under the red umbrella is larger still—one large wet bear (size relationships). The umbrella grows bigger on the pages as the number of animals (meaning of *one-more-than*) and their increasing sizes require. When the rain stops, the animals leave in the order in which they arrived (pattern). After this story, an adult may sequence paper outlines of animals in the order of their appearance in the story. Looking at the sequence together, the adult and the youngster may play the game, "I am Thinking of . . . " (e.g., the adult begins with, "I am thinking of the animal that arrived first to get under the umbrella"; or "I am thinking of the animal that arrived before the kitten; or I am thinking of the animal that arrived after the lamb"). Terms that identify ordinals of *first, second, third*, or such words as *before* and *after* may be emphasized. The youngster responds and identifies the appropriate outline in the sequence. Some boys and girls will enjoy seeing this number story again with the filmstrip-cassette version produced by Weston Woods (Weston, Conn.) Pre-1.

Features: cardinal number identification, number sequence, and size relationships.

Burningham, John. *John Burningham's 123*. Illustrated by the author. New York: Crown, 1986.

Burningham, twice recipient of the Kate Greenaway Medal, uses soft pastel colors and light humor to show boys and girls climbing a large, leafy tree. Ten children may be counted sitting on the branches among the leaves. Numerals and number words are in large type and are easy to read (one-to-one correspondence between the children in this group and natural numbers). What frightens the children out of the tree? What will a young observer predict? K-1.

Features: numerals, number words from one up to ten, accumulation.

Burningham, John. *Ride Off: Learning Subtraction*. Illustrated by the author. New York: Viking, 1983.

For another book suitable for preschool and kindergarten children, there is this number book, where five children try to ride a runaway horse. Predictions can be made and simple relationships of numbers (subtraction) can be learned in this humorous story. As the big horse nears a tree branch, dashes up hill, gallops downhill, stops and bucks, the small riders slip off his back. Without words, the symbols of the subtraction operation on the numbers are the focus. The colorful, attractive illustrations are on heavy cardboard pages that fold out from side to side as well as up and down. To extend the *one-less-than* pattern after the book is read, numeral cards from five down to one are placed on a pocket chart in the classroom or on a table at home. A girl or boy selects one card from a second set of cards with corresponding groups of dots (or other shapes) and places it beside the appropriate numeral card in the chart or on the table. Pre-K.

Features: operation of subtraction with numbers under five, symbols in math sentences, unfolding pages.

Burningham, John. *The Shopping Basket*. Illustrated by the author. New York: Thomas Y. Crowell, 1980.

As Steven, wearing his glasses, walks to the store, an observant listener may review what is needed. First, Mother wants six eggs, five bananas, four apples, and on down to one bag of crisps (potato chips). When Steven leaves the store, a large bear steps in front of him. The bear demands all of the eggs, threatening to squeeze the breath out of Steven. Steven thinks quickly, throws an egg up in the air, and challenges the bear to catch the egg. What can be predicted? The next page shows what happens. Did someone guess that the bear would have egg all over his face? Did anyone notice that one egg is now missing from the rows of pictured items? The objects are shown in a rebus arrangement so the grocery items are seen and counted easily. On his way home, Steven is challenged by other animals, too: a noisy monkey, a clumsy kangaroo, a fat pig, and an elephant with a short trunk. Steven outthinks every one of them. A reader is not told that some of the story is a daytime fantasy, but the illustrations of this Children's Choice book tell a viewer when it is Steven's real day and when it is part of his fanciful imagination. Recommended. Pre-2.

Features: subtraction operation, *one-less* sequence from six down to one, rebuses.

Busy Street. Illustrated. Crystal Lake, Ill.: Rigby, 1988

In this big-book format approximately thirteen by seventeen inches, each situation on the street is numbered. There are full-color illustrations on double-page spreads. For instance, at the number five, a young viewer sees people swimming and diving in the river that runs by the busy street. The rhyming of the words about the numbers may lead to some creative class activities. For reading-along activities, small copies, about six by eight inches, and audio cassettes, are available. Pre-K.

Features: numerals, number words in rhymes, cardinal number identification of objects.

Calmenson, Stephanie. *Ten Items or Less: A Counting Book*. Illustrated by Terri Supes. New York: Golden/Western, 1985.

Young Mandy shops with her mother in the supermarket and rides in the shopping cart up and down the aisles. Mandy and her mother play a counting game called "Ten Items or Less." The meaning of words is given for *items* (groceries) and *express* (fast). Mandy and her mother count one box of cookies, and a package of spaghetti for two items, then a watermelon for three items. Oversize numerals in red are found in the corners of the pages for a young shopper's quick reference as the rest of the purchases are counted up to ten: cereal, raisins, milk, cheese, cat food, a broom, and last, a book about a shaggy, baggy elephant for Mandy. In the express lane, Mandy helps count the items again for the clerk. Pre-K.

Features: numeric narrative from one through ten, oversize numerals in red, and the process of counting shown in print.

Carlson, Nancy. *When Baby Went to Bed*. Illustrated by the author. New York: Viking Kestrel, 1987.

Through simple text and bright illustrations, this board book entertains children as they learn their numbers from one up to ten. Young preschoolers may enjoy the illustrations, framed with a border of stars and crescent moons, of the toddler standing in footed pajamas in the crib and peering out over the side. Shapes of stars or crescent moons can be arranged in different patterns on cards for a boy or girl to identify by numbers. Different patterns for ten and other numbers may be shown. An older child may make as many different patterns as possible for a selected number while drawing with crayons. Pre.

Features: numerals, cardinal number identification from one up to ten.

Charlip, Remy and Mary Beth Miller. *Handtalk Birthday: A Number and Story Book in Sign Language*. Photographs by George Ancona. New York: Macmillan, 1987.

Carrying presents for her birthday, Mary Beth's friends arrive and surprise her. Mary Beth's friends encourage her to guess what is in the boxes. What could be in the box shaped liked a cake? Mary Beth guesses several times but cannot determine that it is a colorful hat. She continues to open the presents, and in the boxes, finds the refreshments for the party: bubble gum, a cake, candy, cookies, ice cream, and punch to drink. Mary Beth's friends sing "Happy Birthday" to her as she makes a birthday wish. Mary Beth's wish is to fly and the illustrations show Mary Beth "flying" by floating up to the ceiling. There are sign language, finger spelling, and full-color photographs. Each word signed in the photographs is shown also in print and helps a reader understand the communication skills of the deaf. Recommended. All ages.

Features: numeric narrative, numerals, number words shown in sign language, and objects at birthday party to count from one up to ten.

Curran, Peggy. *Fire Fighters Counting Book*. Illustrated by Pat Stewart. Chicago: Children's Press, 1983.

This 123 book may be appropriate as a companion book for *Project 123*, and shows how the fire fighters help a community. With this book, a viewer sees the number-numeral relationships in an environment that may be unfamiliar and interesting. For the number one, what object related to fire fighters will be predicted? For ten? A counter should recognize different patterns of grouping for the numbers and the fact that there is no particular way that a number of members in a group of must be arranged. Is any girl or boy ready to show different patterns of grouping for numbers one up to ten while drawing original patterns? K-1.

Features: numerals, cardinal number identification from one through ten.

Cunningham, Aline. *My Counting Book*. Illustrated by the author. St. Louis, Mo.: Concordia, 1973.

My Counting Book is a repetitive text that names the features of a child's body and a child's possessions. The reader sees the numerals and reads at the yellow sentence strips at the foot of the pages. Cunningham's simple illustrations show one head, one mouth, two ears, five fingers on one hand, and ten toes on two feet. Listeners may be ready to predict some of the sentences with number words and repeat the words during a second reading? Older girls and boys (age 7 and up) may be ready to consider measurement in centimeters. With reference to a one tape measure marked in centimeters and displayed by the teacher, each girl and boy first may estimate responses in centimeters to questions based on the illustrations: 1) How wide is your face? 2) How long is your face? 3) How long are your ears? and 4) How wide is your mouth? After the estimates are given, each student receives a centimeter tape measure. Each is asked to draw a face on art paper according to the estimates each gave for width and length and can add other features as needed (Hyde and Bizar, 1989). After the drawings are finished, the teacher demonstrates the use of the ruler or centimeter tape measure to determine a volunteer's actual measurements and records them next to the estimates. In teams of two, the students then use their centimeter tape measures and determine one another's actual measurements and record them. With this information, each student then draws a face according to the actual measurements and adds any needed features. Pre-K.

Features: predictable text, cardinal number identification of body parts.

Ernst, Lisa Campbell. *Up to Ten and Down Again.* Illustrated by the author. New York: Lothrop, Lee and Shepard, 1986.

These illustrations, which look like photographs mounted in a family's photo album, show nine children and two adults on a picnic. First, the *one-more* sequence is presented. A duck sees two cars, from which emerge three dogs. Then four boys and five girls throw six balls. Other animals are curious about the outing: as the three dogs play through the illustrations, frogs gather near the pond to see what is going on, and squirrels in branches take a look at the event—and a closer look at someone's camera. The picnic food is set out and ready to eat but at the numeral 10, storm clouds arrive. The storm sends everyone hurrying to gather their belongings and a countdown begins in a *one-less* sequence until the one lonely duck is left all alone again. An observant viewer may notice the shapes of the raindrops (hooks) and the power of the wind that sends the illustrated pattern of leaves sideways on the pages. At the foot of each page is the numeral and the object name. Somewhere on each page are the appropriate number of objects to find in boxes. There is a review on the final double-page spread that shows each numeral and the object that was counted in squares. For a second ending, the back end-pages show other ducks joining the lonely duck as the rain continues. An older girl or boy preparing original illustrations may appreciate such touches as the duck swimming to the lower corner of the picture and crawling into the border of the illustration. Recommended. Pre-1.

Features: matching, cardinal number identification, numeral recognition, sequence from one through ten and back, and a review.

Farber, Norma. *Up the Down Elevator.* Illustrated by Annie Gusman. Reading, Mass.: Addison-Wesley, 1979.

As the characters step inside the open elevator door, a viewer may count those who push the button to go up in the elevator, one by one and then as a total group. Recto pages offer large black and white illustrations with highlights of color framed with borders of repetitive patterns of numerals and number words. For example, the scene for numeral 1 is surrounded by a border with repeated numeral 1's in bright green. On the page for numeral 2, the illustration of a chef with a crocodile stew and a blacksmith with a stallion's shoe is bordered in purple. The alternating border colors continue with green, then purple. Numeral 3 is for a waitress, a sailor, and an animal trainer. Numeral 4 is for a busboy, doorman, golfer, and trumpeter. Other unusual characters in this elevator are a beeman, a milkman, a locksmith, and a shepherd. Numerals always are found in bold type within the illustrations. Similar repetitive beginnings are seen in the text with words, "When the elevator stopped at 1 . . . " (2, 3, and so on for each floor to 10). At floor 10, the characters all ride together down to floor 1 again (one-less sequence). The final illustrations offer a review of all numerals and number words. While the concept of adding up to groups of ten is appropriate for first graders and some kindergarteners or preschoolers, some of these words may be difficult ones to read. The reading difficulty level seems could be more appropriate for grade two and up, with such characters as a vegetarian, a veterinarian, and a vintner. The elevator riders may set off a discussion about occupations and ways numbers are used in those occupations. Older girls and boys (age 9 and up) may be interested in being given assigned weights for each of the passengers, and asked to add the combined weight of all or the combined weight of selected passengers. Names of passengers and their weights may be written on paper strips and two, three, or four strips drawn from a box to make up a three-digit addition problem to solve. Girls and boys may create their own word problems, e.g., "If the elevator holds a limit of one thousand pounds (1000), which passengers can ride up without going over this limit?" 2 up.

Features: numerals in bold, anaphoric beginnings on pages, repetitive patterns in borders, and review page.

Fisher, Leonard Everett. *Boxes! Boxes!* Illustrated by the author. New York: Viking, 1984.

With more than eighty colorful boxes (color recognition), this one can be used as a counting book. The boxes are shown in different sizes (size relationships) and shapes (geometric shapes) and discussed in a rhyming text as containers for toys, puppy dogs, candy, paints, and other items found in a family's home. Using the overhead projector and box shapes cut from colorful acetate, the teacher may stack the shapes above one another to represent a tower of colorful boxes. Students may copy the color pattern they see on the screen and use crayons to color a tower of outlined boxes on a record sheet. Presented with a second color pattern, the students locate the box on the bottom of a second tower of boxes and color according to the pattern seen on the overhead. For a variation, boxes of two colors may be stacked, their numbers identified, and number sentences recorded. As one example, two blue and three red boxes may be stacked and this sentence written beside the stack: $2 + 3 = 5$. Pre-1.

Features: size relationships, geometric shapes, and cardinal number identification.

Fowler, Rich. *Mr. Little's Noisy 123*. Illustrated by the author. New York: Grosset and Dunlap, 1987.

Mr. Little tries to sleep and the noise begins. One owl hoots, two donkeys bray, and three whistles toot. Frogs croak and lions roar. At twenty, the counting continues by tens to one hundred bees buzzing, until an alarm clock rings and the sound wakes up Mr. Little who thought he wasn't sleeping because he heard so many noises in his dream. Inserted at the foot of each page is a smaller illustration that shows Mr. Little's increasing restlesness through the pages while a larger illustration shows his dream. Mr. Little sleeps on his back, side, and stomach. Pulling his blankets and pillows in different ways, Mr. Little turns his position around, and sleeps with his head at the foot of the bed. A number matrix from one up to one hundred is on the endpapers, providing a preview and a review of numbers (readiness for reading tables or graphs). Perhaps someone can make animal noises and repeat them a selected number of times for counting. K-2.

Features: *one-more* sequence from one through ten, *ten-more* sequence up to one hundred, matrix, and a review.

Gantz, David. *Captain Swifty Counts to Fifty, Isn't That Nifty?* Illustrated by the author. Garden City, N. Y.: Doubleday, 1982.

Some boys and girls may not have heard of Captain Swifty and Moxy, but in this counting book they are famous. Moxy, Captain Swifty, and his parrot, Squawk, have one numeric adventure after another. The first illustrated endpapers introduce girls and boys to some of the episodes to be found in the book. There are objects to be counted—e.g., bees, butterflies, and clocks (matching objects with number names). Inside, there is a treasure to be found, and during the search, a wide variety of objects from pickle jars to snails on the beach can be identified, recognized as a number, and labeled with a numeral symbol. Numerals from 1 to 10 are found in upper left-hand corners of pages near a top hat to show the correct numbers of rabbits hopping out of the hat (cardinal number identification). Each bunny wears a number and the youngster may be interested in knowing that if the numbers represent an order (e.g., representing the first bunny who hopped from the hat), then it is appropriate to use ordinal numbers of first, second, third, and so on, to refer to the bunnies. Captain Swifty and his friends carry on their adventures in the center of the pages with cartoon balloons indicating the objects (groups, sets) to be counted on the page. At the foot of the page, a line is forming with each creature stating its ordinal position. An adult may point out the starting point for counting ordinals in this line. At eleven to twenty, only the numerals are seen. After twenty, the counting goes on by tens up to fifty. K-1.

Features: numeric episodes, object identification, number use, numerals-cardinal numbers relationships from one through ten, ordinals, numerals only to twenty, and the *ten- more* sequence up to fifty.

Gillham, Bill, and Susan Hulme. *Let's Look for Numbers*. Photographs by Jan Siegieda. New York: G. P. Putnam's Sons, 1984.

Gillham, an educational psychologist, and Hulme, an experienced teacher of infants from England, show some of the number-numeral relationships that can be found in a child's daily experiences. Questions may be generated small colorful photographs: "How many muffins did Mom bake in the muffin tin?" "How many blades do you see on this small windmill?" A beginning counter is asked to recognize one part of a whole object and an adult will give guidance if needed. Pre-1.

Features: cardinal number identification.

Gregor, Arthur. *12345*. Photographs by Robert Doisneau. Design by Albert Plécy. New York: Lippincott, n.d.

Chalk-white numerals on a black endpage tell what's to come in this book. For the number one, one lawn bowling pin is left standing in a full-page black and white photograph. One-to-one correspondence is seen for a colorful pink numeral *1* is superimposed over the black and white outline of the bowling pin. The verse tells of the fun of hitting all the pins but one. More rhyming verses concern, for example, five snails who expose their heads and tails and carry their houses like sails; or about seven acrobatic children who build a body pryamid. Final illustrations include eleven candles on a cake and twelve eggs in the grass. Without counting each object, is anyone ready to recognize on sight the number of outlines near the numerals on the verso pages? K-1.

Features: numerals, objects, number words from one up to twelve in rhyming verses.

Hughes, Shirley. *Lucy and Tom's 123*. Illustrated by the author. New York: Viking Kestrel, 1987.

Lucy and Tom, an English sister and brother, are busy doing things. Along with objects to count, such ideas as comparative sizes, the concept of pairs, of odds and evens, and the progression of numbers, all appear as part of Lucy's and Tom's actions in these full-color illustrations, accompanying a number narrative. Tom and Lucy have many things to do and count before going to a tea party in honor of Grandma's 60th birthday (ordinals). Lucy plays with her animals and arranges them two by two. Outside, Lucy and Tom count the birds on a high wire, people at the crosswalk. For Granny's party, there are party treats plus a big colorful cake to count and enjoy. A favorite illustration of a birthday cake may be enlarged or reduced on a copy machine. Features and colors are added to duplicates so the cakes will have different characteristics for a learner to sort: cakes of four different sizes may be used; then cakes of different colors; and cakes with different numbers and colors of candles. Recommended. K-2.

Features: numeric narrative, numerals-numbers relationships, variety of concepts.

Hughes, Shirley. *A Walk in the Park*. Illustrated by the author. New York: Lothrop, Lee and Shepard, 1984.

Grandfather and granddaughter count all the things they find during their walk together in a park. For the number six, an observing boy or girl counts six runners running, and for ten, ten birds swooping in the sky. Is someone ready to recognize the numbers for different groups without counting each object in a group as the pages are turned a second time? Details are easy to see in the watercolor illustrations. Pre-K.

Features: cardinal number identification of objects from one to ten during a walk in the park.

Hutchins, Pat. *The Doorbell Rang*. Illustrated by the author. New York: Greenwillow, 1986.

After Mother bakes one dozen cookies, Sam and Victoria count them and find that they can each have six. As the doorbell rings and rings, more and more friends arrive. Of course, their friends want some of the cookies, so the cookies are divided with the friends. When each boy and girl has only one cookie, the doorbell rings again. Victoria and Sam answer the door unwillingly, but fortunately, it is Grandmother, with trays of additional cookies! Circular cereal pieces may represent cookies when projected on the overhead. The "cookies" may be divided in front of the children as the story is reviewed, and the operation of division is shown on the screen. Recommended. K-2.

Features: recognizing equivalent groups as early experience for division.

Hynard, Julia. *Percival's Party*. Illustrated by Francis Thatcher. Chicago: Children's Press, 1983.

How would you feel if everyone forgot your birthday? How do you think Percival feels when he believes that everyone really forgot his birthday party? Most boys and girls will enjoy the illustrations that show this birthday party more if they know their number-numeral relationships in sequence from one up to ten, since the numerals are out of sequence (numeral recognition). 1–2.

Features: number use, and numeral recognition out of sequence up to ten.

Inkpen, Mick. *One Bear at Bedtime*. Illustrated by the author. Boston: Little, Brown, 1988.

Asked to find and count caterpillars on each page, a young viewer sees a little boy count the animals that accompany him as he gets ready for bed. Along with one bear at bedtime, there are two pigs who wear his clothes, four giraffes who join him in the bath, three kangaroos who bounce on the bed, eight crocodiles who use up all his toothpaste, and, of course, nine hard-to-find caterpillars. This is a before-I-go-to-bed imaginary playtime and counting book with animals of various sizes and descriptions in textured watercolors. Just one bear—the favorite sleeping comparion—begins and ends this circular story. Even though the number words are found in the rhyming lines, the young counter may begin to recognize numbers of groups up to ten without reading the number words and without counting each member in a selected group. Is any girl or boy ready to turn through the pages again and quickly recognize the numbers of imaginary animals? Pre-1.

Features: circular story pattern, cardinal number identification, and *one-more* sequence of objects in groups from one up to ten.

Katz, Bobbi. *Tick-Tock, Let's Read the Clock.* Illustrated by Carol Nick-laus. New York: Random House, 1988.

This book offers clocks that present digital time as well as traditional faces. The paper engineering on the sixteen pages provides movable parts for viewer participation. Pre-1.

Features: digital and standard faces, movable digital wheels, and hands.

Keller, Holly. *Ten Sleepy Sheep.* Illustrated by the author. New York: Greenwillow, 1983.

Twilight blue endpapers add just the right touch of unifying color for this nighttime number book. Lewis cannot sleep and as he counts sheep, the sheep arrive all set for a party in Lewis's bedroom, bringing such personal possessions as a red balloon, drums, hoops, and horns. The fluffy white sheep accumulate, dance, make noise, and have fun. Finally, set-tling down, they ask for drinks of water and stories before bedtime, and before getting into Lewis's bed. Some get under the covers while others rest upon the pillows. Under the bedcover designed with stars, one sheep nudges Lewis over to the edge of the bed for the humor children love. To match numerals with groups in different settings, an interested boy or girl may make an individual set of numeral cards. Pre-K.

Features: cardinal number identification in *one-more* sequence from one up to ten.

Khalsa, Dayal Kaur. *Sleepers.* Illustrated by the author. New York: Crown, 1988.

In this book, the young unnamed character has a refrain, "But I never sleep." Tucked into her bed, she describes the ways that others sleep: her family, animals, a clown, a cowboy, and a fireman. A young viewer finds that Dad sleeps on the sofa, the dog sleeps under the piano, twin aunts sleep sitting up, and Grandma sleeps in the car. With each refrain, the little girl settles deeper and deeper into her comfortable bed, and finally says, "But I never sleep. /Instead I count sheep," and falls asleep by the number eleven (use of numbers, place value reinforcement). The sheep she counts fall asleep, too. The detailed illustrations in bright colors have amusing things for a young viewer to see as well as a rhyming text to hear out loud. Paper plates may be cut in halves with numerals on one half and groups of sheep (or stars) on the other half so an inter-ested boy or girl can practice finding numerals to match with a corresponding number in groups. If the paper plates are cut apart in various directions like pieces of a jigsaw puzzle, then each puzzle-plate becomes a self-checking activity. Pre-K.

Features: rhyming lines and numeric narrative up to eleven.

Knapp, Sonja, and Chris Knapp. *Tea-Time*. Illustrated by Valerie Underwood. New York: Franklin Watts, 1979.

John and Rachel would not eat their food at teatime, so they grew smaller and smaller. Chased by the cat, they hide in a nearby mousehole and walk downhill until they come to a big mouse hall filled with a big table and friendly mice having a party. Joining the party, the children taste one, two, and more, delicious foods. Beneath the framed illustrations in full-color, one sees the oversize numerals accompanying phrases: four ice creams, five sausages, six chocolate eggs. Rachel and John notice they are growing bigger again, so they run along the small passage to find their way out. Arriving home just in time for tea, Mother says, "Now come and eat your tea," and they do! Some British terms may be unfamiliar and can be discussed. With pictures from magazines of good things to eat, an interested listener may cut and paste selected food items on one half of a styrofoam or paper plate and record the appropriate numeral on the other half of the tray. Cut apart in a zig-zag fashion, each tray becomes a tea-time number puzzle to solve. K-1.

Features: numeric narrative, *one-more* sequence from one up to ten.

Kraus, Robert. *Good Night Little One*. Illustrated by Neils Mogens Bodecker. New York: Windmill, 1981.

Large oversize numerals are recognized on the pages as the rhymes are read. With capitalized words and anaphoric beginnings of" Good Night Little One," Kraus supplies short ending phrases in rhyme (patterns): "Day Is Done" (one); "Peek A Boo" (two). Kraus's rhymes provide models for girls and boys interested in creating original lines to rhyme with the number words. *Goodnight, One, Two, Three* (New York: Scroll, n.d.) by Yutaka Sugita complements Kraus's counting book and may be considered for another bedtime counting activity. The young listener may say goodnight to the numbers in the groups of animals, people, and objects from one up to ten. Pre-K.

Features: oversize numerals, number words in rhyming lines.

Kredenser, Gail. *1 One Dancing Drum.* Illustrated by Stanley Mack. New York: Phillips, 1971.

This is a clever, humorous introduction to the numerals, 1 to 10. One bandmaster greets the musicians and their instruments as they gather on a crowded circular bandstand. Each group of musicians wears a different uniform color so it is easy for a young observer to see one dancing drum, two tinkling triangles, or six persnickety piccolos (describing relationships with *one-more-than* or *greater than*). The cartoon-style drawings show that some of the musicians stand on the rooftop of the bandstand; others dangle from trombones; and others stand on the shoulders of fellow musicians. Children enjoy the final double-page spread as they see the musicians in their bright colors tumbling in different directions across two pages as the bandstand falls apart. When the groups of musicians are all mixed up, can all of the members in a particular group (e.g., all of the triumphant trumpets or all of the tootling trombones) be found? Using a collection of musical instruments in the classroom, shapes of musical instruments may be discussed and questions about them asked: "Could classroom musical instruments be arranged by size?" "By the sounds (pitch) the instruments make?" "What other objects in the room might make sounds or beats we can count?" Recommended. Pre-1.

Features: numerals, number words from one up to ten, alliteration, and classifying by attributes.

Kubler, Annie. *Albert Moves In.* Illustrated. Restrop Manor, Eng.: Child's Play, 1985.

An abacus with ten beads is attached to this board book so a young counter may identify a one-to-one correspondence between numbers of objects and the beads. Albert moves into a new house and brings his possessions: one bicycle, two dogs, through four ghosts, and up to ten snails. In the text on the final pages, the review column of all of the numbers of objects is found. K-1.

Features: numeric narrative from one up to ten, and column review in text.

Kubler, Annie. *Counting Kids.* Illustrated. Restrop Manor, Eng.: Child's Play, 1985.

A ten-bead abacus is attached to the sturdy pages of this board book. Through die-cut windows, the beads are moved from left to right to mark a number of objects. Objects are added together or subtracted. For instance, given a certain number of slices of bread, one hungry girl eats two of them. How many slices are left? Friends arriving and leaving make other counting situations. K-1.

Features: objects from one up to ten with addition and subtraction.

Kunhardt, Edith. *Ned's Number Book*. Illustrated by Eugenie. Chicago: Goldencraft/Children's Press, 1981.

Other objects that are familiar to a small girl or boy are seen in this First Little Golden Book. Ned plays with wooden numeral blocks and introduces numbers and their corresponding numerals. When an adult asks for three, can someone select the number of toys needed to make a group of three toys? Pre-K.

Features: numerals and cardinal number identification from one up to ten.

Leighton, Ralph and Carl Feynman. *How to Count Sheep without Falling Asleep*. Illustrations by George Ulrich. Englewood Clifs, N. J.: Prentice-Hall, 1976.

With black and white drawings and highlights of green and blue watercolor, this book explores ways to impprove the recording of objects counted and will be appreciated by ages 9 and up. A shepherd notches his crook, one notch for one sheep, as he counts his sheep, but cannot unnotch the crook if a sheep runs away. Then he decides to count his sheep by putting small rocks in a sack (one rock for each sheep). When the sack becomes too heavy, the shepherd uses a black rock to replace ten white rocks so the sack will weigh less. His next idea is to chip the number of sheep into a stone using 1 for each white rock and X for each black rock. The shepherd invents a mark that means take away when one sheep dies, then an adding and subtracting machine made by using long strips of rock and sliding parts (a slide rule). As a follow-up activity for older learners (age 9 and up), directions are included for constructing an adding and subtracting machine with cardboard, pencil, ruler, and scissors. Adult guidance may be needed. Advanced 2 up.

Features: numeric narrative, information, directions for making simple slide rule.

Little, Mary E. *123 for the Library*. Illustrated by the author. New York: Atheneum, 1974.

It's time for storytime hour at the library. The numerals introduce the children as they arrive. A young reader counts along as the children are seen in the sketches with colors of blue, black, and orange. Hugh is one, Ben is two, and Rosalie is three. When Ted and Carmen arrive, how many children are ready for the story hour? Can a young viewer see if there is one child in the story for every square shape on Little's pages (correspondence)? Then Sue and Kevin and Polly and Caroline appear. Now, how many children are there? Stacy and Tracy arrive. Is that the number ten? Recommended. Pre-K.

Features: numerals to nine, cardinal numbers from one up to ten, numeric narrative, and a review.

McLeod, Emily. *One Snail and Me: A Book of Numbers and Animals and a Bathtub*. Illustrated by Walter Lorraine. Boston: Atlantic/Little, Brown, 1961.

A small girl's imaginative animals join her in the bathtub. Beginning with one small snail who leaves a silver trail on the tub's edge and ending with ten minnows who have prickly fins, there are increasing numbers in groups of animals to identify. When the animals are shown again in a ten-to-one sequence, they reassemble in different groups. For the number ten, a young counter finds that a group of eight animals and two groups of one animal each are the same total number as a group of five animals, a group of three, and a group of two. Recommended. K-2.

Features: position in a group does not affect number, cardinal number identification, *one-more* sequence from one up to ten, commutativity, *one-less* sequence back to one, and rhymes.

Mendoza, George. *The Marcel Marceau Counting Book*. Illustrated with photographs by Milton H. Greene. Garden City, N.Y.: Doubleday, 1971.

Famous mime, Marcel Marceau, poses with hats that signify different roles and occupations, His miming of a farmer, a cowboy, and so on reinforced by the text. Photographs show a different hat in each illustration with the assortment of hats accumulating through the pages. In the classroom, a collection of real or paper hats can be tried on and counted and occupations mimed.

Features: occupations, accumulation, and *one-more* sequence up to ten.

Mendoza, George. *Norman Rockwell's Counting Book*. Illustrated with reproductions of Rockwell's paintings. New York: Harmony House, 1977.

Any interested viewer—child or adult—could spend many minutes looking closely at the details in these twenty-three paintings. The paintings are shown in colorful full pages and are selected mainly from the published covers of the *Saturday Evening Post*. These are paintings which lend themselves to the use of words about mathematics and counting in the things we see around us. Pre-up.

Features: cardinal number identification of objects in twenty-three paintings.

Merriam, Eve. *Project 123*. Illustrated by Harriet Sherman. New York: McGraw-Hill, 1971.

Words and illustrations both reflect the vitality of city life, and show the noise, rhythm, action, and happenings of life in a housing project. At first glance, does there seem to be too much information for a young reader in the verses as well as in the pictures? Some children may be bothered by the myriad of signs, posters, billboards, and grafitti that are seen in these illustrations of life in a big city. Other children, familiar with this environment, will recognize as realistic the many signs on the basement wall in this housing project and enjoy reading the word *drip* seven times to illustrate the numeral 7. The signs display messages that can be discussed, messages telling the maintenence men to check the faucets in a certain building or to check the incinerators as needed. Other examples may be discussed. K-1.

Features: numerals, number words, and numeric verses from one up to ten.

Moncure, Jane Belk. *My One Book*. Illustrated by Pam Peltier. Chicago: The Child's World, 1981.

A young boy wears a tee-shirt with the word *one* on the front and a cap with the numeral 1 and leads a young viewer through the pages to tell how many objects are seen (e.g., one bowl, one spoon, one tablecloth, and one table), to recognize numerals, corresponding black dots, number words, to count, and to identify cardinal numbers. This is one in a series with the other titles being *My Two Book, My Three Book, My Four Book,* and *My Five Book*. Pre-K.

Features: numeral recognition, one-to-one correspondence, number words, and cardinal number identification.

Morris, Ann. *Night Counting*. Illustrated by Maureen Roffey. New York: Harper and Row, 1986.

In these full-color illustrations, toddlers are plainly drawn and easy to see, and what is to be counted can be seen clearly by a young viewer. The endpapers show twenty gray sheep, each one jumping over a yellow gate. This small book, approximately six by six inches, shows a brother and sister getting ready for bed, seeing one crescent moon, getting two hugs from mother, and three teddy bears. The clock face shows the time is seven o'clock, and a young viewer finds other objects to count. No numerals are shown; phrases begin with capitals but have no ending punctuation. When the children are in their beds, under the covers, sound asleep, one gray sheep remains and leaps over the headboards. Since there are no numerals on the pages, can someone match numeral cards with the numbers of objects on the pages as the pages are turned a second time? Pre.

Features: without numerals, cardinal number identification from one up to ten.

Morse, Samuel French. *Sea Sums*. Illustrated by Fuku Akino. Boston: Little, Brown, 1970.

Morse, a New England poet with a fondness for Japan, and Akino, a Japanese artist, give groups to compare and discuss in the *more-than* relationship from one to ten, and in a *less-than* relationship from ten down to one. As the title suggests, the numerals accompany the sights, sounds, and imagined smells near the sea. As the incoming fog makes objects disappear from sight in its covering grayness, a participating reader may count in a *one-less-than* sequence as the fog covers the objects once seen on earlier pages. Finally, the reader is "the only one." As the fog swirls around hiding all, Morse includes the empty group concept in a poetic way with the words, "nothing at all." Two additional features, the numbers in italics in the text and the rebuses, may motivate a young artist to draw an original seaside figure or figures for a home or classroom number-numeral chart. 1–2.

Features: numeric verses, numerals, number words in italics in text, *one-more* sequence from one up to ten, and *one-less* sequence from ten down to one.

Nordqvist, Sven. *Willie in the Big World: An Adventure with Numbers.* Illustrated by the author. New York: William Morrow, 1986.

Leaving home on a journey, Willie sees a number of different people and animals who give him objects one by one (*one-more-than* relationship). Willie accumulates ten objects, e.g., a globe-of-the-world pencil sharpener, a shoe, and a spool of thread to show different elements accumulating in a group. Then, in repeated subtraction situations, Willie gives all but one object away as he returns home (*one-less-than* relationship). The double-page spread illustrations are in full color and show the accumulating numbers of objects to match the number of Willie's visits. On the ninth stop, Willie visits a duke who has nine apple cores, nine geese, and so on. Adult help may be needed in finding the objects to count among the many details on the pages. 1 up.

Features: numeric narrative, accumulation, *one-more* sequence up to ten, and *one-less* sequence from ten down to one.

Omerod, Jan. *Young Joe.* Illustrated by the author. New York: Lothrop, Lee and Shepard, 1986.

Young Joe, a young black boy of about four years old, counts from one up to ten. In this simple counting book, Joe finds the animals and insects shown in large, colorful, and clear illustrations. Is a girl or boy ready to match numeral cards to numbers of objects in this book? Pre.

Features: cardinal number identification from one up to ten, animal and insect recognition as members of groups.

Patience, John. *The Fancy Dress Party Counting Book.* Illustrated by the author. New York: Derrydale Books/Crown, 1984.

Large, bright numerals are backgrounds for girls and boys who are dressed for a fancy dress party. The illustrations entice a young viewer to turn the pages to see more of this festive occasion from one through ten. Dressed in a fairy costume, a girl waits for the other children to arrive for her special birthday party. The children arrive in their fancy costumes: two capering clowns; three merry musketeers; and nine plundering pirates. On each large double-page spread are colorful numerals, the number words, and the right number of blue circles to correspond with the members of the arriving groups of children. After the number ten, the text poses a question about how many party items can be seen: balloons with faces, candles, children, cupcakes with cherries, doughnuts, gelatin desserts, and so on. K-2.

Features: numerals, number words, one-to-one correspondence, alliteration, numeric narrative, and problems in words.

Peppé, Rodney. *Little Numbers*. Illustrated by the author. New York: Viking, 1984.

Best used in a toddler's private book collection because of its small size, this Little Toy Board book's heavy pages show toys to name and to count. Bright colors stand out on the white backgrounds as a beginning counter counts from one to five colorful wooden dolls that nest inside one another, some bears, a rabbit, a boat, and other toys. He also reminds a young reader that after the toys are out and played with, they should be put away. Pre-K.

Features: cardinal number identification of toys from one up to five.

Riley, Kana. *The Picnic*. Illustrated by Richard Brown. Lexington, Mass.: D. C. Heath, 1989.

As one example of a counting book included in a recent reading series, this book offers several patterns for a young viewer. A black family gets into its van, and travels to a nearby park for a picnic. A pink tablecloth is placed on the wooden table, two red tomatoes are taken from the basket, then three orange carrots, four yellow bananas, and so on. Numerals in bold and isolated objects are found at the tops of pages while the action is seen in the framed, full-color illustrations. A young counter sees numerals in a sequence from one to ten, an increasing number of objects (*one-more* pattern), and the objects in a different arrangement in the large illustration. At the number ten, red ants appear, then nine yellow bees, and eight orange caterpillars. This *one-less* sequence continues as other pests arrive to make the family uncomfortable—mosquitoes, worms, dogs, and one black rain cloud. It is easy to predict that the family will head for home but not easy to predict that they will continue their picnic on the living room floor. Pre-K.

Features: patterns, *one-more* and *one-less* sequences, objects in different arrangements, and numeric narrative from one through ten.

Rowan, Dick. *Everybody In! A Counting Book*. Photographs by the author. Scarsdale, N.Y.: Bradbury Press, 1968.

Ten children are splashing in a pool and are waiting to be counted. From one to ten, the numerals and number words are printed on one colorful page while the facing page shows a large black and white photograph of the correct number of children who play in the water. After ten, there is a photographic review that shows the *one-less* concept across a gold double-page spread. A young reader finds words about who is "next" in the bright red words. Completing these words, a young viewer might loop back in thought to the beginning of the book again. K-1.

Features: *one-more* sequence up to ten, *one-less* sequence back to one, and a review.

Schertle, Alice. *Goodnight, Harriet, My Dearie, My Dove*. Illustrated by Linda Strauss Edwards. New York: Lothrop, Lee and Shepard, 1985.

Hattie walks her nine stuffed animals and dolls past her parents, and counting continues as Hatties offers reasons why each of her toys should join her in bed. As each request is fulfilled, Mother repeats the words in the title to encourage Hattie to go to sleep, a possible refrain for joining in by a young listener. Numerals appear on the outside edges of the pages with the appropriate ones shaded for reference to coincide with the text and the increasing numbers. Since this is a *one-more* sequence, a boy or girl may be ready to answer questions such as "What number comes after———?" Is an observing boy or girl ready to identify the shaded numerals found in the sequences on the pages? Pre-2.

Features: repetitive refrain, *one-more* sequence from one up to ten.

Sendak, Maurice. *One Was Johnny: A Counting Book*. Illustrated by the author. New York: Harper and Row, 1962.

Johnny lives by himself and a listener may count along from one to ten as unwanted callers arrive. A cat chases a rat, a turtle bites a dog's tail, and a monkey delivers the daily mail (*one-more-than* relationships). Wanting his privacy back from these rowdy visitors, Johnny begins to count backwards with an ultimatum that he will eat all of the unwanted callers if they don't leave his house. As these unruly visitors leave one by one, a viewer sees that the barefoot robber takes an old shoe, the tiger takes old clothes to sell, and the dog rides home on a blue sled (*one-less-than* relationship).

Since the animals who follow are being discussed in an order, then ordinals (e.g., third was a cat, fourth was a dog, fifth was a turtle, and so on) should be used by the adult who is reading the book to a young listener. In a classroom, some kindergarten students may enjoy seeing the lines of this counting narrative revealed one line at a time on the overhead. Seeing broken lines (instead of a final word in the line) the students predict the final word used in each line. One teacher explains that the broken lines (or dotted lines) stand for Sendak's word, the one the teacher is hiding. If appropriate, the student may write a one-sentence extension of this pattern about the number eleven and another visitor that might have been included in the number sequence. There is a small edition in Sendak's *Nutshell Library* (Harper and Row, 1962) and a filmstrip-cassette version produced by Weston Woods (Weston, Conn.). Pre-K.

Features: rhyming lines, *one-more-than* sequence up to ten, and *one-less-than* sequence down to one.

Shostak, Myra. *Rainbow Candles: A Chanukah Counting Book.* Illustrated by Katherine Janus Kahn. Rockville, MD.: Karn-Ben, 1986.

On the sturdy pages of this board book, there are two- and four-line verses. The illustrations, showing a little girl celebrating this Jewish holiday, are lively and colorful. One candle is added for each of the eight days of the holiday and makes an eight-night rhyme. As the candles accumulate, the little girl counts their number on the Chanukah menorah (quantities). Pre-1.

Features: verses, *one-more* sequence from one up to eight.

Simon, Leonard. *The Day the Numbers Disappeared.* Illustrated by Jeanne Bendick. New York: Whittlesey House/McGraw-Hill, 1963.

For older children, this book presents the question, "What would really happen if you had no numbers?" To show the students in his classroom how much they need numbers, Mr. Dibbs, the teacher, suggests doing away with numbers. The students earn their numbers back by recreating the ways that people worked with numbers through history. They use their fingers for counting, tally with marks, and record the numbers with some of the letters of the alphabet. Then, the girls and boys practice with an abacus. Advanced 3 up.

Features: information, numeric narrative, and number use.

Sis, Peter. *Waving: A Counting Book.* Illustrated by the author. New York: Greenwillow, 1988.

Mary's mother waves for a taxi, and two bicyclists wave back. Soon, in this cumulative tale with ethnic diversity, girl scouts, mounted police, and others are waving back. Finally, fifteen taxicab drivers are waving at Mary and her mother, but they decide to walk home. An older boy or girl preparing original illustrations for a picture book will be interested in the contrast of the black and gray of the buildings with the bright yellow of the taxicabs, the way the color yellow leads a viewer from page to page to see the number details, and the humor Sis shows in the illustrations. Pre-2.

Features: accumulation, *one-more* sequence from one up to fifteen.

Stanek, Muriel. *One, Two, Three for Fun*. Illustrated by the author. Chicago: Albert Whitman, 1967.

Colorful drawings alternate with black and white ones and show familiar activities. Some children may find aspects of the format confusing when the relationships between the pictures and the printed number concepts are inconsistent. Shouldn't one child be shown playing on the page that is labeled *one* instead of two children shown playing on the page? An adult can point out that the two children on the page are some distance apart. Each child is a group of one. Adult guidance may make useful discussion possible. Pre-2.

Features: numerals, number words, and cardinal object identification.

Sussman, Susan. *Hippo Thunder*. Illustrated by John C. Wallner. Chicago: Albert Whitman, 1982.

Father gives different explanations about what causes the thunder and none of the explanations satisfy his small son. Father says one way to tell how far away the storm is brewing is to count the number of hippopotamuses between the lightning and the thunder (number usage). The father and boy together count the seconds with the words, *"one hippopotamus, two hippopotamus,"* and the boy forgets his unease over the thunder and lightning, and falls asleep. Not designed as a counting book, this is one of the few narratives that presents the process of counting within the text. Pre-2.

Features: numeric narrative, number use, and process of counting shown in print.

Sustendal, Pat. *The Trim-the-Tree Counting Book*. Illustrated by the author. New York: Random House, 1984.

As a little boy trims his holiday tree, the young viewer can help find the number of the musical toy horns, the round ornaments for decoration, and the toy soldiers. How many lights look like burning candles? Other holiday objects may be identified and counted to ten on the full-color pages in this small book. Pre.

Features: cardinal object identification of ornaments on holiday tree from one up to ten.

Tafuri, Nancy. *All Year Long*. Illustrated by the author. New York: Puffin, 1984.

With the help of bright watercolors, young boys and girls may count the months of the year, the days of the week, and the seasons as the names are learned. Numerals and numbers and their use are seen in this book based on the calendar (number use). K-2.

Features: sequences of days, weeks, and seasons.

The Ten Sailors. Illustrated. Crystal Lake, Ill.: Rigby, 1988.

In a large format (approximately thirteen by sixteen inches), this rhyme is written by a first-grade class with their teacher's direction and is best suited for girls and boys from preschool to kindergarten. Rhyming lines tell a simple story about ten sailors and what they do. Sailor Three sat in a tree (numbers used as names). Dressed in a blue uniform, one sailor sits in the top of a palm tree, and beneath it, the sailor's rowboat waits on the sandy shore while a larger ship lies at anchor out in the harbor. Washing hangs out to dry from the rigging. Rhythm and rhyme connect Sailor Four, Sailor Five, and the others with numbers through the pages. When the sailors are being discussed in an order, then ordinals (e.g., third sailor, fourth sailor, and so on) should be used by the adult when reading the book aloud. With adult guidance, a girl or boy may identify a starting place beginning with the first sailor and insert ordinals in the proper places in the text. Pre-K.

Features: rnyming lines, number use, *one-more* concept from one up to ten.

Thayer, Jane. *Little House: A New Math Story Game*. Illustrated by Don Madden. New York: William Morrow, 1972.

A boy or girl comes in out of a blizzard and into the little house, and the simple illustrations reinforce concepts of *more, less,* and *same.* The little house and the travelers who occupy it may remind a reader of a Scottish adding story-song, *Always Room for One More*, written by Sorche Nic Leodhas and illustrated by Nonny Hogrogian. K-2.

Features: numeric narrative, *one-more* sequence, math terms.

Thompson, Susan L. *One More Thing, Dad.* Illustrated by Dora Leder. Chicago: Albert Whitman, 1980.

Caleb gets ready for his walk by collecting one orange and two sandwiches, and he also needs other things: a thermos, a celery stick, an insect jar, and his blue blanket. Should he take Obie, his tiger-striped cat? Should he wear his coat and his yellow scarf? At the number ten, Caleb, needs one more thing—his Dad as a walking companion, and Obie, the tiger cat, on a black leash. Preparing for an imaginary walk, a girl or boy may list or dictate all of the things in sequence from one up to ten that will be taken along. In a classroom, the listeners may respond to the question, "How many steps would it take to get from here to there for a classroom walk?" (teacher identifies the distance). One volunteer walks the distance and counts the steps aloud and the teacher records the number of steps. After other volunteers count their steps, they may discuss the difference they find in the number of steps counted by the walkers (nonstandard measurement). K-1.

Features: numeric narrative, *one-more* sequence from one up to ten.

Wells, Rosemary. *Max's Toys: A Counting Book.* Illustrated by the author. New York: Dial, 1979.

Max wants to play with Emily, the doll with the crown and long gown, who belongs to Max's sister, Ruby. Max won't play with his two soldiers, his house with three windows, or his four animal pull-toys, and he is so upset he kicks over a tower of nine building blocks and crashes ten cars of his toy train off the tracks. Ruby offers to trade her doll, Emily, for the all of Max's toys. How many toys will Emily receive? Max looks like a plump little rabbit (but is he really?), and is a favorite character of some young children. This story book is tiny in size, and illustrations are printed in clear bold colors. Young children will like it (a sibling's message of "This toy is mine!") and will begin counting the toys on each page. At home or school, available toys can be counted and arranged and rearranged in groups. Westbrook (1986) points to this book as an example of counting books that deals positively with the issue of sex roles since it shows a young male character who trades his toys for his sister's doll. Recommended. Pre.

Features: humor, numeric narrative, numeral recognition, and cardinal number identification.

Wilmer, Diane. *Counting*. Illustrated by Nicola Smee. New York: Macmillan/Aladdin, 1988.

This is a concept board book about counting in the family. A child's fingers provide a first counting experience in the full-color illustrations. The family members (a toddler, a kindergartener, an older brother, a dog, a cat, and an oversize stuffed teddy bear) with some humor, are seen in eleven other titles in this series. Pre-K.

Features: sequence of numbers beginning with one are shown in familiar family scenes.

Wood, Kay. *Ernie and Bert's Counting Book*. Illustrated. New York: Random House/Children's Television Workshop, 1977.

Part of The *Sesame Street Little Library,* this small counting book, approximately three by four inches, shows Bert and Ernie cleaning their closets. Numerals are in boldface type in the phrases beneath the illustrations. Either Bert or Ernie holds the objects from one rubber duck, two accordions, three fire engines, to ten slinky toys. After ten, objects are not grouped to show a set of ten or to show any additional objects beyond ten. Rather, such things as twelve twiddle-flies are all over one page, thirteen gloves are placed on a doorknob, Bert's head, and the floor on another page, and fourteen footballs bounce all around the room on still another. Turning the pages a second time, a young girl or boy may be ready to identify the numerals found in bold type on the pages. Pre.

Features: numerals in bold up to fourteen, cardinal number identification, and place value recognition.

Yeoman, John. *Sixes and Sevens*. Illustrated by Quentin Blake. New York: Macmillan, 1971.

Barnaby rafts with Mother's big box up the river. Large watercolors show Barnaby first picking up a small kitten and then two active mice as passengers. Will the kitten chase the mice? Barnaby searches in the big box and finds a striped sock to use as a confining berth for the kitten. He continues to pick up strange cargo and each group of new passengers presents him with another problem to solve. For instance, Barnaby has to keep the mice out of the wigs of the schoolmistresses; he has to keep the school mistresses from frightening some small schoolboys; he has to keep the boys from pulling the tails of the monkeys, and so on. Parrots, dogs, green snakes, frogs, and grasshoppers—all may cause traveling problems, but these passengers are calm until a rainstorm occurs. When it is over, among other troubles, the kitty is out of the sock; the mice have escaped the jar; and the parrots perch on the hats of the schoolmistresses. However, Barnaby restores calm and arrives safely at Limber Lea where ten people wait to greet and to collect the ten groups of passengers. Is anyone ready to identify numerals appropriate for each group of arriving passengers? Is an older boy or girl interested in talking about cause-and-effect situations as each group arrives? Recommended. Pre-up.

Features: numeric narrative, number words, accumulation, cardinal number identification, recognizing members in groups, and problem solving.

Youldon, Gillian. *Time*. Illustrated by the author. New York: Franklin Watts, 1979.

Time is a wordless book of full-color double-page spreads with only the time of day showing in the corners of the pages and on the traditional (not digital) clock faces in the illustrations. The clock in the bedroom shows 7:00 and a little girl wakes up. Stars and a crescent moon are seen outside the window, but when the half page is turned, the scene changes to one of sunshine and singing birds. At 10:00, the little girl and her mother shop at the market; at 12:00, Mother buys the little girl a new dress; at1:00, they are in the kitchen preparing for the little girl's birthday party. At 3:00, friends arrive for the party, play together until 5 :00, and leave at 6:00. With simulated clock faces, boys and girls may turn the hands to the corresponding time as the pages are reviewed and tell about their own activities. Pre-K.

Features: numeral use on face of clock, time-telling.

Zolotow, Charlotte (Shapiro). *One Step, Two . . .* Illustrated by Roger Duvoisin. New York: Lothrop, Lee and Shepard, 1955.

A young counter identifies the number of steps that it takes to reach a round white pebble, a laundry line filled with towels and dresses. At the numeral 12, this small girl returns home for lunch. Six steps take her to the hurdy-gurdy monkey, ten steps bring her to the red geraniums in the window, and twelve steps bring her home again, as her steps increase after each object is seen. Tired from the walking, she falls asleep in her mother's arms at home. A young boy or girl may tell of numbers of things seen during a remembered walk. If space is available, the numerals and dots or slant marks for the numbers may be recorded in sequence as the youngster mentions them and placed on a personal sequence chart. One preschool teacher follows up with two story-rhymes from *Fold-and-Cut Stories and Fingerplays* (Fearon/David S. Lake, 1987) by Marj Hart. The first rhyme, "Five Hats," counts to five, complements Zolotow's story, and tells about one little girl who puts on a hat and goes out to play on a sunny day. The second rhyme, "One Small Noodle," counts to five as small noodles (fingers) appear in openings in a paper plate. The words are repetitive and allow a young listener to join in quickly with, "Mother's running to the store, Mother, Mother, give me more." Patterns for the finger holes in a paper plate and for the five hats to be placed on a child's fingers are included. Pre-K.

Features: numerals, sequence from one up to twelve and back to one, numerical narrative.

Farm and Country Life

Barr, Catherine. *Seven Chicks Missing*. Illustrated by the author. New York: Henry Z. Walck, 1962.

The story and simple illustrations show the baby chicks giving in to curiosity. As Mother Hen takes them about, the chicks vanish one by one to investigate the things that puzzle them. A young boy brings them back to their mother. This is a *one-less* story first—then a *one-more* story—a sequence not usually seen in counting books. Madame Cluck, a mother grouse ,crosses the yard with her seven grouse chicks behind her. Going toward the construction of the ranch house being built, she comes near two chidren who are watching the workmen build part of a wall. The young listener may want to chime in with Madame Cluck's croon of "OOooh, OOooh," as she shows off her chicks. The chicks scurry off one by one and a countdown can begin as the chicks scatter and hide. Now with no chicks in sight, Bill drops grain around the yard to entice them back. One by one (*one-more* sequence), the chicks come out and follow the trail of grain to the terrace and to Madame Cluck who continues her walk with all her chicks following. A young girl or boy hears the pattern that begins with seven and shows *one-less* chick with each short action and then sees a second pattern, the *one-more* pattern as the chicks return. Numerals are in bold type within the text. With the chicks easily seen and counted, this story presents number use since the chicks are referred to as chick Number 7, Number 2, and so on, and these names are capitalized in the story. But to show the order in which they hide, ordinals (e.g., second was the chick who hid between rocks; third was the chick who goes under a ramp, and so on) should be used by the adult when reading the book aloud. With or without adult guidance, a young reader may identify a starting place beginning with the first chick who hides and insert ordinals in the proper places in the text. Pre-K.

Features: numerals in bold, numbers as names, numeric narrative with *one-less* sequence from seven down to one and *one-more* sequence from one up to seven.

Francoise (Seignobosc). *Jeanne-Marie Counts Her Sheep*. Illustrated by the author. New York: Charles Scribner's Sons, 1951.

Francoise Seignobosc introduces the numbers with bright colors in the illustrations that alternate with black and white sketches. Jeanne-Marie, a little French girl, and her sheep, Patapon, show objects to count. A young listener can count some of the things that Jeanne-Marie wishes she could buy. Does a youngster recognize the numerals that are placed in the text of the story? Is any girl or boy surprised by the ending? For a second visit with Jeanne-Marie, a teacher may invite the children to see the illustrations again when the pictures are projected on a screen with a filmstrip/cassette set. In addition, the paperback version of the story is available for classroom use and is accompanied by a read-along cassette tape. Both items are available from Random House School Division. Recommended. Pre.

Features: numerals in text, cardinal numbers from one up to three to identify.

Freschet, Bernice. *Where's Henrietta's Hen?* Illustrated by Lorinda Bryan Cauley. New York: Putnam Publishing Group, 1980.

Henrietta gathers one white egg for her breakfast each morning, but one day Henrietta's hen is missing. In lightly colored illustrations, Henrietta's search takes her to visit the crowing rooster, the mooing cow, and the grunting pig. Finally, Henrietta sees her red hen snuggled in the haystack. Without disturbing her, Henrietta walks away quietly and waits . . . for the hen to return with eight baby chicks, all peeping, and following their mother. Recommended. Pre-K.

Features: numeric narrative, cardinal numbers from one up to eight.

Friskey, Margaret. *Chicken Little: Count-to-Ten*. Illustrated by Katherine Evans. Chicago: Children's Press, 1946.

In this version, and in the Spanish one, *Pollito Pequenito Cuenta Hasta Diez*, Chicken Little tries to learn how to drink water from an ever-increasing group of animals. From one cow, two gray elephants, nine puppies to ten brown foxes, the animals all try to help Chicken Little learn to drink, but none of them succeed (*one-more-than* pattern). The number words and the numerals are in the right-hand corners of the pages for reference if needed. A young girl or boy may giggle at the suggestions given to help Chicken Little and offer an original suggestion, too. Can anyone predict how Chicken Little will learn to drink water? Recommended. K-1.

Features: numeric narrative, numerals, number words from one up to ten, increasing sequence of numbers of animals in groups.

Friskey, Margaret. *Mystery of the Farmer's Three Fives.* Illustrated by Lucy Hawkinson and John Hawkinson. Chicago: Children's Press, 1963.

First, the farmer sees three ducks in the corner of the yard and two ducks in the middle of the yard. When the ducks move around, the farmer sees another arrangement of five: four ducks in the middle of the yard and one by the fence (recognizing equal groups when all the ducks in one group are exactly the same as ducks in the other group). When one duck escapes through an opening in the fence, the farmer decides to trade the ducks for four pigs. Then the pigs are traded for three goats, the goats for two colts, and the colts for one quiet cow who gives milk and cream for the farmer's wife. With the milk and cream, the farmer and his boy trade again for the five ducks, four pigs, three goats, and two colts. Can any boy or girl count all of the animals as they are shown with corresponding shapes on a feltboard? When the animals are arranged into groups of five (recognizing equivalent groups when groups have the same number of different animals), can a boy or girl circle a group with his or her hands? The children may count along as the teacher or a student volunteer shows groups of five: five ducks; three goats and two colts; and four pigs and one cow. When the teacher rearranges the animals as different members in groups of five (the mystery), do the children still recognize the groups? When the animal shapes are rearranged again, is any boy or girl ready to see five threes? Using toothpicks to arrange into squares to represent a fenced area and dry beans to represent the groups of five animals, children may glue beans in different arrangements of five and fence in each arrangement with the toothpicks. Number sentences may be written to represent each arrangement. 1–2.

Features: position in groups does not affect number, equivalent groups of five, and commutativity.

Hawkinson, Lucy. *Picture Book Farm.* Illustrated by the author. Chicago: Children's Press, 1971.

In this book, Hawkinson opens with a farm scene. There are animals, people, and areas of the farm to notice. The pages are turned to see parts of the opening farm scene again. In these pages, a young viewer takes another look at objects or the features of objects. The boy or girl may be asked to see a certain number of objects and to tell the number of things seen. K-1.

Features: cardinal number identification from one up to ten.

Hoban, Tana. *Where Is It?* Photographs by the author. New York: Macmillan, 1974.

One white bunny wonders where to find something special. The bunny looks behind a large rock, across the field, through the tall grass, up a tree truck, in clover, then says, "Close my eyes, count to ten." Is the bunny playing a game of hide and seek (number use)? The bunny looks around and says: "Count again." Finally, behind a tree, the bunny's search is over; the something spcial is a basket of carrots and cabbage. The green unifying color emphasizes the setting of the book, a meadow and the surrounding woods near a farm. Pre-K.

Features: shows use of numbers in narrative.

Ipcar, Dahlov. *Brown Cow Farm: A Counting Book.* Illlustrated by the author. Garden City, N.Y.: Doubleday, 1959.

Five brown cows greet a young viewer in this setting that shows winter at the farm of Farmer Brown, his horse, and his hounds. On double-page spreads, the tones of tan and brown show the groups of animals to count: cats, ducks, and geese. The numerals, 1 to 10, are in the lower corners of the pages. When spring comes, each animal reproduces up to ten offspring to show all of the numbers from twenty to one hundred. Small children may identify some familiar animals: kittens, puppies, bunnies, and chicks; others may be introduced to the names of unfamiliar ones: calves, piglets, goslings, poults, and ducklings. Two summary pages at the end of the book show all of the animals on this very large farm, and challenge readers to count them. For some children, the animals may be easier to see and count with the enlarged pictures on the filmstrip/cassette set from Weston Woods (Weston, Conn). 1–2.

Features: numerals, number words from one up to ten, *ten- more* sequence up to one hundred, and a review.

Ipcar, Dahlov. *Ten Big Farms*. Illustrated by the author. New York: Knopf, 1958.

Ipcar describes some farm activities and takes a boy or girl to visit ten big farms along with a family that is looking for a farm to buy. Ipcar shows multiples of chickens on the first farm, fruit on the second farm, and horses on the third farm. The family in the story continues to look for a farm they like as they see tobacco plants, cows, beef cattle, pigs, and wheat on the successful farms they visit. After finding sheep on the ninth farm and vegetables on the tenth (one-to-one correspondence between objects and natural numbers), the family buys a neglected farm, and is glad to be settled in the country. Reference to the farms in the discussion may introduce ordinals. K-1.

Features: use of ordinals and cardinal number identification from one up to ten.

Kilroy, Sally. *The Baron's Hunting Party*. Illustrated by the author. New York: Viking Kestrel, 1988.

Baron Bertie and his friends begin a wild ride through the countryside to hunt for numbers of things to count. The baron collects (and counts) all the objects found during this outing. In doing so, there is confusion for everyone. The text is simple and characters offer additional dialogue during the hunt. Using information from the illustrations and from the text, is any listener ready to recreate the order in which objects were found and counted during this hunt? Pre-3.

Features: numeric narrative, simple text, dialogue, and objects from one up to ten.

Krüss, James. *3x3 Three by Three*. Illustrated by Eva Johanna Rubin. Translated by Geoffrey Strachan. New York: Macmillan, 1963.

Krüss, a Hans Christian Andersen Award recipient, makes a contribution to counting with this book, aiming at the concept of grouping and showing groups of three in various ways (recognizing equivalent groups). Krüss's merry chase is a pleasure to hear with its three-line verses and it is humorous to see in Rubin's large, colorful, full-page illustrations. A young viewer sees three hunters chase three dogs. The dogs chase three foxes who chase three cats. The cats chase three mice. Once the hunters catch the dogs, events return to normal, and finally, the mice snuggle down to sleep in their beds. With paper shapes of the animals for a girl or boy to classify, an adult may ask, "Can we group hunters, dogs, foxes, cats, and mice together? Why? Why not?" Recommended. Pre-2.

Features: verses and numeric narrative with equivalent groups of three.

Lindbergh, Reeve. *The Midnight Farm*. Illustrateed by Susan Jeffers. New York: Dial, 1987.

From the book's cover, children could predict that this story will be about a boy and a horse. Once read, *The Midnight Farm* will be identified as counting book and a rhyming book. The endpapers at the beginning of the book are in daylight and the ones at the end are in moonlight. The opening scene looks down on the farm (is it the narrator guiding a horse down the path to the farmhouse?) and the title pages show a close-up of the farmhouse with a horse standing in the yard (did the narrator just arrive at the farmhouse?). Inside the house, a mother holds her son as they sit on his bed at the end of a day. Poetic words describing the dark with no moon or sun as "the heart of the dark" are read. Before going to bed, mother and son take one last look around the farm and they say goodnight to the animals: one old dog; two white cats; three in a raccoon family; and four geese. The words, "in the dark," are repeated at the end of each double-page spread, a refrain the young listener will recognize and repeat with the adult. After the walk, the boy is tucked into bed and dreams about the animals he saw. Recommended. Pre-2.

Features: cardinal number identification of farm animals with number words in rhyming lines from one up to ten, repetitive words.

A Little Book of Numbers. Illustrated. New York: Simon and Schuster, 1980.

Some of the nutritious produce grown on a farm can be seen on these small pages, approximately five by five inches. From one pumpkin for baking a Halloween pie and two sliced purple onions to make you cry to nine grapes on a leafy vine and ten cherries on a plate, many members of the vegetable and fruit food group can be identified. There are carrots, radishes in a bunch, peas in a pod, and apples in a basket to name, read about in rhyming lines and count. Pre.

Features: cardinal number identification of groups of food items from one up to ten.

McMillan, Bruce. *Counting Wildflowers*. Illustrated with photographs by the author. New York: Lothrop, Lee and Shepard, 1986.

Photographs of flowers are on these pages with numerals from one through twenty. Discs are shown with the appropriate number of flowers filled in with their color. Number words begin with capitals. Each photograph carries a caption with the common name of the flower so young readers may use this for a first field guide. Older readers may use the end material for reference, with a complete list of the flowers shown in the book, their scientific names, and where to find them. During a discussion after reading time at school, teachers can present information to students about a Fibonacci sequence, patterns of numbers in nature, the basic one of *1,1, 2, 3, 5, 8, 13*, etc. This sequence can be discovered when observing flowers in McMillan's book, or in a similar book about flowers. For information about Fibonacci and patterns, see *Patterns: What Are They?* (Lerner, 1969), written by William Shimek and illustrated by Charles Stevenson. Shimek and Stevenson use blueprints, recipes, and weather trends to point out how we use patterns in the world around us each day. These are patterns that can be discussed, recorded, and graphed. Recommended. Pre-3.

Features: numerals from one up to twenty, number names in capitals, corresponding discs for matching, common and scientific names of wildflowers.

Mendoza, George. *Counting Sheep*. Illustrated by Kathleen Reidy. New York: Grosset and Dunlap, 1982.

In this Children's Choice book, an old shepherd regularly counts sheep when he falls asleep and is troubled by dreams of one to twenty sheep having unusual adventures. These sheep conduct a frog's choir and pose as artists' models. They romp at the seashore and dance in a chorus line. Most children will enjoy the colorful complementary illustrations which alternate with black and white pictures showing sheep doing such unusual things as skydiving, ice skating, and running a marathon. In addition, some children will enjoy acting out the shepherd's restless turns. Recommended. 1–2.

Features: numeric narrative, number use, and cardinal identification of numbers from one up to twenty.

Miller, Jane. *Farm Counting Book*. Photographs by the author. Englewood Cliffs, N.J.: Prentice-Hall, 1983.

Miller's bright red harvest reaper takes a boy or girl right into a farm setting. On the colorful pages, a variety of farm animals and objects appears. Kittens, pigs, swans, and sheep are not only counted, but are rearranged and can be counted again. There are bright red numerals beside the number words that are spelled out for word recognition. After this introduction to numbers, there are some informative sentences about farm animals to read. When some of the objects are rearranged, a one-to-one correspondence can begin. There are also two cats. How many bowls of milk will the two cats need if each one wants one bowl? To guide a young viewer, other questions are asked about the objects in the photographs: How many horseshoes on the wall? How many eggs? How many strawberries? Is there enough for all? Are there the same number as in a previous photograph? This photographic essay introduces basics in mathematics. Recommended. K-1.

Features: numerals in red, number words, informative sentences, farm objects in photographs to identify, and one-to-one correspondence.

Page, Robin, designer. *Count One to Ten*. Illustrated by the designer. New York: Museum of Modern Art, 1987.

Page's book teaches girls and boys to count using a flip-over design and accordion action pages that unfold to twenty-four inches. Numbers from one through ten are shown in digits, words, and symbols. Opening this colorful tall book, one finds three rows of small pages in red, white, and bright blue. Turning the first small red page from right to left to see the numeral 1, a viewer finds one yellow banana on the small white page in the second row. Below, the young reader sees the word in capital letters, ONE, on the first small blue page. This arrangement continues through ten as a child counts apples, oranges, pears, lemons, limes, strawberries, and cherries. Listeners may consider the question, "Which fruit would you buy?" Pictures of fruit to buy are drawn on small squares of art paper, signed, collected, and attached to a graph with headings of names of fruit. Discussion of learners' comments about what the graph tells them may be written on paper and loaned to a child (along with the graph) for discussion at home. Pre-up.

Features: numerals, number words in capitals, names of fruits from one up to ten, and a review.

Russell, Sandra Joanne. *A Farmer's Dozen*. Illustrated by the author. New York: Harper and Row, 1982.

One small farmer welcomes the arrival of a wife, a baby, and nine animals. There is rhyming text of two lines for each of the colorful illustrations. Beginning with the text about a farmer working in the sun and being the only one and ending with words about a farmer's dozen, this book offers colorful illustrations bordered in red on recto pages and rhyming words on verso pages. Around the small illustrations are groups of objects to represent numbers of things shown with numerals. A pattern on the page consists of the numeral 1, one pumpkin, repeated around the borders. The illustration shows the farmer standing between rows of corn and vines of pumpkins. A similar pattern for numeral 2 is seen: first, the numeral 2, then two ears of golden corn. The pattern continues for other numerals with groups of vegetables. On the final page, a boy or girl counts the farmer's dozen (wife, baby, and animals) and then, one dozen vegetables. Since illustrations of vegetables—carrots, onions, potatoes, and sweet peas—are small, this one is best suited for one-to-one reading and for face-to-face talking about naming the vegetables, recognizing them, and the work of the farmer needed to grow the vegetables. Some selections—artichokes, eggplant, and yellow squash—may be unfamiliar names for children. With a note to parents, children are invited to bring a sample of their favorite vegetable to class on a selected day, to be discussed and categorized. Pre-1.

Features: numeric narrative, accumulation, vegetables for cardinal number identification from one up to twelve with number words in rhyming lines, patterned borders of vegetable-numeral-vegetable.

Smith, Donald. *Farm Numbers 123: A Counting Book.* Illustrated by the author. New York: Abelard-Schuman, 1970.

For number one, the illustration shows one dog near the numeral *1* on a plain background. There are no distractions for the viewer. On a facing page, the dog has moved and is now in a doghouse. Using this technique of movement, a youngster is led toward the concept of rearrangement of members in a group. From two cats on a brown background to two cats in the barn where one cat walks the rafters and the other rests on a hat, a youngster may count, count again, and gain reassurance about the quantity of number. There are additional animals to count—horses, pigs, cows. Discussion about the animals found on this farm may help a child classify: "Is this animal like any other animal you have seen? Like one you saw at the zoo? Like one in your animal book? Is this animal like the one you saw on your walk? What are some of the things that are alike in these animals?" Recommended. K-1.

Features: classifying, numerals, number words, and rearrangement of members in a group from one up to ten.

Stobbs, JoAnna, and William Stobbs. *One Sun, Two Eyes and a Million Stars*. Illustrations by William Stobbs. London: Oxford University Press, 1983.

Textured backgrounds take readers through a day of things to recognize in the countryside. From page to page, the items accumulate and carry over into a rearrangement on the next page. At the page for the number eighteen, eighteen lights go on in a nearby house. All of the cows, geese, and sheep are seen again. At nineteen, the litle girl enters the house, climbs the stairs to see the next number of things in this *one-more-than* sequence—twenty dolls in her room. Once in bed, she sees the stars in the night sky from the bedroom window. A million stars? Some viewers may want to turn back the pages to see if they can locate the farm objects found outside that are used again as decorating items inside the farmhouse. Some creative storylines about numbers can be told about each of the illustrations. K-1.

Features: accumulation, rearrangement of members in groups from one up to twenty.

Sugita, Yutaka. *One to Eleven*. Illustrated by the author. London: Evans Brothers, 1971.

This number-numeral book introduces numerals through 11. The objects aid in counting sequentially in the *one-more* pattern, and give the oportunity to identify simple objects. Sugita's one character appears in all of the colorful illustrations and provides a discussion base about numbers of things. The character becomes a figure around which a youngster can tell short number stories in brief sentences. Pre-K.

Features: numerals, number words, and objects from one up to eleven.

Wahl, John and Stacey Wahl. *I Can Count the Petals of a Flower*. Illustrated by the authors. Reston, Va.: National Council of Teachers of Mathematics, 1976.

Beautiful photographs of flowers are seen with the numbers one through sixteen. A viewer counts the petals on a white calla lily (one), an orange crown of thorns (two), and a white snowdrop (three). Through the number ten, each page shows a corresponding numeral, a sketch of the petal shapes, and a photograph of the flower. Then, counting begins with different flowers: lily of the Nile (one petal); Chinese dogwood (four); and a black-eyed Susan (twelve). A nature walk to observe flowers and to count the petals is a natural extension of this book—an activity which helps youngsters see math in their outside surroundings. Inside, a child with small broccoli flowerlets (heads) may group and regroup them into various joining and separating situations. Given groups with a varying number of objects or elements, will anyone be able to assign the cardinal number to each group? If a youngster is interested further, the broccoli may be placed in water for several days and observed to see if small yellow flowers will bloom. 1-up.

Features: numeral recognition, corresponding numbers, shapes, and one-to-one correspondence from one up to sixteen.

Monsters and Other Creatures

Asch, Frank. *Little Devil's 123*. Illustrated by the author. New York: Charles Scribner's Sons, 1979.

In this accumulation of devils, one to twenty-five, some of the devilish details are humorous ones. Colors of blue, brown, green, pink, and yellow define the devils in groups of five, while they sail paper airplanes, blow bubbles, pour tea, and eat ice cream. After climbing over, on, up, and down the numeral shapes, the devils form a stacked balancing act for a finale at twenty-five. Which boy or girl can sequence paper shapes of these colorful devils following the pattern of blue, brown, green, pink, and yellow? One shape is removed from the pattern while eyes are closed; when the pattern is looked at again, the adult asks, "What color is missing?" The youngster is invited to replace the colored shape in the pattern and may take a turn removing a shape while the adult's eyes are closed. To emphasize numbers of different colored objects, the learner may receive a clear sandwich bag which holds a handful of circular cereal shapes of different colors and a record sheet with headings naming the colors. Beside each heading is a row of squares. The learner selects one cereal piece, notes the color, and records it by coloring in one square in the appropriate row. 1-up.

Features: equivalent groups of five, color sequence in patterns, and accumulation up to twenty-five.

Calmenson, Stephanie. *Ten Furry Monsters*. Illustrated by Maxie Chambliss. New York: Parents Magazine Press, 1984.

When Mother Monster leaves, she gives clear instructions to her ten furry monster children that they should not leave the park. While she is away, the ten little monsters decide to entertain themselves and, monster by monster, they all hide somewhere. A young viewer who looks at these bright, lively, full-color illustrations with counting rhymes carefully may find all ten of the friendly, furry monster children in their hiding places, with numerals on their shirts (numeral usage). Can someone find the monster with the big blue ears and fuchsia horns who hides behind a tall birdbath? Is that another monster hiding in the shrubs? If there is difficulty, some adult guidance may be needed. Pre-K.

Features: numeric narrative, numeral recognition, number use, *one-less* sequence from ten to one, and *one-more* sequence from one to ten.

Cooke, Tom. *The Count's Counting Book.* Illustrated by the author. Paper engineering by Ib Penick. New York: Random House/Children's Television Workshop, 1980.

Featuring Jim Henson's Muppets, this is a Sesame Street pop-up book. Castle doors of sturdy paper open to show one "countmobile." There are two yellow busy birds behind large sacks of bird seed. Three eggs crack, but not enough to fully show what is inside. A participating reader pulls a tab to see four flying bluejays. Later, other tabs reveal five train cars with passengers, six riders on a roller coaster, seven remarkable rabbits, and eight trashy treasures. After ten, a paper-engineered wheel turns to display the objects to count (early experience in reading charts and graphs). The turning of the wheel simulates projecting a movie of the members in groups and the Count watches this number movie. Is someone interested in responding as an adult turns the pages again and asks such questions as, "Are there more flying bluejays or train cars? Are there more beautiful bats or twirling twiddle bugs (estimation)?" Numbers of members in the groups may be shown with markers. Pre-K.

Features: cardinal number identification from one to ten and a review.

Davidson, Avelyn. *Ten Little Goblins: Math Rhymes to Read Together.* Illustrated. San Diego: The Wright Group, 1986.

The attraction of rhymes gives meaning to the concept of ten. Numeric goblins live in the woods among the trees, wearing clothes like caps with long floppy points and soft shoes with pointed toes that turn up (just like the shoes of elves). Hairless and skinny, these goblins have pointy chins, large noses, and still larger eyes, and wave their long narrow fingers. The readers discover numbers of things up to ten in a big-book format, approximately thirteen by seventeen inches. For complementary reading, there are additional small books available for individuals. K-1.

Features: rhymes in verses and number words from one up to ten.

Hawkins, Colin. *Take Away Monsters: A Pull-the-Tab Book.* Illustrated by the author. New York: G. P. Putnam's Sons, 1984.

Wearing hats, showing their cat-like paws, and baring lots of teeth, these monsters illustrate subtraction facts. For example, a girl or boy sees the sentence: 3 - 1 = ———. With this sentence, fuzzy monsters appear in each of three windows on the page. To separate (subtract) a member of the group, one pulls a tab, so the shutters of a window close up, and one monster disappears behind the shutters. How many monsters are left? Similarly, a youngster subtracts all combinations of numbers up through five and sees one subtraction situation happen in each colorful illustration. On another page, three monsters hide from each other in a cabinet. Two get shut inside the cabinet when the tab is pulled to show that: 3 - 2 = 1. On other pages, the monsters count treasures, line up in jail, sing songs, play games, and disappear under the lid of a piano. The learner may record the number sentences on paper after each tab is pulled. Pre-2.

Features: operation of subtraction with groups of five, symbols in math sentences.

Holt, Virginia. *Nine Little Popples.* Illustrated by J. M. L. Gray. New York: Random House, n.d.

Popples look somewhat like puppies and act like people, colored in pink or blue, with short rhymes to be read. One little popple swings and five popples play tricks. Six are in a fix and seven are in a row. Eight popples play in the snow while nine snuggle up tight to rest for the night. Pre.

Features: numbers in rhyming lines from one up to nine and cardinal number identification.

Hyman, Jane. *Gumby Book of Numbers.* Illustrated with photographs. New York: Doubleday, 1986.

Gumby, a green clay figure, moves from television to a book to help introduce a preschooler to numbers. Full-color photographs from television episodes star Gumby (and Pokey, his clay horse and friend). Gumby's adventure introduces numbers through a road race. A preschooler may match objects seen during the race to corresponding numerals. Of course, Gumby wins the race. Pre-K.

Features: numerals on endpapers, framed full-color illustrations, object-numeral relationships, and brief text.

Irons, D. *Even Steven*. Illustrated. Crystal Lake, Ill.: Rigby, 1987.

In a cartoon format and full color with word bubbles, two metal robots, one standing tall in shining silver, and the other appearing short in shining gold, take turns dividing up cans of oil so each robot will have an even share. The gold metal robot in his turn divides the oil unfairly, saying, "Three for me and one for you. This is fun for me to do." With cries of unfair from the silver robot, the two do the division again. Available only in a set of four titles published by Rigby. Volunteers may move markers to recreate the actions of the robots as they try to divide the oil cans so each will have a fair share. 1–3.

Features: numeric narrative and equivalent groups for early experience for division.

Irons, D. *The Mean Machine*. Illustrated. Crystal Lake, Ill.: Rigby, 1987.

Riding on a tank track with wheels, a purple mean machine with a cab shaped like jaws and headlights as eyes roams the countryside looking for things to zap away with its mounted laser-zap ray. It subtracts things in groups. A young reader finds words about the mean machine with, "It will amaze you and me. For when it sees six, it will zap out three." Aiming at six clouds in the sky, the machine zaps out three in a explosion of white. Eight green planets revolve in a yellow sky and the rhyming lines continue: "The mean machine will do even more. When it sees eight, it will zap out four." Four planets are zapped in an explosion of white. Rhyming lines provide a pattern for children to write their own subtraction lines about a original situation, and with visual clues helps boys and girls review subtraction facts. This title is available only in a set with the other titles of *Ten Silly Sheep, The Wizard's Wand,* and *The Queen of Hearts,* and has follow-up activities accompanied by teachers' notes, blackline masters, and an audio-tape of hands-on activities for students to finish by themselves. 1–3.

Features: numeric narrative, rhyming lines, and subtraction review.

Krahn, Fernando, and Maria De La Luz Krahn. *The Life of Numbers*. Illustrated by Fernando Krahn. New York: Simon and Schuster, 1970.

A personified numeral 1 won't play with a personified numeral 0 because zero is "none." Searching for another numeral as a friend, numeral 1 meets strange numeral-beings: 2s take the shape of swans; 3s parade with banners; 4s serve as soldiers; and 5s form a pyramid act at a circus. Later, returning home, Numeral 1 meets zero again. Side by side, they sit on a mountaintop as other numerals climb a hillside to play with them. Some teachers have asked questions about this final illustration: when the numerals 1 and 0 come together to show 10 , will anyone think of the joining of inappropriate groups? For instance, will a child visualize a mental image of a group of one and an empty group with no members or elements? If so, can we say that this illustration accurately shows the identity of ten (one group of ten ones) for a young counter? For added information about the child's mental images of groups, an adult can encourage a boy or girl to identify the number of objects (or elements) in a group found on randomly selected pages in the book or in a group of objects in the room. Which numeral symbol will be selected for each group? Adult guidance may be needed. 1–2.

Features: numeric narrative, personified numerals, and recognition of numeral shapes.

Leedy, Loreen. *A Number of Dragons*. Illustrated by the author. New York: Holiday House, 1985.

Ten little dragons rush out to play and their number decreases by one as the pages are turned (*one-less-than* relationship) and they run away from toads, dance down a road. Eventually, all of the dragons are gone (empty set concept). Later, the dragons increase in number until all of them are at home with Mother Dragon once more (*one-more- than* relationship). Purple numerals are located in the top corner of every page and tell a viewer the number of dragons to count in each illustration (cardinal number identification; number-numeral correspondence). After seeing this book, a child may want to use numerals decorated with a purple crayon to label numbers of things at home and at school. Recommended. Pre-K.

Features: numerals in purple, *one-less* sequence from ten down to one, and the *one-more* sequence from one up to ten.

Mayer, Mercer. *Little Monster's Counting Book*. Illustrated by the author. Racine, Wis.: Golden/Western, 1978.

With his ears like bat wings, his round body, claws for feet, and sharp teeth shining in his pointed yellow bill, Little Laff is a fun-to-watch monster in Mayer's colorful illustrations. Other monsters, the Trollucks, wear hats, ties, and flags. At the numeral 10, there is a countdown rhyme of "Ten Little Weedles," to be chanted in the manner of "Ten Little Indians." To get to the numeral 21, there are eggs to be counted, laid by a blue monster bird. The eggs are grouped in fives and are easy to count. At 21, the baby monster birds emerge from their eggs. Children enjoy reading the number words, recognizing the numerals, and listening to Mayer's text about all of the monsters in the full-color illustrations. To see the illustrations enlarged on a projection screen, there is a read-along filmstrip (Listening Library, 1 Park Avenue, Old Greenwich, CT) showing Professor Wormbog, the Trollusks, and the Yalapappus to encourage participation in counting again. K-1.

Features: numeric narrative, numeral recognition, number words, cardinal number identification, and counting by fives.

Meddaugh, Susan. *Too Many Monsters*. Illustrated by the author. Boston, Mass.: Houghton Mifflin, 1982.

This one is about one hundred monsters who live in a dark, dark forest. Ninety-nine green monsters are mean, gloomy and greedy, but Howard, a lavender monster, is nothing like them. Howard chases a butterfly up a tree into the sunshine at the tree tops. The other monsters chase Howard up the tree. When the tree breaks, they fall back into the darkness of the forest. Ninety-nine flowers are in the opening left by the fallen tree. Howard plays in the flowers and with other creatures of the forest. K-2.

Features: numeric narrative and place value up to one hundred.

Moncure, Jane B. *Magic Monsters Count to Ten*. Illustrated by Rosemary Fudala. Chicago: The Child's World, 1979.

With a red numeral 1 on its blue metallic chest, a robot introduces young children to Moncure's assortment of monsters to count. Fudala's full-color illustrations will entertain those with a special interest in monsters or in other different creatures as the rhymes are read aloud. Pre-K.

Features: numerals and number words in rhymes from one up to ten.

My Peter the Pixie 123. Illustrated. New York: Crown, 1981.

In this pop-up book, Peter the Pixie lives with his friends which include such animals as pigs and dogs. When Mr. Snail, the wizard, grants Peter's wish to be tall, there are other living things to count—five chickens, six birds, seven dwarfs, eight bees, and ten mice. This is a good book for the game, "How many?" To begin, an adult asks, "How many animals on this page? Estimate or guess first. Then let's count." Pre.

Features: numeric narrative and cardinal number identification from one up to ten.

Nolan, Dennis. *Monster Bubbles: A Counting Book.* Illustrated by the author. Englewood Cliffs, N.J.: Prentice-Hall, 1976.

From zero to twenty, numbers of bubbles float through the air. Bubble-blowing monsters fly through the bubbles, try to dodge them, and play in the air in the midst of them. There are such monster personalities as a flying monster with a bulbous nose and a snake-like tail. Several pink and blue bubbles floating above one fat monster's head give an opportunity to count two, then three. At four, a flying reptile joins the group, and a monster blows more bubbles with both hands. After twenty, all of the bubbles are gone, and Nolan's scene returns to show zero, the number of things in an empty group. One natural extension of this book is to make bubbles outside with soap bubble mixture and count as they float away. If numbers of bubbles are to be shown in an illustration, a young artist may enjoy cutting circular shapes of bubbles from clear sandwich bags. White liquid glue applied with a toothpick will hold the bubble shapes to art paper. Recommended. Pre-K.

Features: wordless book, concept of zero, and cardinal number identification from one up to twenty.

Pavey, Peter. *One Dragon's Dream.* Illustrated by the author. Scarsdale, N.Y.: Bradbury, 1978.

Preparing for bed, one large red-brown dragon settles down with his counting dreams, in which numbers of animals appear. There are full-color illustrations to show the scenes in which he attends his own trial, is sentenced by stern storks, and then is taken off to jail by some slippery seals (cardinal number identification). After elephants smuggle the dragon out of jail, the turtles tow him home. When the dragon awakes, he wonders if his dream predicted a real experience. A viewer is invited to look at the scene out the dragon's bedroom window to see the line of animals through the window and respond to, "Was this all a dream?" The story may be a focus of activity (e.g., repeating the alliterative lines as tongue twisters or introducing the lines for listening, reading, and writing activities). Recommended. 2 up.

Features: numeric narrative, alliteration, and cardinal number identification from one up to ten.

Irons, D. *The Pixies' Toyshop.* Illustrated. Crystal Lake, Ill.: Rigby, 1987.

Before the arched wooden door of a granite block toyshop, a pixie welcomes children looking for toys. The pixie's colorful costume (much like that of a court jester) includes a red collar and a tabard, (half green, half yellow), with elongated points around the hem. This pixie wears soft slippers, sharply pointed, with the toes turned up and the tops folded down. One slipper is green and the other yellow. A boy and girl visit the toyshop and look in the windows. As they see numbers of toys, the children say, "Six bells are what we see. Some for you and the same for me" and "Eight trucks are what we see. Some for you and the same for me." This rhyme is one to take into the classroom as children, in pairs, face the top of an overhead projector. Repeating the rhyme with: "_____(number) _____(object) are what we see. Some for you and the same for me," two children divide selected numbers of objects on the overhead projector while their classroom friends watch the operation on the numbers. Their procedure may be verified and the final quotient announced. 1–3.

Features: numeric narrative, rhymes, cardinal number identification to ten, and equivalent groups for early experience in division.

Rand, Ann and Paul Rand. *Little 1*. Illustrated. New York: Harcourt Brace and World, 1962.

The Rands' rhyming sentences personify the numeral 1. This numeral 1 wears a red hat and walks on small feet. The numeral wants to play and to be a part of another numeral group. When numeral 1 joins two yellow pears, he recognizes the addition sentence: $2 + 1 = 3$. Joining other groups, 1 greets buzzing bees, waiting umbrellas, and searching ants. Later, one bright red hoop shows the numeral 1 that they can stand together to form the numeral 10. Seeing this illustration, some teachers ask the same question about this book that they ask about several others: When the numerals 1 and 0 stand together in the illustration, what might be a child's mental construction about the number ten? Will any boy or girl think of the joining of two groups, one group with only one member (rather than ten members) and the second group as an empty group? Adult guidance needed. 1–2.

Pattern: numeric narrative, personified numerals, addition sentences, place value, and math symbols for addition.

Randell, Beverley. *Ten Big Dinosaurs*. Illustrated by Dyan Prujean. San Diego: The Wright Group, 1987.

Written with rhyme, repetition, and rhythm, here is an amusing big book of ten dinosaurs. Dressed in jogging suits, the bright green dinosaurs engage in different nonsense activities. Suggestions for related counting activities are found on the back cover. To complement this big book, individual small readers are available from the publisher. 1–3.

Features: numeric narrative, rhymes, number words from one up to ten.

Ross, H. L. *Not Counting Monsters*. Illustrated by Doug Cushman. New York: Platt and Munk, 1978.

One monster reads a book while it walks down a country path. Resembling a blue dodo bird, a second monster peers at him from over a stone wall. The counter is to remember that monsters "won't count" in some of the later counting situations. First, one can count the monsters at their reunion, at gas pumps, as chefs, and as boy scouts. But reviewing each scene again, we see that some objects are monsters and some are not. For instance, in the illustration of the mailboxes, one sees that some of the mailboxes are real and others are monsters posing as mailboxes. On a clothesline, some of the clothes are really articles of clothing and others are monsters hanging on the line. Other monsters masquerade as boats, birds, chickens, and sheep. For reinforcement and to ensure one's accuracy, answers can be found in the left-hand and right-hand corners of the pages. K-1.

Features: cardinal number identification from one up to ten, classifying by attributes, and a self-check for answers.

Satchwell, John. *Counting*. Illustrated by Katy Sleight. New York: Random House, 1984.

In *Counting*, a book in the Early Math Concept series, boys and girls meet a friendly green monster. The monster grows from a blob outlined in green into a recognizable monster with all of his monster parts. As the monster gradually appears, there are numerals to recognize, number words to read, and the names of the monster parts to repeat (arms, legs, head). On a culminating page, there is a review of the sequence of numerals, 1 through 10, which shows the counting sequence again. Pre-K.

Features: numerals, number words, parts of a whole, and a review from one up to ten.

Sendak, Maurice. *Seven Little Monsters*. Illustrated by the author. New York: Harper and Row, 1977.

Larger than the house from which they emerge, Sendak's seven monsters each have a distinct appearance. One monster wears oversize shoes and a coat reminiscent of one worn by Frankenstein's monster. Two more monsters sport devilish horns. A third one reminds one of the Wild Things, while a fourth monster wears sprouting wings. Another has the face of a Halloween mask and the last monster, the seventh, prefers traveling on all fours at times. This last monster has a very, very, long nose. In this Children's Choice book, the seven monsters frighten some tiny people in a tiny Lilliput-like village. With Sendak's counting rhyme, a listener hears about the soldiers' attempts to capture the monsters as they advance. Sendak offers number words about the advancing monster who goes up (flying), another monster who goes down (crawling), and a third monster who goes creeping into the small, small town (*one-more-than* relationship). The use of ordinals may be substituted in the appropriate places in the text. If interested, a learner at school may draw and color the largest monster possible on art paper, cut out the shape, and contribute the monster, along with the other monsters created by friends, to an activity of arranging the monsters in order from tallest to shortest. Adult guidance needed. Recommended. K-2.

Features: *one-more* sequence from one up to seven in rhyming lines.

Shepherd, Ray. *The Count's Poem.* Illustrated by Tom Cooke. Chicago: Goldencraft/Children's Press, 1978.

One teacher asks if the children know of any more books about numbers that have characters from Sesame Street. With this request, a familiar figure appears in the classroom. It is the Count, a 123 character from the "Sesame Street" television show. More words about numbers are found in this poem. A boy or girl begins this tale by vicariously crossing the blue moat and entering the Count's castle in this Golden Tell-A-Tale reader. The number names may be repeated aloud as the rhyming words from the Count are heard. Pre-1.

Features: numeric narrative, rhyming lines, and number names.

Slater, Teddy. *Molly's Monsters.* Illustrated by Mary Morgan. New York: Putnam/Grosset and Dunlap, 1988.

Tucked in bed, one little girl counts the monsters as they move through her dreams. There is one gruesome glog, two toothsome trogs, and up to ten glitches with tails like dragons and noses like witches. Young viewers may match some of the characteristics of the monsters with those of animals they recognize and notice that the rhino-monster pokes his head through the window, an alligator-monster crawls out from under the bed, and a gorilla-like-monster peers over the headboard of the bed. At the number ten, Molly disperses the monsters by turning on the light (which gives them a fright). The *one-less* sequence is reviewed as they leave in the order in which they arrived. Pre-1.

Features: *one-more* sequence of one up to ten and *one-less* sequence down to one, accumulation.

Stange, Deborah and Rappaport, Ira. *Fuffles Getting To Know Colors, Numbers and Shapes.* Illustrated by the authors. New York: Modern Publishing/Unisystems, 1985.

Every strange creature in this small book has two features (faces). They are Fuffles, and all present objects to count. Number words are in colors and all capital letters. Lucille Dicken (a yellow chicken-like creature) holds two eggs. Shamel (shaped like a camel) makes four footprints in the sand. Six bishes (fishes) are all yellow and hide in a bush (not in seaweed). Snyder Spider wears eight sneakers. For a prediction activity, an adult may pronounce one of the names of the Fuffles and ask a boy or girl to guess what that selected Fuffle might look like before seeing the illustration in the book. Pre-K.

Features: number words in capitals and cardinal number identification.

Tester, Sylvia R. *One Unicorn: A Counting Book.* Illustrated by Arnoldus J. Gruter. Chicago: The Child's World, 1977.

Tester explains some of the folklore origins of the unicorn and other mythical animals in this counting book. The full-colored illustrations are large, clear, and distinct. Thunderbirds fly through zig-zags of black lightning, green frogs change into princes, and curving snakes perform their dances. At the story for the number ten, tigers illustrate the Asian myth about how the first tiger came to be in the world. After the number ten, Tester provides more explanations. From the myth of the unicorn and Aesop's fable about the tortoise and the hare to Hans Christian Anderson's story about the emperor and the nightingale, Tester retells folklore beliefs for the interested reader. 2 up.

Pattern: folklore and numeric narratives from one up to ten.

Wallner, John. *Milton the Monster You Can Count On.* Illustrated by the author. Los Angeles: Price/Stern/Sloan, 1985.

When a wicked witch changes a mouse into a monster, the mouse needs the young reader's help to break the spell. The reader is invited to push the monster's tummy (it holds a squeaker) to make the monster squeak for the appropriate number of times the objects are seen in the illustrations—two birds, three eggs, four ducks, and on up to ten mouse relatives (*one-more* sequence). The mice celebrate when the witch's spell is finally broken and Milton is transformed back into a mouse. Pre-K.

Features: *one-more* sequence, cardinal number identification from one up to ten, and one-to-one correspondence.

Wood, A. J. *A First Book of Counting*. Illustrated by David Anstey. Dorking, Eng.: Templar Publications, 1986.

Decorated endpapers introduce a boy and girl to the characters to come in this book, the dinosaurs. In the first double-page illustration, one dinosaur watches two dinosaurs dance. The number words are spelled out up through nine and ten where nine dinosaurs pound drums to wake up ten dinosaurs asleep in a big bed. The first double-page spread is linked to the second by text and by scene. The first part of the sentence is read and illustrated on the first spread and the last part of the sentence is completed and illustrated on the following second spread. In addition to this linking, oversize numerals are inserted in the illustrations. 1–2.

Features: oversize numerals, number words in text, linked sentences across illustrations from one through ten, *one- more* sequence, and cardinal number identification.

Mysteries and Puzzles

Anno, Masaichiro and Mitsumasa Anno. *Anno's Mysterious Multiplying Jar*. Illustrated by Mitsumasa Anno. New York: Philomel, 1983.

Anno and his son help a reader understand the concept of factorial, an idea that is difficult for some. This easy-to-understand story has beautiful illustrations that show this fairly advanced math concept. One magic jar multiples until the product becomes quite large. The number is so large that the illustrator must represent the number with 10! (ten factorial). Here is supportive pictorial information for an emerging math specialist who is ready for the concept. Recommended. Advanced 2 up.

Features: concept of factorial and addition as multiplication.

Brown, Marc. *One, Two, Three: An Animal Counting Book*. Illustrated by the author. Boston: Atlantic Monthly Press/Little, Brown, 1976.

The endpages, with their bright red-orange numerals framed in brown and white squares, show the counting that is to come on the pages ahead. One textured elephant hides the numeral 1 in his tough, bristly hide and begins the counting on the first double-page spread. The repeated numerals on each succeeding animal's body-shape. For example, the numeral 4 is seen as part of a pattern on one alligator's scales and as part of the mouths of two other alligators. But where is the numeral 4 on the fourth alligator? Do all five fish have a numeral 5 somewhere in their fin designs? Does each monkey's tail form a numeral 6? A careful observer finds all of the numerals through 20 on the animals. The large illustrations show his humor: an alligator wears glasses, one monkey stands on his head, and several reindeer balance on top of other reindeer. On the bright, concluding pages, all of the animals hold up white cards to show red numerals in a *one-more* sequence for review. 1–2.

Features: hidden numerals for numbers of animals from one through twenty, and a review.

Carle, Eric. *Let's Paint a Rainbow*. Illustrated by the author. New York: Philomel, 1982.

In this board book, the puzzling task (to some) of counting by twos is addressed, and introduces eight colors to make a rainbow. With rhyming lines, one man and one woman invite children to paint a rainbow and to use first the colors of purple and blue (two), then yellow and green (four), brown and orange (six), and last, red and pink (eight). As each set of two colors is presented, one sees the colors increase through die-cut windows. Cans of paint and stripes in the rainbow can be counted to eight. Before the last page is turned, a girl or boy may predict the object that the painters are painting (a rainbow cat). Pre-K.

Features: counting by twos up to eight, die-cut windows, rhyming lines.

Carle, Eric. *My Very First Book of Numbers*. Illustrated by the author. New York: Thomas Y. Crowell, 1974.

This book presents the challenge of matching the squares on the top portion of the divided page with a corresponding portion that shows colorful fruits in groups from one through ten. Spiral binding makes the pages of this counting book easy for a viewer to flip back and forth for matching the shapes on these puzzle pages. What is the shape that a viewer wants to find? What is the appropriate number? Which portion of the pages should be turned, the top or the bottom? Without any words in this book, how may a girl or boy find out if a match has been made? For instance, the numeral 2 identifies two black squares. These squares, in turn, match two colorful bananas on the split cardboard pages. What can be done to verify a match? Pre-K.

Features: matching, one-to-one correspondence from one through ten.

Charlip, Remy and Jerry Joyner. *Thirteen*. Illustrated by the authors. New York: Parents Magazine Press, 1975.

Thirteen picture stories develop separately and simultaneously in pale colors on double-page spreads. Any one of the thirteen stories may be followed as the pages are turned. For example, the first spread shows the first scene in each of the stories. The second spread shows the second scene in each of the stories. "Countdown," for instance, begins with the numeral 13 on the first page, 12 on the second page, and so on. In another story, about a sinking ship, the ship sinks lower and lower . . . to the bottom of a bottle of water and not to the bottom of the sea. Other children may choose the story of "Cinderella" or the episodes in 'Paper Magic." Can anyone who see the pattern of these pictures in sequence and unravel the secret of this unusual page arrangement without a clue? There is a preview of coming attractions on each page in a small framed insert which reproduces the actions in all thirteen stories found on the succeeding page. With this clue, some students will discern the pattern in this wordless book. At the foot of each page is another story about a caterpillar. On the first page in the left corner, the caterpillar is on the leaf, which moves page after page, toward the right margin. The caterpillar struggles in the water as the leaf floats to the center, then swirls along, is used as a raft by the caterpillar who floats on the leaf to dry land in the right-hand corner. As fall becomes winter, and the ground is covered in snow, the viewer sees the caterpillar's cocoon. When spring arrives, a butterfly emerges and flies off the page, all alone on a white background to signal the end of the stories (sequence). 2 up.

Features: sequence of events in thirteen picture stories.

Children's Television Workshop. *The Sesame Street 1, 2, 3 Storybook.* Illustrated. New York: Random House, 1973.

Hiding inside *The Sesame Street 1, 2, 3 Storybook* is a mystery story entitled, "Sherlock Hemock and the Mystery Stranger." Hemlock counts two unusual shoes, two evil-looking hands, and then two beady eyes. Who is this mysterious stranger? Hemlock turns on his light to find out, and discovers that he has been shining his flashlight into his own mirror and counting body parts from its reflection. At home, girls and boys may enjoy watching the "Electric Company" television show or finding some two-dimensional fun on the pages of the *Electric Company Color and Learn Book, Letters and Numbers* (Crown, 1985). With the two-color illustrations, these pages offer activities for connecting the dots, completing puzzles, coloring the objects, and other pencil-on-paper tasks. K-1.

Features: numeric narrative, concept of two.

Demi. *Demi's Count the Animals.* Illustrated by the author. New York: Putnam Publishing Group, 1986.

A brightly illustrated counting book features a collection of animals to count from one through one hundred. For example, four tigers are shown for the numeral 4. The numeral is shown in black with an accompanying word for the number. The tigers spring across a double-page spread in a tiger race. Demi asks a viewer to count the tigers and then, in a one-to-one correspondence activity, to count the tails of the tigers. There is an appealing, rhymed text, the animals are shown in double-page spreads, and a challenge is offered: Who can count to one hundred by twos? Recommended. Pre-2.

Features: rhymes from one through ten and beyond, hidden animals, counting by twos, and cardinal number identification from one up to one hundred.

Gantz, David. *The Wacky World of Numbers.* Illustrated by the author. New York: Macmillan/Checkerboard Press, 1987.

If a child likes humorous characters and events, then Gantz's cartoon world may be just the book for reviewing numbers. Some of these questions about the full-color illustrations may be puzzling but enjoyable ones to figure out. For some examples, there are these questions: "What could be worse than a wacky world with numbers? What is worse than an eight

monster nightmare? What could a reader call a nine-tentacled octopus?"
1–2.

Features: humorous numeric questions, and number use.

Harada, Joyce. *It's the 0123 Counting Book*. Illustrated by the author.
San Mateo, Cal.: Heian, 1985.

Sometimes, the mixture of hidden objects in the pictures of this number book can present puzzling problems. Some effort is required to find
the right number of objects before one sees the quantity of a group. A
large numeral and an appropriate number of dots appear with each illustration. At the numeral 6, a viewer counts such items as six penguins, six
party hats, and six packages. Additional counting exercises lead the
counting from eleven up to twenty. For larger numbers, there is a colorful matrix on the endpages which shows all of the numerals from 0
through 109. 1–2.

Features: oversize numerals, corresponding dots, cardinal number
identification, hidden pictures, and a review matrix from 1 up to 109.

Hoban, Russell. *Ten What? A Mystery Counting Book*. Illustrated by
Sylvia Selig. New York: Charles Scribner's Sons, 1975.

For all children who have been wishing for a number mystery book,
the wait is over when an adult shows this one. Opening the covers begins
a search for ten of something and the two yellow-billed bird sleuths who
join in appear baffled on every page. From one mysterious message to
two agents up to nine windows in buildings and ten paws reaching toward
ten lollipops, a young viewer identifies and counts a wide variety of
objects in every illustration. For instance, at the numeral 7, the search
continues through seven houses while seven police cars wait nearby.
Seven chairs are outside on the sidewalk and seven large butterflies
hover, ready to be counted.

Some teachers ask questions about this book. For some children, is
there too much to see on each page? Or does it matter that there seems
to be no one central focus point for each of the illustrations? Should the
settings change with each illustration when presenting counting information to a young boy or girl? Still other teachers ask, Since this is a mystery
story, shouln't there be more of a plot, a story-line? Despite these questions by adults, certain children remain loyal to this book, helping the
two bird detectives search and search again for the missing ten of something. 1–2.

Features: wordless mystery, numerals and objects for numbers from one up to ten.

Hoberman, Mary Ann. *The Looking Book*. Illustrated by Jerry Joyner. New York: Knopf, 1973.

Ned loses his cat, Pistachio, on the first page and looks through all of the pages to find his pet. Within the bordered illustrations and among the thumbprint numerals, Ned searches and searches. Ned looks under the numeral 2, climbs on a 3 to reach an apple tree and rests on the top of an 8. Some clues in the text ask a reader to turn to such pages as 22, then 5, and back to 24 to help the search. A bookmark in the book is suggested so the place won't be lost. And where does Ned finally find Pistachio? The cat is found in a box on page 28, the same box that was seen on the first page of the book. Does the reader see it? If not, the reader is asked to look again: the box is near Pistachio's food dish. 1–2.

Features: long numeric narrative and use of numerals.

Howe, Caroline Walton. *Counting Penguins Zero to Nine: A Wordless Picture Book*. Illustrated by the author. New York: Harper and Row, 1983.

In the illustrations, a girl or boy counts the black and white penguins as they play throughout the day and looks for a corresponding gray numeral hidden in each setting. 358

There is one penguin who skates all alone. Two penguins dance. The number of penguins grows with each page as they sled, fish, swim, and ski until there are nine in the group ready for a night's rest after their day of play. At the foot of each illustration there is a red numeral and the corresponding number word in black, the only text in this almost wordless book. The lack of text makes this a natural for miming the actions of the penguins. For the numeral 8, notice the different sizes of penguins. Which ones are small, average, or large? Does someone see a penguin who appears different from the others? Varieties are identified on the title page. If all of the penguins left on an ice floe, would a young mathematician see an empty group or set? K-1.

Features: numerals in red, number words in black lowercase, hidden numerals in illustrations, concept of zero, and penguins to count from one up to nine.

Hutchins, Pat. *1 Hunter*. Illustrated by the author. New York: Greenwillow, 1982.

Dressed in a desert helmet, khaki shirt, walking shorts, glasses, and boots, the hunter stalks past animals camouflaged in the jungle. A reader puzzles over the pictures to locate the animals that the hunter does not see. The hunter misses two elephants whose thick legs look like the trunks of palm trees, eight monkeys in a tall jungle tree, and nine snakes that are wrapped around another tall palm tree in an encircling design. The hunter walks across floating logs, ignoring the shapes that reveal them as the backs of crocodiles. The number of hiding animals increases with each page. , and enough of each animal is shown so a boy or girl can make predictions before turning pages. After the number ten, the hunter is confronted by all of the animals in groups. Startled by this jungle force, the hunter runs away quickly, losing his glasses, his hat, and his long gun. Reading this book may prepare one for some computer activities based on this story (Millennium Group, 24 E. 22nd St, New York, NY 10010). There are sound effects to enjoy in "A-Hunting We will Go." In "Count the Animals," members from one species of animals may be counted; In "Mixed-Up animals," members from a variety of species may be identified and counted. In "How Many," the animals reveal themselves, are counted, and then the appropriate numeral on the keyboard is pressed to continue. During "Pick and Count," the value of a numeral is identified and the space bar used to enter the correct number of animals that correspond to the numeral. Recommended. Pre-2.

Features: wordless adventure, hidden animals from one up to ten, and cardinal number identification.

LeSieg, Theo. *Wacky Wednesday*. Illustrated by George Booth. New York: Random House, 1974.

Rhyming verse and humorous illustrations point out some of the things that could go wrong on one wacky day. What could go wrong before one gets out of bed in the morning? Is there a brown shoe on the bedroom wall or a brown boot on the bathroom ceiling? Looking out of a bedroom window, one can see the yellow bananas growing on an apple tree or notice the brown worm chasing a bluebird. Inside and outside of the house, there are additional wacky things to see. What wacky things might one see in the bathroom? In the kitchen? Walking to school? In the classroom? On the way home from school through the park? Once a viewer finds the twenty wacky things on the last page, this wacky Wednesday is over. Recommended. K-2.

Features: humorous, rhyming verses from one up to twenty, number use, and classifying.

Livermore, Elaine. *Lost and Found.* Illustrated by the author. Boston: Houghton Mifflin, 1975.

In this one, a boy or girl is asked to join some people in the park, while a busy bird flies off with odds and ends. Can someone find the items that are missing in the sketches on the bright yellow backgrounds? Livermore gives clues: the lost object is seen on a left-hand page and the viewer discovers what is missing on a facing right-hand page. Recommended. K-1.

Features: visual discrimination, numeric narrative, missing objects, and cardinal number identification.

Livermore, Elaine. *One to Ten, Count Again.* Illustrated by the author. Boston: Houghton Mifflin, 1973.

The young viewer must look closely to find such animals as three cows in an overgrown field, four mules who hide behind umbrellas, or seven sheep among the rocks, tall grass, and trees. The city yields more animals. One of the final illustrations is of an empty house. But is it really empty? As an observer looks closely, additional animals are seen in the lines of the drawing. Each group of animals joins another group to fill the house with occupants. One bull rests in the front window, the camels look out of a second-story window, and the monkeys sit on the roof. While certain older children enjoy these illustrations, some adults ask questions about showing the drawings to younger children on the grounds that they might be confusing. Recommended. 2 up.

Features: numeric narrative, visual discrimination, and hidden animals from one through ten.

MacDonald, Suse, and Bill Oakes. *Numblers.* Illustrated by the authors. New York: Dial, 1988.

Each double-page spread is devoted to one numeral with the number's name in an outlined type style, the numeral transformation into shapes shown in a series of framed inserts, and an illustration that shows the use of the transformed numeral to make an object. For example, the numeral 1 stretches itself into the shape of a seal (one part) and the numeral 2 divides and becomes a swan (two parts). A careful observer counts the number of parts for each object: the numeral 4 inflates, replicates, and is seen in the two sails of a sailboat, its hull, and the flying pennant on top of a mast (four parts). Nine numeral nines form the shape of a squirrel. For self-checking, a viewer may use the map of numbers at the end of the book. Some viewers may have problems visually discriminating the transformations where colors are similar and the texture of both the figure and ground make the objects in the illustrations difficult to identify. If so, adult guidance may be needed. Recommended. Pre-1.

Features: from one up to ten, numerals transform into objects composed of similar number of parts, number names, and a self-checking key.

Peppé, Rodney. *Odd One OuT*. Illustrated by the author. New York: Viking, 1974.

The capital last letter gives a hint of odd things to come. Peppé's bright colors help make a game of finding odd things on the large pages. The viewer takes a walk with young Peter on this unusual day. At breakfast, Peter sees an odd amphibian on the kitchen table, a frog which follows him into the garden where Peter sees a traffic light. This light shows up in a traffic scene on the next page. Each odd item gives a viewer a hint about the scene to come. For instance, when there is a school chalkboard in an illustration, one can predict that the next illustration will show a schoolroom environment. A chimpanzee in the classroom is the clue to the following zoo scene. When Peter sees his own familiar bed at a county fair, a young predictor might guess that a nighttime scene will follow to end the day. To introduce some boys and girls to symbols that have meanings, one teacher shows the end pages with the bright, smiling, sun-faces, which could symbolize this sunny, unique day in Peter's life. One teacher separates the illustrations of an extra copy, hands one to each student, and asks each to write as many questions as possible about what is seen in the picture. Students can trade illustrations and questions and upon receiving the "new" illustration, each begins to answer in writing the questions about the illustration. For still more objects to name and count and recognize, there is *Rodney Peppe's Puzzle Book* (Viking, 1977). In this one, there are eleven intricate and humorous full-color picture puzzles to discuss with others. Recommended. K-1.

Features: visual narrative, classifying by finding things that do not belong in illustrations.

Testa, Fulvio. *If You Take a Pencil*. Illustrated by the author. New York: Dial, 1982.

A young artist picks up a pencil and imagines what to draw. Children enjoy the full-color illustrations and count as they see two children draw a cat, then two, and then three. A close look at the pictures reveals other groups to count. For example, on one of the pages, three cats are surprised and agitated by a small boy's animal mask. A young observer may look for other objects in groups of three on this same page. Are those three leaves on the floor? Are there three pottery pieces in the bookcase? What other puzzles can be found? The three cats watch four birds as the numbers accumulate. Arriving on an island, the two children find twelve treasure chests. What could be predicted about their contents? All chests are empty except the last one, which holds a pencil, to complete the circular pattern of the story. Can someone tell an original number story about one of the illustrations? Who would like to take a pencil and draw a picture with numbers of objects? Who is ready to draw a circular story, one beginning and ending with a single object as Testa did? Recommended. 1–2.

Features: circular story pattern, numeric narrative in pictures, objects from one up to twelve.

Vreuls, Diane. *Sums (A Looking Game)*. Illustrated by the author. New York: Viking, 1977.

The eye-catching word, game, introduces the concept of addition in a nonnumerical way. A young viewer plays with a series of shape puzzles in his or her mind and adds different parts together to make up a whole picture. For one example, a viewer sees the front hood of a car, then one fender and wheel, then another fender and wheel, and last, sees the trunk—all in a vertical notation form that uses pictures instead of numerals. Vreuls includes the plus sign to the left of the pictures to encourage a viewer adding the parts together. Then, the viewer turns the page and finds the sum of all of the car parts—a completed sideview of the finished car. There are no words to read in this book but lots of comprehending to do. One felt board activity continues the looking game and begins with such words as, "My car fell apart but I have all the pieces. Who can find the fender? Window? Tire?" The teacher places cut-apart pieces (jig-saw puzzle style) of the illustration of a car in a mixed-up arrangement on the board. The meanings of the $+$ sign and $=$ sign are discussed. Children take turns finding the parts, identifying them, and arranging them to make a whole. Large, colorful illustrations of toys, houses, household objects may be cut apart, and offered as a challenge for another to put back together again. Recommended. K-2.

Features: vertical notation format, object recognition, and adding parts to make a whole.

Youldon, Gillian. *Numbers*. Illustrated by the author. New York: Franklin Watts, 1979.

Different backgrounds or scenes can be created as these slip pages are turned, and how new objects to count appear on these colorful pages. A viewer begins by seeing a barn, a pond, and a horse with the numerals, number words, and object words and chooses which strip to turn. Turning the strip showing the grazing brown horse, the viewer sees two brown cows. More strips take a counter up to ten chickens, ten flowers, ten stars, and then to directions to read: "Count the frogs! Count the carts! Count the gates!" A final double-page spread shows colorful bands for objects from one through ten. In the green band is one pail and the appropriate numeral. This review emphazises the concept or pattern of *one-more-than* as a viewer always sees one object separated from the other objects. For example, in the orange band for eight, seven objects are seen and then one object separated from the others to sum to eight. Each group in this review has one member from one of the groups seen earlier on the strip pages. For example, for the number three, a pail, a rabbit, and a tree, are found, and for the number four, a pail, a rabbit, a tree, and a dog. Reminiscent of the illustrations by Bruna and Pienkowski in their 123 books, these outlined objects are easy to see, and to count. Recommended. Pre-1.

Features: strip pages, numerals, number words, object words, *one-more-than* concept, and a review.

Transportation

Carle, Eric. *1, 2, 3 to the Zoo*. Illustrated by the author. New York: Collins, 1968.

The numerals are easy to recognize on this train that is going to the zoo. A mouse rides along and meets groups of animal with numbers from one through ten. Across the double-page illustrations march a series of animals into circus cars—one elephant, two hippos, three giraffes, and up to ten birds (accumulation). On the bottom left-hand corner of each page, a small version of the train cars on the previous pages enables the beginning counter to count the animals in the cars up to the present page (one-to-one correspondence). Both cardinal and ordinal relationships are reinforced. Pictures are bright and large. In black at the foot of each page, Carle shows the train getting longer and longer as each page is turned. The final illustration shows the animals all in place at their new home, the zoo. In "Features: Choosing for Children Under Three," an article from the "Children's Book Council," Frank Self cites this book as an example of the way clarity of the meaning of the content of a book can come from four major sources: from the contrasts in and among the subjects on the pages; from the placement and size of illustrations; from the use of color or black-and-white; and from the way illustrations directly convey movement, feelings, and ideas. What movement, size of objects, feelings, ideas, or contrasts between the animals does a young viewer want to talk about after seeing these colorful illustrations? To count the numbers of objects with another animal often seen at the zoo, there is *The Very Fussy Monkey* (Philomel, 1982). Pre-1.

Features: one-to-one correspondence from one up to ten.

Carle, Eric. *The Very Long Train: A Folding Book.* Illustrated by the author. New York: Thomas Y. Crowell, 1972.

A boy or girl unfolds the page that shows a colorful engine to see one rhino on a flatbed train car. Next are two blue elephants, three brown camels, and four chimpanzees. There are many other groups of animals to count on this long train. This unfolding book can become a frieze for the room. When it is turned over, a reader finds the names of the animals and the numerals that represent the members in the groups, an introduction to vertically written numerals. Along with the collage illustrations and bright paintings, a reader sees the words that tell the sums of the animals on the cars of the train (numeral recognition). Pre-1.

Features: numeral recognition, animal names, and vertical notation.

Cole, Joanna. *Fun on Wheels.* Illustrated by Whitney Darrow, Jr. New York: William Morrow, 1977.

First, a viewer counts one bear on a small unicycle, then three men on a motorcycle, and one girl on a tricycle. When the page is turned, there are more wheels and riders to count. Are there four wheels on that bright pink wagon? How many wheels does the juggler throw into the air? How many wheels are seen on the lion's cage-car? Not only do Cole and Darrow give wheels to count but also information about what wheels can do. For example, there are wheels that help feed people (meals on wheels) and wheels that help move boats, coats, and floats. Other things can be placed on wheels, e.g., chairs and airplane stairs rolled to the plane's door. Then, there is a pizza wheel to slice, a ferris wheel to ride, and wheels to spin at a fair. Not designed as a counting book, this lacks numerals and number words; however, the use of numbers is shown along with numerous wheels to count. 1–2.

Features: number use and groups of wheels to count.

Crews, Donald. *Bicycle Race*. Illustrated by the author. New York: Greenwillow, 1985.

Warming up for a bicycle race, twelve riders show their numbers in different colors. Once the race starts, the riders take different positions in the race. Who is ready to order the position of the riders and read the list of numbers at the foot of each page that shows the positions of the bikers for that page? If interested, a young counter can use number words as names and indicate, "Rider number four is first" or "Rider number seven is second." In telling the positions of the other bikers this way, the counter uses both cardinal number words and ordinals. Some readers may be interested in a brain teaser such as this one: If you had three bicycles, one red, one blue, and one gray, and wanted to ride them in a different order each day, how many days would it take? Or this one: The blue bicycle is between the red and gray. The gray bicycle is in front of the brown one. The brown one is not first in the line. Can you arrange the bicycles in line? Some adult guidance may be needed. 1 up.

Features: colors, numerals, number words, number use, and ordinals.

Ehrlich, Amy. *The Everyday Train*. Illustrated by Martha Alexander. New York: Dial, 1977.

Through the pages of this book, the reader joins Jane in greeting the train that travels on the tracks near her home each day. What does a young viewer find? First, there are many types of train cars to identify. Second, there is the sound of the engine and the wheels on the tracks to mimic in a creative way. Can one count all of the train cars just as Jane does? What color is predicted for the color of the train's caboose? 1–2.

Features: number use.

Green, Suzanne. *Little Bookmobile: Colors, Numbers, and Shapes on Wheels*. Illustrated by Daisuke Yokoi. New York: Doubleday, 1988.

Numbers is one of three board books in a pull-string case shaped like a wheeled vechicle. Inside are illustrations of ten familiar vehicles. A young preschooler may identify such objects as motorcycles and school buses while counting up to ten. Pre-K.

Features: board book, object-numeral relationship from one up to ten.

Hayward, Linda. *The Little Engine That Could 123*. Illustrated by John Nez. New York: Grosset and Dunlap/Playvalue Books, 1986.

Adapted from the classic story (Platt and Munk by Watty Piper), this is a participation book for an interested girl or boy to color. Two double-page spreads show numbers of things for the numeral shown in the upper left-hand corner of the page. Accumulating patterns are seen. For the numeral *1*, a viewer sees one engineer and one engine. In the corner beside the numeral is one outlined engine. For the numeral 2, there are two dolls in the gondola car, two bears and two giraffes. Three toys are found in a boxcar, and other numbers of toys in a refrigerator car, flatcar, hopper car, passenger car, baggage car, mail car, and up to ten balloons in the caboose. Use of numerals is found on a final page. A line drawing of the engine features numerals beside parts of the engine, so one can identify the engine parts. The numeral 4 identifies the dome; 2, the smokestack; and 5, the whistle. Familiar and less familiar words include headlight, bell, cab, cowcatcher, driver wheel, and pilot wheels. Adult guidance needed. K-1.

Features: numerals, numbers of toys from one up to ten, and use of numbers as legend for diagram.

Magee, Doug. *Trucks You Can Count On*. Photographs by the author. New York: Dodd, Mead, 1985.

The words of the title have a double meaning: one can rely on tractor-trailers to serve people in different ways and one can learn to count with the objects on a truck. There are such items to count as three windshield wipers and four fog horns, part of the exciting world of tractor-trailers. Recommended. Pre-K.

Features: numeral-number correspondence of objects found on trucks.

Meeks, Esther K. *One Is the Engine: A Counting Book*. Illustrated by Joe Rogers. Chicago: Follett, 1972.

Here, a father helps a small boy count the train cars as they roll by. As each car is seen, facts are introduced. Above the train cars are the numerals to indicate the number of the car (number use). Adult guidance will be needed for discussion of much information gained from the text:

does someone know that the diesel engine burns oil to generate electricity, a force that causes the motors to turn the wheels? Can one say what a flatcar might be used for? Or the refrigerator car? Who sees that the tank car is one that can be filled with liquid (measurement of liquid)? What are some of the liquids the car might carry? What is the name of the car with the open top (gondola car)? Why a young listener think that a piggyback car is called that? At the number ten, the last train car is seen—the caboose—a car that serves as a home for the conductor and for the rear-end brakeman. 2 up.

Features: numeral use and numbers as names.

Collections of Unrelated Objects

Fewer than Ten

Grender, Iris. *Playing with Numbers*. Illustrated by Geoffrey Butcher. New York: Pantheon, 1975.

For the child who is ready for some activities of counting, grouping, and one-to-one correspondence, here is Grender's manipulative retelling of the number sequence, one through five. A young viewer matches a numeral to a number and then a number to a numeral. The heavy pages of the book and Butcher's use of color in the clear, simple illustrations make this appropriate for a preschooler. For a complementary story, one preschool teacher selects "Five Little Snowmen" from *Paper Stories* (Fearon/David S. Lake, 1984) by Jean Stangl. This counting story-rhyme is repeated as five snowmen are cut from paper during the story and then shown to the young children as an ending. Stangl includes objects to cut for "The Funny Shape Family" (basic shapes and counting to five), "Six Little Girls and One Valentine" (counting to six, Valentine's Day), and "Hickety Pickety" (counting to twelve). Pre.

Features: board pages, numerals, and numbers from one up to five.

Kessler, Ethel and Leonard Kessler. *Two, Four Six, Eight: A Book about Legs*. Illustrated by Leonard Kessler. New York: Dodd, Mead, 1980.

In these illustrations, boys and girls, animals, and insects run by so a viewer can count their legs by twos. In over half of the illustrations, one sees two-legged creatures; in twenty-five percent, four- and six-legged animals; and in about a fifth, eight-legged insects are shown. An adult may want to cover up the text with post-it tape so the viewer can concentrate on counting by twos from the bright pictures. If catalogs, magazines, or newspaper advertisements are saved, these items may be used for a cutting and pasting activity to make an individual book about things to count by twos. Pre-1.

Features: numeric information and counting by twos.

Marshall, Roy, and Korky Paul. *The Pop-Up Numbers Books: Addition and Subtraction*. Illustrated by the authors. New York: E. P. Dutton, 1984.

Animals and objects spring from the book in lively, humorous color as the pages are turned. The pop-ups illustrate the addition and the subtraction sentences. For instance, in the *Pop-Up Number 2 Book: Subtraction,* a young viewer sees a plane disappear behind a cloud, frogs who jump from lily pads, and fish that swim into a whale's mouth. For children who are moving along into multiplication and division, there are pop-up books for those math topics, too, with *Pop-Up Number 3 Book: Multiplication* and *Pop-Up Number 4 Book: Division.* 1 up.

Features: paper engineering, addition and subtraction operations, math symbols, horizontal notation format, and math sentences.

My 123 Pop-Up Book. Illustrated by J. Pavlin and G. Seda. London: Brown Watson, n.d.

With its cover illustration by Hildegarde Bone, this book conveys the *one-more* concept in understanding numbers and their relationships. First, one brown rabbit pops up next to another rabbit in a cabbage patch. Numerals in boxes show the addition sentence with $1 + 1 = 2$. The rabbits are near three cabbages. A second sentence shows $2 + 1 = 3$. One more is always added to the previous number. As the young viewer turns other pages, different objects pop from the illustrations: four cars drive down a street past one parked car to show $4 + 1 = 5$; three houses are near one house to show that $3 + 1 = 4$. Other objects that stand out are seven bright butterflies, eight circus dogs performing tricks, and nine colorful birds in a group. Key words are near objects and found in bold type. K-1.

Features: numerals to nine, *one-more* concept, horizontal notation format, addition symbols, key words, and math sentences

Numbers Pop-Up Book. Illustrated. London: Ramboro, 1985.

In this oversize book, two children talk about their summer adventures while on each page, the center illustration pops up when the page is turned. At Miss Maypole's house, Jane and Tracey climb up the old stairs by candlelight to the attic. In the attic, one black bat flies at them and then out the window. Back downstairs, the children settle down to hear Miss Maypole tell of her adventures. In nine pages, this book is a short lead into telling other original adventures. The smaller illustrations show objects to count from one Japanese lady to two children to nine birds and have nothing to do with the storyline unless a boy or girl, interested in storytelling, wants to relate some of the things seen on the pages to the telling of original number stories. K-1.

Features: numeric narrative and cardinal number identification from one up to nine.

One to Ten: Baby's First Book. Illustrated. Japan: Grosset and Dunlap/ Zekeisha, 1978.

In this small board book, clear objects are outlined on colorful backgrounds. A young viewer sees one balloon flying, two children running, seven candles on a chocolate cake, and eight lollipops that taste good. Pre.

Features: cardinal number identification from one up to eight.

One Up to Ten

Adams, Pam. *Ten Counting Beads*. Illustrated. Restrop Manor, Eng.: Child's Play, 1985.

Ten colorful counting beads are strung on a shoestring and attached to the book. When the beads are removed from the shoelace, they are used to measure the objects found on the sturdy pages in this board book. A young mathematician is asked to measure the height, width, and length of objects, using the beads as measurement units. A child selects objects to measure and announces how tall the tree in the illustration seems to be, how wide the selected toy, or how long the favorite animal. Pre-1.

Features: colorful objects to measure with nonstandardized units.

Adler, David A. *Three, Two, One, Number Fun*. Illustrated by Sharon Geller Metal and David A. Adler. Garden City, N.Y: Doubleday, 1981.

Bright colors of blue, green, red, and yellow attract a young child's eyes to these math activity pages. Some of the activities such as "The One Less Than" are not for beginners. However, there are some easier activities, ones which ask a beginner to count, show numbers in groups, and give examples for the numbers, one through ten. Students, second grade and up, may enjoy the "Soccer Field" math activity or the "Dominoes." 1–2.

Features: cardinal number identification up to ten, matching, one-to-one correspondence, and viewer participation activities on the pages.

Adler, Irving, and Ruth Adler. *Sets and Numbers for the Very Young.* Illustrated by Peggy Adler. New York: John Day Company, 1969.

In this book, the Adlers give boys and girls a variety of number-numeral relationships to explore. An interested youngster traces numerals, matches sets of cats and mice, and determines one-to-one correspondence. Some helpful notes to parents and teachers are included. 1–2.

Features: numeral recognition, matching, one-to-one correspondence, and child participation activities on the pages.

Allen, Robert. *Numbers: A First Counting Book.* Illustrated with photographs by Möttke Weissman. New York: Platt and Munk, 1968.

Bright, clear, colorful photographs reinforce a beginning concept about the way that numbers develop in sequence. Can someone recognize a number of items in a short row as the same number of items in a long row? To interact further with the idea that size and location do not affect the number of members in a group, paper cut-outs of objects of various sizes may be placed on a felt board. One teacher quickly constructs a simple rectangular grid with colorful lengths of yarn on the classroom felt board. With the help of the children, each horizontal length is identified with numerals at the left-hand side. Each vertical length is identified with letters at the top of the board. Paper cut-outs of large and small animals are placed one at a time on the grid. The teacher models the reading of the grid to locate the position of the cut-out. The girls and boys take turns and each place a cut-out on the grid, choose someone from the class to locate the cut-out by reading the grid, and then identify a friend to place another cut-out on the grid to continue this location activity.

In three parts, this book offers one-to-one correspondence from one to ten, quantity in a group while answering the question, "How many?" and conservation of number where a boy or girl sees that the size of objects shown do not affect the cardinal number of a set. Recommended. K-2.

Features: cardinal number identification, position of member of group does not affect number, conservation of number, one-to-one correspondence.

Anderson, Sara. *Numbers*. Illustrated by the author. New York: E. P. Dutton, 1988.

This offers numbers from one up to ten in brightly colored pages of sturdy board in different lengths. With no number words to read, a preschooler sees the numbers of objects increase as the pages become wider and wider with each turn. On each spread, a boy or girl finds cut-paper objects to count and shapes to match in a one-to-one correspondence activity. For instance, at the number five, a viewer identifies the numeral 5, counts five windows, five bricks in a wall, and matches each of the corresponding five squares to one of the windows or one of the bricks. Does anyone notice only one object seen in each of four windows and no object seen in the fifth window? Pre.

Features: numeral recognition, cardinal number identification from one up to ten, and one-to-one correspondence.

Baby Learns to Count. Illustrated. Los Angeles: Modern Systems/Division of Unisystems, n.d.

Found in a green cardboard slipcase, several small books (approximately three inches square) offer counting of various groups of objects: one bee, two pandas, and three balls. Groups offer fruits and vegetables, pets, things in the garden, toys, things that go, and zoo animals. Bright colors of primary ones red, blue and yellow predominate. Pre-K.

Features: classification by topics and cardinal number identification from one up to ten.

Bound, Linda. *Numbers and Colors*. Illustrated by the author. New York: Starlog Press, n.d.

A girl or boy may flip through the pages of this one to see the accordion-style pages and their scenes on white backgrounds. The counting begins with one dog and two kittens and ends with nine bees and ten balloons. When the book is flipped over, a boy or girl sees more numbers in groups of things as well as an emphasis on accompanying colors. For instance, the word blue appears on the paper cover of a crayon at the foot of an illustration and then the color is shown again on the object, the bluejay. When a youngster is ready to review these two variables of colors and numbers again, there is another book to consider: *1 Is Red* (Golden/Western, 1974). This Tell-a-Tale reader is written by Eileen Daly and illustrated by Eugenie. Pre-K.

Features: cardinal number identification from one up to ten, colors, and accordion-style pages.

Bruna, Dick. *I Know about Numbers*. Illustrated by the author. New York: Methuen, 1981.

Bruna's bright colors of blue, green, orange, and yellow help a girl or boy see all of the objects that relate to the numerals in the math sentences. For example, one sees two orange socks and two yellow socks and reads that $2 + 2 = 4$. There are counting as well as adding experiences. The number of spoons add up to seven, blocks add up to eight, and there are ten colorful drawing pencils.

For anyone who understands numbers in groups and can conserve number, there are objects in groups that show the corresponding math sentence. For instance, four blue shovels are shown with one red shovel for the sentence $4 + 1 = 5$. Ten strawberries are arranged in groups and the math sentence is $7 + 3 = 10$. Using paper strips and a paper punch, a learner may punch the appropriate number of holes for the numerals in the math sentences and record the sentence under the punches. To see commutativity for $4 + 1 = 5$, the strip may be turned over, the order of the punches may be noted $(1 + 4)$ and the math sentence recorded: $1 + 4 = 5$. 1–2.

Features: numeral-number relationships, addition sentences summing to ten, and commutativity.

Chwast, Seymour, and Martin Moskof. *Still Another Number Book*. Illustrated by Martin Moskof. New York: McGraw-Hill, 1971.

This book uses one page to show the concept of the number one with an illustration, two pages to show the concept of the number two and so on. For the numeral 3, three large colorful flowers represent the addition sentence that is shown: $1 + 1 + 1 = 3$. A butterfly is seen on the last flower in the counting sequence, which leads to turning four pages to see four butterflies and the accumulating number sentence of $1 + 1 + 1 + 1 = 4$. The last butterfly lands on a dog's nose so dogs are counted in the next sequence, and counters finish with ten jugglers. On a final review page, the objects are shown in black and white outlines in small inserts beginning with ten jugglers and ending with one boat in a sequence which shows the *one-less* pattern. A frieze of colorful numerals from 1 to 10 is seen at the top of the page for easy reference. K-1.

Features: from one through ten, one-to-one correspondence, *one-more* sequence, and a review of *one-less* sequence from ten down to one.

Conran, Sebastian. *My First 123 Book*. Illustrated by the author. New York: Macmillan/Aladdin, 1988.

Each number is shown on a single or a double-page spread. In the illustrations are familiar objects to count (cardinal number recognition). Bright illustrations and a simple text combine to show numerals and numbers of objects. For a one-to-one correspondence activity, there are brightly colored, finger-sized dots to touch for tactile reinforcement. With simple text and some humor, a small boy and his tiger cat lead the way to numbers through each illustration. A reader touches and counts along. Pre-1.

Features: humor in simple text, one-to-one correspondence with objects from one up to ten, and colored dots to touch.

Counting See and Say. Illustrated. Harrison, N.Y.: Tuffy Books, 1986.

Single colorful objects on the pages introduce a young boy or girl to one cap to wear, then two sneakers. There are numerals and object words. The objects are familiar ones, e.g., pails, buttons, keys, and drinking mugs up to ten fingers. Pre.

Features: numeral recognition, object and cardinal number identification from one through ten.

Crews, Donald. *Ten Black Dots*. Illustrated by the author. New York: Greenwillow, 1986.

In this reprint of a 1968 book, boys and girls see what one can do with ten black dots: the basic shape of one dot forms a sun or a moon; two dots make the eyes of a fox and so on. There is a text that rhymes and introduces all of the objects from one to ten. At the end of the book are a series of black dots to count. Since the black dots are shown within the shapes of objects of different sizes, does any viewer seem confused about which object is larger or smaller as the pages are turned? Which objects does the viewer want to compare and discuss? Moving from the shapes of the black dots to the shapes of the round openings on computer paper tracks, an interested boy or girl may cut a desired number of openings to add to original art work. The youngster may use the discarded paper tracking strips torn from computer paper pages to count the openings as circle shapes. Fences, rafts, buildings, tree trunks, and other objects may be designed with strips showing groups of two, five, ten, and other numbers. Given strips, a boy or girl may circle groups of two, four, and six. To illustrate simple addition or subtraction sentences, sections of computer strips that contain the right number of openings may be pasted beneath the number sentences. The circle openings on the strips may be numbered to make inexpensive number lines. For another variation, the strips may be used to make daisy chain decorations with a specified number of circles in each chain. Dipped in watercolors and left to dry, the strips then may be cut into small sections and pasted into patterns of color in chains (e.g., two circles of red, two blue, two yellow, two red, and continuing on the chain). Painted or not painted, the strips are useful in making a collage or several three-dimensional objects to paste on a child's original art work. Pre-K.

Features: basic shapes, rhyming text, one-to-one correspondence, cardinal number identification from one to ten, and a review.

Frederico, Helen. *The Golden Sturdy Book of Counting 123*. Illustrated by the author. Racine, Wis.: Golden/Western, 1969.

On colorful backgrounds of blue, yellow, and purple, and inserted in a large numeral shape on a tall, thin page are such objects as a ladybug, a lion, and a worm. Each identifying numeral holds the appropriate numbers of object in groups, and the viewer is challenged to find them. For instance, a large pink numeral 2 is the background for groups of two cats, two jack-o-lanterns, and two ships. On the last spread, Frederico asks one to find more numbers of objects beginning with one tall tree to complete a final sequence and review up to ten. Pre-K.

Features: oversize numerals, numbers of objects in groups, equivalent members in groups, and a review from one up to ten.

Giganti, Paul, Jr. *How Many Snails?* Illustrated by Donald Crews. New York: Greenwillow, 1988.

In a sequence to ten, a young viewer is asked to count the objects and to examine them to find those with a particular attribute (subgroup or subset). For an example, a young girl or boy may count the dogs and then count them again to find how many are spotted. After the cupcakes are counted, the counting begins again to locate the ones with icing. When eight snails are counted, the viewer looks again to find the snails with stripes. Looking again, one may notice that some of the bodies of the snails are of different colors or see the stripes in the shells are of different colors (attributes of members in groups). Is anyone ready to identify original subgroups in these groups of objects? if so, this identification may turn into a number challenge to friends with the question, "How many?" This book requires visual discrimination that goes beyond a beginner's counting skills. 1–2.

Features: sequence from one up to ten, cardinal numbers, attributes, and subgroups.

The Gold Star Numbers, Shapes and Colors Book. Illustrated. Copyright by Dean's International Publishing Company. New York: Modern Publications/Unisytems, 1980.

This book has bright endpages of green, purple, and yellow with pages that show an object-numeral-number word arrangement. The numerals are in sequence in the lower left-hand corners of the pages for easy reference when needed. Selected objects to count are fish, flowers, pigs, and rings. Pre-K.

Features: numeral recognition, number words, and cardinal number recognition from one through ten.

Hefter, Richard. *One White Crocodile Smile: A Number Book.* Illustrated by the author. New York: Strawberry Books/Larousse, 1974.

Seeing oversize, three-dimensional numerals, boys and girls find the white crocodile smile on the green crocodile in each illustration. After seeing one green crocodile smiling, with text, one turns the page to find two red beds, an accumulating text and objects in the illustrations. Crocodiles are found in or near the objects: in one of two beds; posed at the top of one of three green trees; near one of four brown doors, so a young reader learns shapes of numerals, color words, names of objects, and a repeating pattern of words (accumulation). Capitals and periods are shown at appropriate places in the repetitive phrases. Unfamiliar combinations are seen: five pink opera-singing wives, seven orange feet, nine black lines, and ten blue policemen named Ben. At ten, all of the objects are aligned in rows on the first review page, without numerals; on the next page, only numerals are seen, with no objects. Then on a third page of review, selected groups of objects in the *one-less* pattern are shown along with numerals. The book is a circular one, ending as it begins with one green crococdile and the white crocodile smile, and is full of bright colors, huge numerals, childlike drawings, and acccumulating words. Numerals are arranged to match specific things in pairs, vertically, horizontally, or in simple graph forms. Boys and girls can enjoy the verse, the easy-to-count objects, and the inventive format of numeral presentation. As early as first grade, a student may construct a simple table to represent a situation when there is not enough information to give a number as a firm answer. One example of a problem that would lead to the construction of a table is: Carl has four fewer crocodiles than Carla. How many crocodiles does Carl have? In this problem, there is not enough information to give a number as an answer so it is appropriate to construct a table as a way to record answers for a number of possible situations. An adult constructs a model:

Carla 4 5 6 7 8 9 10

Carl 0 1 2 3 4 5 6

Discussion occurs about the information in the table. An adult shows how to read the table. For instance, if Carla has four crocodiles, then Carl has zero. If Carla has eight crocodiles, then Carl has four.

Available in Spanish, it is *Una Blanca Sonrisa de Cocodrilo: El Libro de Los Numeros* (Barcelona, Spain: Editorial Juventud, S.A., 1980) and is translated by Concepcion Zendera. Pre-1.

Features: oversize numerals, accumulation, repetitive words from one up to ten, and a review.

Hoban, Tana. *123*. Illustrated with photographs by the author. New York: Greenwillow, 1985.

A concept book with photographs for a very young boy or girl, ages one to three. A colorful rectangle, cylinder, and square may attract a young viewer to the cover for a first looking and learning experience with counting objects on pages in a book. The board pages are filled with full-color photographs of the things that babies see and use as they play and explore. Recommended. Pre.

Features: recognition of basic geometric shapes on board pages.

Hooks, William H., Betty Boegehold, Barbara Brenner, JoAnne Oppenheim, and Seymour V. Reit. *1 to 10, More Counting Fun*. Illustrated by Joel Schick. New York: Barron's Publishing, n.d.

For anyone interested in paper and pencil activities, every page has an activity, one that is illustrated in full-color that alternates with another one in black and white. There are questions to answer, tracing to do, and dot-to-dot activities. Pre-K.

Feature: numeral recognition, number use with participation activities.

I Can Count. Illustrated. Loughboro, Eng.: Ladybird Books, 1985.

Colorful pages will entertain very young girls and boys as well as help present the numerals and numbers of things. A beginning counter finds soldiers in red uniforms, yellow teddy bears, and green frogs. There is a *123 Teaching Frieze* (Ladybird Books) that complements the book. The frieze can be displayed as a poster or a wall chart. Accompanying Ladybird activity books are *Learn to Count, Learn to do Sums* and *Counting* (all 1978). Pre-K.

Features: numeral-number relationships, numeral recognition, and cardinal number identification.

Izawa, Tadasu. *My First Book of Numbers.* Illustrated by the author. Japan: Zekeiska Publishers, n.d.

As the pages are turned in this sturdy book, a young viewer counts one boy, two puppies who tug for socks, and three playful kittens. The counting ends with ten crayons used for coloring pictures. If board books similar to *My First Book of Numbers* are being collected for a preschooler, there is another recent publication, with a collection of familiar objects on board pages: *I Learn Numbers* (Bantam, 1987) with no cited author.

Features: cardinal number identification from one up to ten.

Jacobs, Warren. *The Young New Zealander's First Book of Counting.* Auckland, New Zealand: Kowhai Publishing, 1984.

Clear, colorful photographs show familiar objects such as roller skates, boats, puppies, balls, and pencils. Different colored backgrounds contrast with flowers, bananas, and strawberries. Getting acquainted with the culture of New Zealand, a young American youngster finds lollies (colorfully wrapped candies), milk bottles, and jars of homemade jam. Numerals and number words in English and Maori are found in the corners of verso pages with objects to count on recto pages. If interested, an eager young linguist may show an ability to count in a language different from his or her first language and learn the Maori number words: *tahi* (1), *rua* (2), *toru* (3), *wha* (4), *rima* (5), *ono* (6), *whitu* (7), *waru* (8), *iwa* (9), and *tekau* (10). At ten, there are hats representing different roles in work and recreation: a panama straw hat, a baseball cap, a navy captain's hat, a bike rider's helmet, and a pink straw hat decorated with ribbons. Pre.

Features: sequence from one to ten with English-Maori number words.

Kawai'ue'w, Keiki Chang. *Let's Learn to Count in Hawaiian: Coloring and Activity Book*. Illustrated. Honolulu: Island Heritage, 1988.

Black and white outlines of objects from one to ten are found. Outlined numerals are oversize and located in corners of pages. Objects fill the pages. Each Hawaiian number word is read along with a pronunciation guide. One ('elahi) canoe and two ('elua) dolphins begin the sequence and nine ('eiewa) coconut trees and ten ('ume) pineapples end it. Sentences about the objects are at the foot of the pages. A participating youngster is asked to write the numbers in Hawaiian from one to ten. A final page offers numerals, number words, and the appropriate number of flowers to count to show the *one-more* sequence.

Features: oversize numerals, Hawaiian objects, Hawiian number words from one up to ten, and pronunciation guide.

Lippman, Peter. *Peter Lippman's Numbers*. Illustrated by the author. New York: Putnam/Grosset and Dunlap, 1988.

This one is a pull-tab surprise book which means a child's pull of the cardboard tab propels four daredevils, one each from four cannons, or causes six plants to bloom into six flowers. Beginning with one green hat, each page offers a number of surprising things to count. There is one-to-one correspondence (e.g., one mouse for each opening in a slice of cheese). Pre-1.

Features: cardinal numbers from one up to ten and one-to-one correspondence.

Numbers. Illustrated. Loughboro, Eng.: Ladybird Books, 1979.

Prepared for a young boy or girl living in Africa, this counting book is appropriate for a number-numeral review by anyone with an interest in African children and the selected objects from Africa that are shown on the pages. Pre-K.

Features: numeral recognition and cardinal number identification of objects in Africa from one to ten.

Piénkowski, Jan. *Numbers*. Illustrated by the author. New York: Harvey House, 1975.

Piénkowski's illustrations show the numbers one through ten, present the symbols for the numerals, and rearrange numbers of things in different settings. A yellow and black leopard introduces a young girl or boy to the numeral 1 to begin the counting in these bright and lively pictures. After one reads the words, *one leopard,* and sees the symbol for the numeral 1, one notices the leopard again in a jungle setting on the facing page. At the numeral 4, the four ducks swimming in a stream can be counted, then are rearranged in a different setting on a facing page. Can all of the beads that are shown on the counting frame on the endpapers be counted? Since there are different combinations of ten to see, is anyone ready to count one and nine to arrive at ten? Two and eight? Three and seven? K-1.

Features: numerals, number words, object words, position of member of group does not affect number, and conservation of number.

Richards, Elspeth and Frances Fernyhough. *Fun with Numbers*. Illustrated by Angela Kerr. New York: Doubleday, 1986.

With bright colors in the illustrations, this book invites a primary girl or boy to interact with the pages. Using the pages, one may play games, complete puzzles, trace objects and numeral shapes and select other activities about numbers from one up to ten. Pre-1.

Features: activities for numbers from one up to ten.

Rizzo, Fran. *123 Numbers*. Illustrated. New York: Modern Publishers/ Unisystems, 1982.

Cat-loving girls or boys can find objects from one rubber ball and two balls of yarn to nine frogs and ten fish, all of them of interest to a cat. Can one find the yellow cat on each page of this book? Pre.

Features: cardinal number identification from one through ten.

Ruben, Patricia. *True or False*. Illustrated with photographs by the author. New York: Lippincott, 1978.

One large black and white photograph is shown on each page along with a question to be answered true or false. Some of the questions are counting problems. For instance, a boy or girl sees five dancers and the words, "there are ten legs in this picture." Other photographs will refer the young viewer to simple geometric shapes. Borders with such shapes may be made for a child's bulletin board. Using strips of colorful construction paper, approximately eighteen by three inches, an older child or adult folds the strip over twice from end to end and following a pattern may cut the strip while holding it in the center. Patterns for borders with diamonds, circles, and ovals, chains with circles, chains with squares, chains with diamonds, diamonds and squares, diamonds and hexagons, bars and octagons, and others, are available in *Instant Borders: Cut-Out Patterns to Enhance Bulletin Boards* by Anthony Flores (Fearon/Pitman, 1979). Pre.

Features: sentences beneath photographs ask for a response of true or false as confirmations.

Seymour, Peter. *Numbers.* Illustrated by Linda Weller. New York: Macmillan, 1984.

In the preface Seymour asks a young viewer to find out how many objects are on the pages. The fact that *one* is a name and *1* is a symbol is explained. As the tabs are moved around each picture one learns about numbers of objects in groups from one to ten. First, two puppies in a wagon are seen. Words are read in sentences and then again inside the cutout openings. When the tab is turned again, different pictures appear in the windows of the pages. For instance, three seals (group 1) balance four balls (group 2). As the tab is turned, a viewer sees one of the groups again. What prediction can be made? Will it be three seals or four balls in a different arrangement? This repetition adds reinforcement to a child's ability to recognize members of groups in an arrangement different from a previous grouping. After a final counting of nine flowers and ten butterflies, there are more wheels with directions for counting more objects. How many clowns are found? How many fish are seen? Pre-1.

Features: numerals, number words from one up to ten, sentences, objects rearranged, position of member in group does not affect number, and conservation of number.

Tallarico, Tony. *Finger Counting.* Illustrated by the author. Harrison, N.Y.: Tuffy Books, 1983.

Tallarico announces that there are ten fingers to count with. On each page, the appropriate number of fingers are portrayed to show one, two, and so on up to ten. Each numeral is the center of two double-page spreads. The first spread for the numeral 1 shows one child and one apple. On the second spread, number words and object names are added beneath the illustrations (e.g., one child and one apple, two children and two pears). After five, there are other objects to count in addition to fingers. Pre-K.

Features: numerals, number words, object names, and cardinal number identification from one through ten.

Tallarico, Tony. *Numbers*. Illustrated by the author. Harrison, N.Y.: Tuffy Books, 1982.

Through the die-cut openings on the sturdy pages, a boy or girl sees objects to count, a color of an object, or a part of a numeral. From one bird and two building blocks to ten cups, one finds numerals, objects, and words about the objects that tell the action (e.g., four tricycles zoom, six fish swim, seven balloons float, and eight bears hug one another). Looking through a window in this book, which is shaped like a tote bag, a young viewer can see two blocks used for building something and three birds which can sing in trees. Complete sentences offer capitals and periods in appropriate places. Oversize red numerals appear in word balloons on each page above the character who is speaking. Die-cut openings let one peek through and predict what is to come. Will it be a numeral six or a nine? Will the objects be four tricycles, five leaves, six fish or nine cars for driving? At ten, the viewer is asked to find one mouse hiding in one of the cups. Pre.

Features: die-cut openings, oversize numerals in red, number words from one up to ten, sentences with capitalization and punctuation, cardinal number identification, and prediction.

Wildsmith, Brian. *Brian Wildsmith's 123s*. Illustrated by the author. New York: Franklin Watts, 1973.

Shapes and bright colors in this 123 book have a geometric approach. As a young boy or girl turns the pages quickly, he or she catches glimpses of entertaining colors—bright blue, fuchsia, green, and purple. Turning the pages more slowly a second time, the viewer has time to notice the basic shapes of a square, a circle, and a triangle, which Wildsmith relates to numbers. Who can count the number of shapes that it takes to form the red-eyed owl with his colored feathers, his bright yellow feet, and attractive blue beak? Facing each large illustration is a numeral to identify and a corresponding number word to read in capitals and in lowercase letters. Looking at the shapes, it may not be clear what the question means or the arrow pointing to the object with the words, "How many?" Careful looking is needed and some adult guidance. If a boy or girl recognizes the basic shapes and is ready for scissor work, the following may be cut (with assistance) from felt or medium-weight pellon (lining material for clothing from yardage store): rectangle, square, circle, small square, small rectangle, triangle. The young player selects the name of a figure to make and replicates the construction or creates a new construction for the figure. When the figure is completed to the player's satisfaction, the player says the rhyming lines for the activity and repeats, "This one's not hard to make. This one's made of basic shapes.——— (number) pieces are all it takes." The player counts the number of basic shapes needed to construct the figure, and after returning the shape pieces from the figure into a pile by naming each basic shape, may select another name of a figure to make and continue the activity. K-1.

Features: numerals, number words in capitals and lowercase letters, and basic geometric shapes as parts of whole objects.

Greater than Ten

Bruna, Dick. *I Can Count*. Illustrated by the author. New York: Methuen, 1975.

On the small pages, Bruna's bold objects begin with one white candle on a bright blue page, two ribbons in a small girl's braided hair; and three red apples on a green background. A young viewer counts to twelve to see one dozen red ties on a flying kite's tail. Simple and clear, Bruna follows the pattern of one numeral and one matching number of objects on each double-page spread. Pre-K.

Features: numeral-number relationships and cardinal number identification from one up to twelve.

Bruna, Dick. *I Can Count More*. Illustrated by the author. New York: Methuen, 1972.

Bruna continues counting numbers of things from thirteen to twenty-four. Again emphasizing black outlined objects as in *I Can Count,* This begins with a clown juggling yellow balls on an orange background and continues with fourteen white raindrops falling through a gray sky. After counting all of the objects shown in bright colors of green, blue, orange, and yellow, one reaches the final illustration of twenty-four flying pennants on a sea-blue background. These objects can be seen again in a poster format with Bruna's *123 Frieze* (New York: Methuen, 1968). When this frieze is placed at a child's eye level, the objects can be touched and talked about with friends. With this arrangement, a boy or girl can easily point to such objects as four blue tablespoons, five rabbits, or six red stockings that hang on a line to dry. Pre-K.

Features: numeral-number relationships and cardinal number identification from thirteen up to twenty-four.

Budney, Blossom. *A Cat Can't Count*. Designed and illustrated by Willliam Wondriska. New York: Lothrop, Lee and Shepard, 1962.

Endpapers with oversize black or turquoise numerals from one to ten and number words show what's to come on the following pages. Rhyming lines introduce a young reader to counting with number words in capitals in blue. Accompanied by numerals, figures of children are the first objects to count. Then, five animal homes, including a beehive, are counted along with six things to fix; and seven objects in places where they belong (e.g., a ship at sea). It continues with eight pounds of weight (one pound of pelican feathers), nine things that shine, such as new coins, and ten trips to take—including a trip to the mountains. Included is a review of other objects from one raisin on a bun to ten men. Budney points out other ways to count using special tools like rulers (to measure inches), cups and spoons (to measure ingredients for baking), thermometers (to measure temperature), scales (to measure pounds), clocks (to measure time), calendars (to measure days), and all kinds of meters (to find out how far, how fast, how long, how loud, or how high). Showing figures from 1 to 357 in a final review, words explain that numbers never stop for even a zillion is not the top. 2 up.

Features: oversize numerals and number words in color from one up to ten, rhyming lines, classifications, and a review.

Cartwright, Mary. *One Two Three*. Illustrated by the author. New York: Rand, 1981.

Here is where a boy or girl finds numerals that seem to appear in three dimensions. For example, a three-dimensional numeral *1* looks like a slice of birthday cake and complements the objects in this group with its one member, a complete birthday cake. The numeral 6 looks as if made from wood, the same wood seen in the beach chairs for the six resting zebras. The numeral 7 is painted with flowers, similar to the ones seen on the seven china teapots. On each large page, the selected numeral becomes smaller and is replicated with mirror images to form a colored border around each illustration. As the full-color pages are turned, the illustrations show a variety of toys, animals, and useful items to count. A viewer counts by ones to twenty, then sees twenty-five ducks in a bathtub. There are thirty wooden blocks for playtime and forty brightly colored birds. The counting goes up to seventy-five tulips and one hundred toy soldiers dressed in red uniforms. 1–2.

Features: oversize, three-dimensional numerals, cardinal number identification from one to one hundred, *one-more* sequence from one up to twenty, and numerals replicated in patterns in borders.

Curry, Peter. *Peter Curry's 123*. Illustrated by the author. Los Angeles: Price/Stern/Sloan, 1981.

Curry gives boys and girls several pages of object-numeral-number word arrangements. For instance, a young viewer sees one bright orange sun, the numeral 1, and reads the word one written in lowercase letters. Curry's objects could be the beginning of patterns in number sentences (e.g., "I see———[number]———[name of object]"). Some of the things to see are purple socks on a clothesline, jewels in a crown, and white stars in a black sky. For a final review, Curry shows the numerals from 1 to 20 at the end of the book. K-1.

Features: numerals, number words, objects, anaphoric sentences from one up to twenty, and a review.

Doolittle, Eileen. *World of Wonders: A Trip through Numbers*. Illustrations by author and Starr Ockenga. Boston: Houghton Mifflin, 1988.

A circus ringmaster takes girls and boys on a tour to unrelated places to see animals, dolls and soldiers, both antique and modern. Numerals are shown in roman and arabic style, with the number words, and again to show the corresponding time on the face of a traditional clock. In each photograph a viewer sees numbers of things to count from one to twelve. For an older girl or boy, the pages offer more objects to identify (e.g., the twelve days of Christmas, objects that refer to children's literature, and lines from songs). For self-checking, an interested viewer may turn to the back to find a black and white key to the photographs. 1 up.

Features: time-telling, roman and arabic numerals, cardinal numbers from one up to twelve, and references to songs and children's literature.

Fisher, Leonard Everett. *Number Art: Thirteen 123s from around the World*. New York: Four Winds, 1982.

A sophisticated history and story of the design of numerals. For each of thirteen ways to record numbers of things, Fisher illustrates the numeral forms in two colors from different cultures: Arabic, Armenian, Brahmin, Chinese, Mayan, Roman, and others. There is an informative text for each notation system. 2 up.

Features: numerals and informative text for thirteen cultures.

Gillen, Patricia Bellan. *My Signing Book of Numbers*. Illustrated. Washington, D.C.: Gallaudet University Press, 1987.

Here are 56 pages of full-color illustrations to help girls and boys learn numbers in sign language. For the numbers from zero through twenty, there are objects (toothbrushes) and creatures (turtles, butterflies) to count. Signs for numbers to one hundred by tens are included. Each number and appropriate sign is found in the corner of the page. There are written explanations about the way to form each sign at the end of the book. Pre-up.

Features: objects, numbers, and sign language from one up to twenty, by tens from twenty to one hundred, and instructions for forming each sign.

Hoban, Tana. *Count and See*. Illustrated with photographs by the author. New York: Macmillan, 1972.

Black and white pictures of such items as birthday candles, cookies, and firefighters' hats illustrate the numbers. Facing the illustrations are the numerals, the written words for the numerals, and groups of black dots in patterns on green backgrounds. The large black and white illustrations are on the recto pages. A boy or girl counts, matches numbers of objects to numbers of dots, and may identify higher numbers to 100. Full of clear photographs, this book helps establish correspondences with numbers one through fifteen. Recognizing numbers of things in illustrations, a girl or boy may locate objects in discarded magazines, cut out numbers of things to paste on index cards and make and color the appropriate number of coresponding dots. Recommended. K-1.

Features: numerals, number words, one-to-one correspondence from one up to fifteen, and higher number recognition.

Howard, Katherine. *I Can Count to One Hundred . . . Can You?* Illustrated by Michael J. Smollin. New York: Random House, 1979.

For picture representations of large numbers, an adult might suggest this one. For assistance in counting, there are framed numerals and number words in the corners of the pages. Changing his costume on the pages, a mouse is the narrator. The text explains the illustrations. Adult guidance may be needed as a young counter sees a plant with four flowers and leaves and stems for the number one, and for three finds many objects (not all totaling three). At the number five, one counts five mice plus the narrator mouse. Twenty though thirty are introduced with addition concepts. There are no separate illustrations for the groups, thirty through one hundred. A final double-page spread spread shows counting by tens in colorful rows up to one hundred, an array that might be too crowded with digits for some young children. 1–2.

Features: framed numerals, cardinal number identification from one up to ten, addition from twenty through thirty, *ten-more* sequence up to one hundred, and a review.

Ivanovsky, Elizabeth. *Counting 123*. Illustrated. New York: Crown, 1986.

Ivanovsky's collection begins with one each of a sun, pumpkin, and bell and ends with twelve beads, pears, and pigs. Interesting objects are seven dwarves, seven dots on one domino, four hooves on one colt. All of the number words are spelled out for word recognition. The sturdy board illustrations are in full-color and have borders. A boy or girl reviews all of the numbers of things again on the last double-page spread where all of the group members may be counted a final time (early experience in reading tables or graphs). Pre-K.

Features: numeral, number word, cardinal number identification from one up to twelve, and a review.

Law, Felicia and Suzanna Chandler. *Mouse Count*. Illustrated by John Farmon. London: Octopus Books, 1980.

In forty-four colorful pages, there is a wide variety of activities for children. Boys and girls match numerals with numbers, guess how many are in a selected group, and learn a number rhyme. In some activities, the young reader is asked to make a one-to-one correspondence, to review the concept of balance, and to read a numeral story in a comic strip format. Relying on Farmon's illustrations, a boy or girl may play a game of "Mouse and Ladders," read "Little Red Riding Puss," divide numbers, review odd and even ones, and finally, complete a magic square. 2 up.

Features: numeral-number relationships, one-to-one correspondence, odd and even numbers, and participation activities.

Oxenbury, Helen. *Numbers of Things*. Illustrated by the author. New York: Franklin Watts, 1968.

Oxenbury's counting book is entertaining because it has humorous, colorful illustrations. Oxenbury's question, "How many?" is answered by numbers that range from one golden lion to ten animals who are close to a nearby ark. After ten, the groups increase by ten. Twenty balloons fly high at the end of strings and fifty ladybugs use their separate sets of six legs to walk in serpentine lines across the pages. In the last illustration, an astronaut walks on the cold crisp surface of the moon and perhaps initiates a viewer's question about how many stars there are in the dark blue sky or poses the consideration of the concept of infinity. The illustrations are clear, distinct, cheerful, and change settings easily among the circus, home, playground, park, and the zoo. Boys and girls can count by tens from ten to fifty and join the child on the last page who asks, "How many stars?" Recommended. Pre-1.

Features: numeral-number relationship, cardinal number identification, *one-more* sequence from one up to ten, and the *ten-more* sequence to fifty.

Pragoff, Fiona. *How Many: From 0 to 20?* Illustrated with photographs by the author. New York: Doubleday, 1987.

Figures from 0 to 20 are found in the corners of these bright colorful photographs of familiar objects. There is an additional counting aid—domino squares with corresponding dots. As the numerals ascend, the objects and the black dots increase. Sometimes, this becomes a confusing format. Placement of the domino squares changes from page to page. One key takes one page, two children face one another on two pages, and three utensils take a page. A cake cut into fourths shows the number four. Seven yellow chicks must be counted across two pages, with the numeral 7 on the verso page and the domino dots on the recto page. Eight colorful knobs of green, blue, and red are located on one white dresser. Five pairs of socks are counted to show ten single stockings, and there are eleven bananas in one bunch and three domino squares to show the corresponding eleven dots. Twelve wristwatches are on two arms and eighteen balls in a clustered grouping makes counting individual balls difficult. Some are hidden in the cluster. Pre.

Features: numerals from zero up to twenty, cardinal number identification, and one-to-one correspondence.

Reiss, John J. *Numbers.* Illustrated by the author. New York: Bradbury, 1971.

With items formed from bright glazed papers, Reiss shows girls and boys an arrangement of numeral-number word-object on every page. How many toes are ready to wiggle? What is the number of yellow grapefruit on the pink page? Who will count the pigeons in their coops? Is there someone who can count by tens up to the one hundred legs on the colorful centipede? Is anyone interested in seeing what one thousand raindrops look like as the drops all fall from the sky? Sometimes the number of things that matches the appropriate numeral are part of one whole object: for the numeral 3, one sees three lights in one traffic light, and for 5, five arms of one starfish. At other times, objects, such as seven ravens, are easy to count. Over ten, a group of ten objects is not separated consistently from the additional objects. For example, when the viewer sees seventeen marbles, a group of ten is not separated from the rest. After twenty, an increase by groups of ten is shown and the counting moves to thirty. Drawings are simple and bright but adult guidance may be needed. Recommended. K-1.

Features: numeral-object-number word arrangement, *one-more* sequence from one up to twenty, and the *ten-more* sequence up to one hundred.

Robinson, Shari. *A First Number Book.* Pictures by Sal Murdocca. New York: Platt and Munk, 1982.

A similar earlier edition was entitled *Numbers, Signs and Pictures: A First Number Book* (Platt and Munk, 1975). On the large pages of this paperback version, a boy or girl sees the numbers as a code, is asked to tell how many, and puts numbers in order. Some numeric alliteration is heard in counting to ten with the words about one rhino who rhumbas, two tigers who are toothless, and ten teapots which toot with steam. This book is not a first number book since it includes addition, subtraction, multiplication, and division, and one unusual presentation is the mention of *twice:* one tall troll who is twice as tall as one small troll. As a final activity, a reader counts up to one hundred with all of the totems that are shown on several totem poles. 1–2.

Features: numeric alliteration to ten, cardinal number identification up to one hundred, numeral-number relationships, and participation activities of addition, subtraction, multiplication, and division.

Schwartz, David M. *How Much is a Million?* Illustrated by Steven Kellogg. New York: Scholastic, 1985.

For someone who would like to explore numbers further, this gives information about the concept of one million. Adventurous thoughts start with statements about the size of a fishbowl needed to hold a million fish—it would be as big as a stadium; or about a million children standing on top of one another to form a human tower, which would extend past the moon; and then point out how long it would take to count to one million—twenty-three days. Is a boy or girl ready to mark off twenty-three days on a calendar? 1–2.

Features: numeric information, concept of one million, and number use.

Tallarico, Tony. *How Many?* Illustrated by the author. Harrison, N.Y.: Tuffy Books, Inc., 1983.

Tallarico's book is small and sturdy and emphasizes the concept of *one-more* to make a succeeding number in a sequence. For example, the math sentence of $1 + 1 = 2$ is shown visually with two children and again with two crayons in the illustrations. One more of something is added each time a new math sentence is presented. A viewer counts caps, lollipops, stars, valentine hearts, flowers, and mittens up to the number fifteen. Pre-K.

Features: cardinal number identification from one up to fifteen, *one-more* sequence, addition sentences, and symbols.

Wyse, Anne, and Alex Wyse. *The One to Fifty Book.* Illustrated by Canadian children. Toronto: University of Toronto Press, 1973.

A boy or girl opens this book to see a colorful pigeon and then turns the other pages to see the rest of the double-page spreads in black and white drawings. The authors give a numeral, the number word, and the name of the object on one page while artwork by a young Canadian child is shown on the facing page. Young children will enjoy seeing these pictures that have been created by other children—particularly the drawings of the beetles, birds, and the dreams of Christmas with deep-green holiday trees. I-2.

Features: numeral-number relationships and names of objects from one up to fifty.

Appendix: Selected Counting Books

Understanding	Selected Book	Author/Artist
Counting Process	*One Duck, Another Duck*	Charlotte Pomerantz with Jose Aruego and Ariane Dewey
Correspondence		
one-to-one		
black dots to objects	*Count and See*	Tana Hoban
shapes to objects	*My Very First Book of Numbers*	Eric Carle
	1,2,3 to the Zoo	Eric Carle
pages to objects	*Still Another Number Book*	Seymour Chwast with Martin Moskof
Number sequence		
one to three	*Jeanne-Marie Counts Her Sheep*	Françoise
	3X3 Three by Three	James Krüss and Eva Johanna Rubin
	We Came a-Marching . . . 1 2 3	Mildred Hobzek and William Pené Du Bois
one to five	*The Chicken Book*	Garth Williams
one to six	*The Shopping Basket*	John Burningham
one to seven	*Seven Little Rabbits*	John Becker and Barbara Cooney
	The Very Hungry Caterpillar	Eric Carle

	Where's Henrietta's Hen?	Bernice Freschet with Lorinda Bryan Cauley
one to ten	*All in the Morning Early*	Sorche Nic Leodhas and Evaline Ness
	Always Room for One More	Sorche Nic Leodhas and Nonny Hogrogian
	Anno's Counting House	Mitsumasa Anno
	The Balancing Act: A Counting Book	Merle Peek
	Chicken Little: Count-to-Ten	Margaret Friskey
	Farm Counting Book	Jane Miller
	Handtalk Birthday: A Number and Story Book in Sign Language	Remy Charlip with Mary Beth Miller and George Ancona
	An Invitation to the Butterfly Ball: A Counting Rhyme	Jane Yolen and Jane Breskin Zalben
	Lucy and Tom's 123	Shirley Hughes
	Max's Toys: A Counting Book	Rosemary Wells
	The Midnight Farm	Reeve Lindberg with Susan Jeffers
	Moja Means One: Swahili Counting Book	Muriel Feelings and Tom Feelings
	A Number of Dragons	Loreen Leedy
	Numbers	Gillian Youldon
	One Dragon's Dream	Peter Pavey
	1 Hunter	Pat Hutchins
	1 One Dancing Drum	Gail Kredenser with Stanley Mack
	One Snail and Me: A Book of Numbers and Animals and a Bathtub	Emily McLeod and Walter Lorraine
	123 for the Library	Mary E. Little
	Over in the Meadow	Ezra Jack Keats
	Over in the Meadow	John Langstaff and Feodor Rojankovsky

	Over in the Meadow: An Old Nursery Counting Rhyme	Paul Galdone
	Pooh's Counting Book	Alan Alexander Milne and Ernest Howard Shepard
	Roll Over!	Mordicai Gerstein
	Roll Over: A Counting Song	Merle Peek
	Sixes and Sevens	John Yeoman and Quentin Blake
	Teddy Bears 1 to 10	Susanna Gretz
	Ten Apples Up on Top	Theo LeSieg and Roy McKie
	Trucks You Can Count On	Doug Magee
	Two Lonely Ducks: A Counting Book	Roger Duvoisin
	Who's Counting?	Nancy Tafuri
one to twelve	*Anno's Counting Book: An Adventure in Imagination*	Mitsumasa Anno
	Can You Imagine . . .? A Counting Book	Beau Gardner
	Counting Carnival	Feenie Ziner and Paul Galdone
	One Old Oxford Ox	Nicola Bayley
	Peter Rabbit's 123	Beatrix Potter
	So Many Cats!	Beatrice Schenk deRegniers and Ellen Weiss
one to twenty	*Babar's 123*	Laurent De Brunhoff
	Counting Sheep	George Mendoza with Kathleen Reidy
	Counting Wildflowers	Bruce McMillan
	Dancing in the Moon: Counting Rhymes	Fritz Eichenberg
	Little Wolf and the Upstairs Bear	Lilian Obligado

	Monster Bubbles: A Counting Book	Dennis Nolan
	1 Is One	Tasha Tudor
	Wacky Wednesday	Theo LeSieg and George Booth
one to thirty	*The April Rabbits*	David Cleveland and Nurit Karlin
one to fifty	*The Bears' Counting Book*	Jocelyn Wild and Robin Wild
one to one hundred	*Animal Numbers*	Bert Kitchen
	Count and See	Tana Hoban
	Circus Numbers: A Counting Book	Rodney Peppé
	Numbers	John J. Reiss
	Richard Scarry's Best Counting Book Ever	Richard Scarry

Back to One

seven to one	*Seven Little Monsters*	Maurice Sendak
	Seven Little Rabbits	John Becker with Barbara Cooney
ten to one	*Ten, Nine, Eight*	Molly Bang

Counting Forward and Back

one to five, five to one	*The Rooster Who Set Out to See the World*	Eric Carle
one to ten, ten to one	*One Was Johnny: A Counting Book*	Maurice Sendak
	Up to Ten and Down Again	Lisa Campbell Ernst
	Who's Counting?	Nancy Tafuri
Factorial	*Anno's Mysterious Multiplying Jar*	Masaichiro Anno and Mitsumasa Anno
Infinity	*Numbers of Things*	Helen Oxenbury

Measurement

| money | *26 Letters and 99 Cents* | Tana Hoban |

Operations		
addition	*Pigs Plus: Learning Addition*	John Burningham
subtraction	*Ride Off: Learning Subtraction*	John Burningham
	Hip, Hippo, Hooray!	Betsy Lewin
addition and subtraction	*One More and One Less: A Concept Book*	Giulio Maestro
division	*The Doorbell Rang*	Pat Hutchins
Ordinals		
first to tenth	*Harriet Goes to the Circus: A Number Concept Book*	Betsy Maestro with Giulio Maestro
first to thirtieth	*The April Rabbits*	David Cleveland
Puzzles	*Demi's Count the Animals 1 2 3*	Demi
	Ten What? A Mystery Counting Book	Russell Hoban with Sylvia Selig
	1 Hunter	Pat Hutchins
	Numblers	Suse MacDonald with Bill Oakes
	If You Take a Pencil	Fulvio Testa
	Sums (A Looking Game)	Diane Vreuls
	Numbers	Gillian Youldon
Rearrangements	*Farm Numbers 123: A Counting Book*	Donald Smith
	Numbers: A First Counting Book	Robert Allen and Mottke Weissman
Shapes	*123*	Tana Hoban
Visual discrimination	*Lost and Found*	Elaine Livermore
	Odd One OuT	Rodney Peppé
	One to Ten, Count Again	Elaine Livermore

References

Abram, Sandra L. "The Effect of Computer Assisted Instruction on First Grade Phonics and Mathematics Achievement Computation." Ed. D. diss., Northern Arizona University, 1984.

Almy, M. *Young Children's Thinking*. New York: Teachers College Press, 1966.

American Library Association. *Realities: Educational Reform in a Learning Society*. Chicago: American Library Association, 1984.

Ashlock, Robert B. "Teaching the Basic Facts: Three Classes of Activities." *Arithmetic Teacher* 28 (October 1971): 359-64.

Ashlock, Robert B., and Carolyn Washbon. "Games: Practice Activities for the Basic Facts." *Developing Computational Skills*, Yearbook of the National Council of Teachers of Mathematics. Reston, Va.: The Council of Teachers of Mathematics, 1978.

Babbitt, Beatrice Clare. "The Contribution of Concepts and Computation to Children's Problem Solving Performance in Mathematics." Ph. D. diss., University of California, Los Angeles, 1986.

Baroody, Arthur J. "Children's Difficulties in Subtraction: Some Causes and Questions," *Journal for Research in Mathematics Education* 15 (May 1984): 203–13.

―――. "Children's Difficulties in Subtraction: Some Causes and Cures." *Arithmetic Teacher* 32 (November 1984): 14–19.

Baroody, Arthur J., and Kathleen E. Gannon. "The Development of the Commutativity Principle and Addition Strategies in Young Children." Paper presented at the Annual Meeting of the American Educational Research Association, Montreal, Canada, April 11–14, 1983.

―――. "The Use of Economical Mental Additional Strategies by Young Children." Paper presented at the Annual Meeting of the American

Educational Research Association, Montreal, Canada, April 11–14, 1983.

Barron, Pamela Petrick, and Jennifer Burley. *Jump Over the Moon: Selected Professional Readings*. New York: Holt, Rinehart and Winston, 1984.

Bauch, Jerald P., and Huei-hsin Joyce Hsu. "Montessori: Right or Wrong about Number Concepts?" *Arithmetic Teacher* 35 (February 1988): 8–11.

Bauer, Caroline Feller. *Handbook for Storytellers*. Chicago: American Library Association, 1977.

Beckerman, Terrill M., and Thomas L. Good. "The Classroom Ratio of High-and Low-Aptitude Students and Its Effect on Achievement." *American Educational Research Journal* 18 (Fall 1981): 327–37.

Bell, Kathy. "Learn Counting from Storybooks." *Reading Teacher* 41 (May 1988): 972.

Blackwell, Janet M. "When 2 + 2 Ain't 4." *Language Arts* 53 (April 1976): 422–24.

Blazejewski, Edward Joseph. "The Effects of Two Microcomputer Instructional Programs Upon Mathematical Achievement of Intermediate Elementary Students." Ed. D. diss., Lehigh University, 1984.

Brattesani, Karen, and others. "Using Student Perceptions of Teacher Behavior to Predict Student Outcomes." *Research in Education* (July)1981.

Brenner, Richard Alan. "Elementary School Students' Abilities to Read and Solve Arithmetic Word Problems: A Study of Prerequisite Skills." Ph. D. diss., University of California, Los Angeles, 1981.

Brown, L. J. "Developing Thinking and Problem-solving Skills with Children's books." *Childhood Education* 63 (December 1986): 102–7.

Brown, Sam Ed. *One, Two, Buckle My Shoe: Math Activities for Young Children* Illustrated by Julia Libonn. Mt. Ranier, Md.: Gryphon House, 1982.

Burke, Eileen M. *Early Childhood Literature: For Love of Child and Book*. Boston: Allyn and Bacon, 1986.

Butler, Dorothy. *Babies Need Books*. New York: Atheneum, 1982.

California State Department of Education. *Handbook of Planning an Effective Mathematics Program*. Sacramento, Calif.: California State Department of Education, 1982.

———. *Problem Solving Teams in California: Appropriate Responses by School Site Staff to Students Who Are Difficult to Teach and Manage.* Sacramento, Calif.: California State Department of Education, 1984.

Campbell, Patricia F. "What Do Children See in Mathematics Textbook Pictures?" *Arithmetic Teacher* 28 (January 1981): 12–16.

Canton City Schools. Department of Government Programs. *X-TRA*, 2 (May). Canton, Ohio: Canton City Schools, 1976.

Carlson, Ann D. *Early Childhood Literature Sharing Programs in Libraries.* Hamden, Conn.: Library Professional Publications, 1985.

Carmody, L. "A Theoretical and Experimental Investigation into the Role of Concrete and Semi-Concrete Materials in the Teaching of Elementary School Mathematics." Ph. D. diss., Ohio State University, 1970.

Carpenter, T. P., and J. M. Moser. "The Acquisition of Addition and Subtraction Concepts." In *Acquisition of Mathematical Concepts and Processes,* edited by R. Lesh and M. Landau. New York: Academic Press, 1983.

Cebulski, Larry A., "Children's Errors in Subtraction: An Investigation into Causes and Remediation." *Research in Education* (September) 1984.

Chambers, Dewey Woods. *Children's Literature in the Curriculum.* Chicago: Rand McNally, 1971.

Charles, Desiree Ann Dyer. "A Longitudinal Study on the Growth of Addition and Subtraction and Related Concepts in Children, Their School Arithmetic Experiences, and Their Teachers' Perceptions of Their Abilities." Ph. D. diss., State University of New York at Buffalo, 1984.

Chiosi, Lou. "Fractions Revisited." *Arithmetic Teacher* 31 (April 1984): 46–47.

Clements, M. A. "Careless Errors Made by Sixth Grade Children on Written Mathematical Tasks." *Journal for Research in Mathematics Education* 13 (March 1982): 136–44.

Coody, Betty. *Using Literature with Young Children, 3d ed.* Dubuque, Iowa: William C. Brown, 1983.

Cook, Ruth E., and Brent D. Slife. "Developing Problem-Solving Skills." *Academic Therapy* 21 (September 1985): 5-13.

Cooper, Harris. "Homework." in *Research on Teaching Monograph Series*. White Plains, N.Y.: Longman Publishing, 1989.

Copeland, Richard W. *How Children Learn Mathematics, 3d ed.*, New York: Macmillan, 1978.

Cordeiro, Patricia. "Playing with Infinity in the Sixth Grade." *Language Arts* 65 (October 1988): 557–66.

Cox, Christopher J. "Questions to Provoke Discussion." *Mathematics in School* 12 (May 1983): 4–5.

Cullinan, Bernice E. "Teachers' Choices 1983." *Language Arts* 61 (April 1984): 418–24.

Cullinan, Bernice, and Carolyn Carmichael, eds. *Literature and Young Children*. Urbana, Ill.: National Council of Teachers of English, 1977.

Cullinan, Bernice E., Mary K. Karrer, and Arlene M. Pillar. *Literature and the Child*. New York: Harcourt Brace Jovanovich, 1981.

Cunningham, James W., and Hunter Ballew. "Diagnosing Strengths and Weaknesses of Sixth-Grade Students in Solving Word Problems." *Journal for Research in Mathematics Education* 13 (May 1982): 202–10.

———. "Solving Word Problem Solving." *Reading Teacher* 36 (April 1983): 836–39.

Davidson, James E. "The Language Experience Approach to Story Problems." *Arithmetic Teacher* 37 (October, 1977): 28-37.

Davison, David M., and Daniel L. Pearce. "Using Writing Activities to Reinforce Mathematics Instruction." *Arithmetic Teacher* 35 (April 1988): 42–45.

Dickson W. Patrick. "Little Programs for Little Kids." *Family Computing* (November 1983): 64–68.

Dickson, W. Patrick, and Karin Borgh. "Software for Preschoolers." *Family Computing* (November 1983): 66–68.

Duncan, James Edwin. "The Heuristics Utilized by Fifth Grade Students in Solving Verbal Mathematics Problems in a Small Group Setting." Ph. D. diss., University of Arizona, 1985.

Dunkley, M. E. "Some Number Concepts of Disadvantaged Children." *Arithmetic Teacher* 12 (May 1965): 359–61.

Engelhardt, Jon M. "Using Computational Errors in Diagnostic Teaching." *Arithmetic Teacher* 29 (April 1982): 16–19.

Evans, Christine Sobray. "Writing to Learn Math." *Language Arts* 61 (December 1984): 826–35.

Fallon, Michael. "Eighth Grade Math Scores Just Aren't Measuring Up." *Sacramento Union* (January 13, 1985): B1.

Farr, Pamela. "Trends in Math Books for Children." *School Library Journal* (October 1979): 99–102.

Favat, F. Andre. *Child and Tale: The Origins of Interest.* Urbana. Ill.: National Council of Teachers of English, 1977.

Fennema, E. "The Relative Effectiveness of a Symbolic and a Concrete Model in Learning a Selected Mathematical Principle." *Journal for Research in Mathematics Education* 3 (1972): 233–38.

Ferguson, Anne M., and Jo Fairburn. "Language Experience for Problem Solving in Mathematics." *Reading Teacher* 38 (February 1985): 504–7.

Finn, Chester E., Jr.. *What Works: Research about Teaching and Learning.* Department of Education Publication no. 82-110. Washington, D.C.: U. S. Government Printing Office, 1987.

Fischler, Rosamond Welchman. "Mathematics from Children's Literature." *Arithmetic Teacher* 35 (February 1988): 42–47.

Fuson, Karen C. "Research into Practice: Subtracting by Counting Up with One-Handed Finger Patterns." *Arithmetic Teacher* 35 (January 1988): 29–31.

Fuson, K.C., and J. W. Hall. "The Acquisition of Early Number Word Meanings: A Conceptual Analysis and Review." In *The Development of Mathematical Thinking,* edited by H. P. Ginsburg. New York: Academic Press, 1983.

Fuson, K. C., J. Richards, and D. J. Briars. "The Acquisition and Elaboration of the Number Word Sequence." In *Children's Logical and Mathematical Cognition,* edited by C. J. Brainerd. New York: Springer-Verlag, 1982.

Ganz, Alice. "Writing as a Problem-Solving Experience." *Language Arts* 60 (September 1983): 737–39.

Gelman, R., and C. R. Gallistel. *The Child's Understanding of Numbers.* Cambridge, Mass.: Harvard University Press, 1978.

Ginsburg, H. P. *Children's Arithmetic: The Learning Process.* New York: D. Van Nostrand, 1977.

——— . "Children's Surprising Knowledge of Arithmetic." *Arithmetic Teacher* 28 (September 1980): 42–44.

Glazer, Joan I., and Gurney Williams III. *Introduction to Children's Literature.* New York: McGraw-Hill, 1979.

Hall, Cheryl Ann. "Children's Literature: Using Predictable Text as the Basis for Beginning Reading." Master's thesis, California State University, Sacramento, 1985.

Hall, Margaret Ellen. "Kindergarten Children's Knowledge of the Mother Goose Rhymes." Master's thesis, Sacramento State College, 1969.

Hall, Robert J. "Orthographic Problem-Solving." *Academic Therapy* 20 (September 1984): 67–75.

Hamrick, Kathy B. "Are We Introducing Mathematical Symbols Too Soon?" *Arithmetic Teacher* 28 (November 1980): 14–15.

Harsh, A. "Teaching Mathematics with Children's Literature." *Young Children* 42 (Summer 1987): 24–29.

Hart, Kathleen, and Daphne Kerslake. "Avoidance of Fractions." *Research in Education* (August1983).

Hart, Marj. *Fold-and-Cut Stories and Fingerplays.* Belmont, Calif.: David S. Lake, 1987.

Heald-Taylor, Gail. "Predictable Literature Selections and Activities for Language Arts Instruction." *Reading Teacher* 41 (October 1987): 6–13.

Hiebert, James. "Why do Some Children Have Trouble Learning Measurement Concepts?" *Arithmetic Teacher* 31 (March 1984): 19–24.

Holcomb, Jean. "Using Geoboards in the Primary Grades." *Arithmetic Teacher* 25 (April 1980): 22–25.

Hollis, Loye Y. "Mathematical Concepts of Young Children." *Arithmetic Teacher* 29 (October 1981): 24–27.

Holt, Michael, and Zoltan Dienes. *Let's Play Math.* New York: Walker and Company, 1973.

Hopkins, Lee Bennett. *Selections from Books Are by People.* New York: Scholastic Book Service, 1970.

––––––. "Profile: An Interview with Garth Williams." *Language Arts* 53 (October 1976): 806–9.

Horner, Charlotte M., and Cleborne D. Maddux. "The Effect of Logo on Attributions toward Success." *Computers in the Schools* 2 (Summer/Fall 1985): 45–54.

Hsu, Huei-Joyce. "An Integrated Model for Learning Number Concepts at the Preschool Level in Taiwan." Ph. D. diss., Peabody College at Vanderbilt University, 1987.

Huck, Charlotte S., Susan Hepler, and Janet Hickman. *Children's Literature in the Elementary School, 4th ed.* New York: Holt, Rinehart and Winston, 1987.

Hutchinson, James W., and Carol E. Hutchinson. "Homemade Device for Quick Recall of Facts." *Arithmetic Teacher* 24 (January 1978): 54–55.

Hyde, Arthur A., and Marilyn Bizar. *Thinking in Context: Teaching Cognitive Processes Across the Elementary School Curriculum.* New York: Longman, 1989.

Immerzel, George, and Don Wiederanders. "Ideas." *Arithmetic Teacher* 17 (December 1971): 576–84.

Jamison, D., P. Suppes, and S. Wells. "The Effectiveness of Alternative Instructional Media: A Survey." *Review of Educational Research* 44 (1974): 1–67.

Jones, Billie M. "Put Your Children in the Picture for Better Problem-Solving." *Arithmetic Teacher* 30 (April 1983): 30–33.

Kahn, Emily, and Robert W. Wirtz. "Another Look at Applications in Elementary School Mathematics." *Arithmetic Teacher* 30 (September 1982): 21–25.

Kalin, Robert. "How Students Do Their Division Facts." *Arithmetic Teacher* 31 (November 1983): 16–20.

Kane, Martin. "Cognitive Styles of Thinking and Learning, Part Two." *Academic Therapy* 20 (September 1984): 83–92.

Katz, Janet Lea. "Early Number Concepts, Skills and Strategies in Children At-Risk and Not At-Risk for Academic Achievement." Ed. D. diss., Columbia University Teachers College, 1986.

Kennedy, Leonard M. *Models for Mathematics in the Elementary School.* Belmont, Calif.: Wadsworth, 1967.

———. *Guiding Children to Mathematical Discovery, Fourth Edition.* Belmont, Calif: Wadsworth, 1984.

Kennedy, Leonard M., and Ruth L. Michon. *Games for Individualizing Mathematics Learning.* Columbus, Ohio: Charles E. Merrill, 1973.

Klausmeier, H. J. "Using Research: Improving Problem Solving." *Wisconsin Journal of Education* 96 (1964): 15–16.

Klingberg, Doris. "Profile: Eric Carle." *Language Arts* 34 (April 1977): 445–52.

Kosc, L. "Developmental Dyscalculia." *Journal of Learning Disabilities* 7 (1984): 164–77.

Lamme, Linda Leonard, ed. *Learning to Love Literature: Preschool Through Grade Three*. Urbana, Ill.: National Council of Teachers of English, 1981.

Landauer, Edwin G. "Counting Using License Plates and Phone Numbers: A Familiar Experience." *Mathematics Teacher* 77 (March 1984): 183–87.

Lettieri, Frances M. "Meet the Zorkies: A New Attribute Material." *Arithmetic Teacher* 24 (September 1978): 36–39.

Leutzinger, Larry Paul. "The Effects of Counting On the Acquisition of Addition Facts in Grade One." Ph. D. diss., University of Iowa, 1979.

Lickteig, Mary J. *An Introduction to Children's Literature*. Columbus, Ohio: Charles E. Merrill, 1975.

Liedtke, Werner. "One Point of View: Let's Talk about Talking Mathematics." *Arithmetic Teacher* 35 (April 1988): 2.

Liedtke, W. W., and L. D. Nelson. "Activities in Mathematics for Preschool Children." *Arithmetic Teacher* 21 (November 1973): 536–41.

Lowell, K. *The Growth of Understanding Mathematics: Kindergarten Through Grade Three*. Toronto, Ont.: Holt, Rinehart and Winston, 1971.

Lucas, J. S. "The Effect of Attribute-Block Training on Children's Development of Arithmetic Concepts." Ph. D. diss., University of California, Berkeley,1966.

McCracken, Robert A., and Marlene J. McCracken. *Stories, Songs, and Poetry to Teach Reading and Writing: Literacy through Language*. Chicago, Ill.: American Library Association, 1986.

Manna, Anthony L. "1986 Notable Children's Trade Books for the Language Arts." *Language Arts* 64 (November 1987): 767-68.

Marshall, Patricia. "Homework and Social Facilitation Theory in Teaching Elementary School Mathematics." Ph. D. diss., Stanford University, 1983.

Marshall, Patricia. "Meta-Analysis of the Research Literature on Homework in Elementary and Secondary School Mathematics." Paper presented to University Association of Research Scholars, California State University, Sacramento, Spring 1985.

——— . *Math Plans for K-6 Teachers.* Sacramento, Calif.: California State University, Sacramento, Department of Teacher Education, 1988.

Mastain, Mary Steele. "A Parents' Guide to Reading." Master's thesis, California State University, Sacramento, 1982.

Mathews, Eugene. "A Study of the Relationship between Student Achievement in Mathematics and Performance Evaluation and Other Variables." Ph. D. diss., University of South Carolina, 1981.

Matthews, Julia. "A Subtraction Experiment with Six and Seven Year Old Children." *Educational Studies in Mathematics* 14 (May 1983): 139–54.

Maxwell, M. "Games Children Play: Powerful Tools that Teach Some Thinking Skills." In *Thinking: The Expanding Frontier*, edited by W. Maxwell. Philadelphia, Pa.: Franklin Institute Press, 1983.

Montessori, Marie. *The Montessori Method.* New York: Schocken Books, 1964.

Moyer, John C., and others. "Story Problem Formats: Some Interview Results." In *Resources in Education*, Washington, D.C: National Science Foundation, September 1983.

——— . "Story Problem Formats: Some Interview Results." *Resources in Education*, (September) Washington, D.C.: National Science Foundation, 1983.

Muller, Adelyn C., and Ray Kurtz. "Students Like Personalized Word Problems." *Arithmetic Teacher* 28 (May 1982): 13–14.

Nelson, Glenn. "Teaching Time-Telling." *Arithmetic Teacher* 29 (May 1982): 31–34.

Nelson, L. D., and W. Liedtke. *Mathematical Experiences in Early Childhood.* Toronto, Ont.: Encyclopedia Britannica Publications, 1972.

Nelson-Herber, Joan. "Research Into Practice: Cooperative Learning." *Reading Today* 5 (June/July 1988): 16.

Newman, Judith M. "Online: Logo and the Language Arts." *Language Arts* 65 (October 1988): 598–605.

Norton, Donna E. *Through the Eyes of a Child: An Introduction to Children's Literature, 2d ed.* Columbus, Ohio: Charles E. Merrill, 1987.

Omanson, Susan F., and others. "The Effects of Mapping Instruction on Children's Procedural Bugs in Subtraction." *Research in Education* (January) 1983.

Osborne, A. R. "The Effects of Two Instructional Approaches on the Understanding of Subtraction by Grade Two Pupils." Ph. D. diss., University of Michigan, 1966.

Owston, Ronald D. "Systematic Computational Errors and Achievement in Elementary Mathematics." *Alberta Journal of Educational Research* 27 (June1981): 114–20.

Peterson, Penelope L. "Ability X Treatment Interaction Effects on Children's Learning in Large-Group and Small-Group Approaches." *American Educational Research Journal* 18 (Winter 1981): 453–73.

Petty, Walter R., and Julie M. Jensen. *Developing Children's Language.* Boston: Allyn and Bacon, 1980.

Piaget, J. *The Child's Conception of Number.* New York: W. W. Norton and Company, 1965.

Quintero, Ana Helvia. "The Role of Conceptual Understanding in Solving Word Problems: Two-Step Problems." *Research in Education* (July) 1983.

————. "Children's Difficulties with Two-Step Word Problems." *Research in Education* (August) 1984.

Radebaugh, Muriel Rogie. "Using Children's Literature to Teach Mathematics." *Reading Teacher* 34 (May 1981): 902–5.

Rea, R. S., and R. E. Reys. "Mathematical Competencies of Entering Kindergartners." *Arithmetic Teacher* 17 (1979): 65-74.

Reeve, R. A., and A. L. Brown. "Metacognition Reconsidered: Implications for Intervention Research."Technical Report no. 328. Washington, DC.: Department of Education; Bethesda, Md.: National Institute of Child Health and Human Development, Washington, D. C..: National Institute of Education,1984.

Resnick, Lauren B. "Syntax and Semantics in Learning to Subtract." *Research in Education* (February) 1983.

————. "Beyond Error Analysis: The Role of Understanding in Elementary School Arithmetic." *Research in Education* (January) 1985.

Resnick, L. B., and W. W. Ford. *The Psychology of Mathematics for Instruction.* Hillsdale, N.J.: Earlbaum Publishing, 1981.

Riedesel, C. Alan. *Teaching Elementary School Mathematics, 4th ed.* Englewood Cliffs, N.J.: Prentice-Hall, 1985.

Roberts, Patricia L. *Alphabet Books as a Key to Language Patterns: An Annotated Action Bibliography.* Hamden, Conn.: Library Professional Publications, 1987.

Sacramento Bee. "Study: Half of Kindergarteners in Chicago Ill-Suited for School." Sacramento, Calif.: *Sacramento Bee* (June 27, 1988): A8.

Sadowski, Barbara R., and B. McIlvenny. "Diagnosis and Remediation of Sentence-Solving Error Patterns." *Arithmetic Teacher* 31 (January 1984): 42–45.

Schell, Vicki J. "Learning Partners: Reading and Mathematics." *Reading Teacher* 35 (February 1983): 544–48.

Sebesta, Sam Leaton, and William J. Iverson. *Literature for Thursday's Child.* Palo Alto, Calif.: Science Research Associates, 1975.

Secada, Walter G., and others. "The Transition from Counting-All to Counting-On in Addition." *Journal for Research in Mathematics Education* 14 (January 1983): 47–57.

Self, Frank. "Features: Choosing Books for Children One to Three." *Children's Book Council* 41 (January-August 1987): unnumbered pages.

Sharpley, Anna M., and others. "An Examination of the Effectiveness of a Cross-Age Tutoring Program in Mathematics for Elementary School Children." *American Educational Research Journal* 20 (Spring 1983): 103–11.

Sherrill, James M. "Subtraction: Decomposition Versus Equal Addends." *Arithmetic Teacher* 27 (September 1979): 16–17.

Singer, Rita. "Estimation and Counting in the Block Corner." *Arithmetic Teacher* 35 (January 1988): 10–15.

Slaughter, Helen. *Classroom Implementation Study of an Activities-Based Supplemental Mathematics Program: Final Report.* Washington, D.C.: National Institute of Education, 1981.

Slaughter, Helen, and Jean Chilcott. *Classroom Ethnographic Study of an Activities-based Supplemental Mathematics Program.* Washington, D. C.: National Institute of Education, 1981.

Smith, Nancy J., and Karla Hawkins Wendelin. "Using Children's Books to Teach Mathematical Concepts." *Arithmetic Teacher* 28 (November 1981): 10–15.

Snethen, Charles Oliver. "Peer Support in the Teaching of Verbal Problem Solving in Arithmetic." Ed. D. diss., University of Missouri, 1975.

Sowder, Larry, and others. "Format Variables and Learner Characteristics in Mathematical Problem Solving." In *Resources in Education,* Washington, D. C.: National Science Foundation, (May) 1984.

Sower, Gayle Mary. "An Investigation of the Effects of Direct and Functional Reading Instruction upon Mathematical Problem Solving Abilities of Elementary School Children." Ph. D. diss., University of Connecticut, 1980.

Stangl, Jean. *Paper Stories.* Belmont, Calif.: David S. Lake, 1984.

Steffe, Leslie P. *The Effects of Two Variables on the Problem-Solving Abilities of First Grade Children: Teaching Reports #21.* Madison, Wis.: Wisconsin Research and Development Center for Cognitive Learning, University of Wisconsin, 1967.

Steffe, Leslie P., Ernest Von Glaserfeld, John Richards, and Paul Cobb. *Children's Counting Types: Philosophy, Theory, and Application.* New York: Praeger Publishing, 1983.

Stenmark, Jean Kerr, Virginia Thompson, and Ruth Cossey. *Family Math.* Berkeley, Calif.: University of California Printing Department, 1986.

Sutherland, Zena and May Hill Arbuthnot. *Children and Books, 7th ed.* Glenview, Ill.: Scott, Foresman, 1986.

Suydam, Marilyn N., ed. *Motivational Activities for Low (and Higher) Achievers.* Informational Bulletin no.13. Washington, D.C.: National Institute of Education, 1983.

———. "Research Report: Low Achievers."*Arithmetic Teacher* 31 (December 1983): 40.

——— ed. *Solve It with a Calculator.* Informational Bulletin no.14. Washington D. C.: National Institute of Education, 1983.

———. "Fractions." *Arithmetic Teacher* 31 (March 1984): 64.

Suydam, M., and J. Higgins. "Activity-Based Learning in Elementary School Mathematics: Recommendations from Research." Columbus, Ohio: ERIC Clearinghouse on Science, Mathematics, and Environmental Education. ERIC ED 14480 1980.

Thomas, David A. "Reading and Reasoning Skills for Math Problem Solvers." *Journal of Reading* 32 (December 1988): 244–49.

Thompson, Charles E., and John Van De Walle. "Paper Dot Plates Give Numbers Meaning." *Arithmetic Teacher* 28 (September 1980): 3–7.

Threadgill-Sowder, Judith, Larry Sowder, Margaret A. Moyer, and John C. Moyer. "A Case Against Telegraphing Math Story Problems for Poor Readers." *Reading Teacher* 37 (April 1984): 746–48.

Tiedt, Iris M. *Exploring Books with Children*. Boston: Houghton Mifflin, 1979.

Trueblood, Cecil, and Michael Szabo. *Guidelines for Evaluation of Published Metric Materials*. Reston, Va.: National Council of Teachers of Mathematics, 1978.

Van de Walle, John. "The Early Development of Number Relations." *Arithmetic Teacher* 35 (February 1988): 15–21, 32.

Webb, June R., and Leland F. Webb. "Students' Computation Errors." *Today's Education* (April-May 1982): 46–49.

Wells, Carmi Ray. "The Relationship Between Journal Writing and Achievement in Mathematical Measurement and Place Value/Regrouping among Primary School Children." Ed. D. diss., Montana State University, 1986.

Westbrook, Lynn. "A Study of Sexism in the Illustrations of Counting Books." ERIC Silverplatter 4 (1/83–3/88): EJ245785.

Whitehead, Robert J. *A Guide for Selecting Books for Children*. Metuchen, N.J.: Scarecrow Press, 1984.

Whitehead, Robert J., and Karen Van Scoy. *Literature Games*. Belmont, Calif.: Fearon, 1971.

Williams, Judith A. "Partner Prediction." *Reading Today* 5 (June/July 1988): 13.

Williams, Elizabeth, and Hilary Shuard. *Elementary Mathematics Today: A Resource for Teachers Grades 1–8*. Reading, Mass.: Addison-Wesley, 1970.

Winner, Alice-Ann, and Margo D. McClung. "Computer Game Playing—'Turning On' to Mathematics." *Arithmetic Teacher* 29 (October 1982): 38–39.

Witzenburg, Harvey Gene. "Teaching the Telling of Time to Second Graders." Ph. D. diss., The University of Iowa, 1979.

Wilson, Bruce L., and others. "Effect of Task and Authority Structures on Student Task Engagement." *Resources In Education* (October)1983.

Wolfinger, Donna M. "One Point of View: Mathematics for the Young Child—not Arithmetic." *Arithmetic Teacher* 35 (February 1988): 4.

Woodward, Ernest. "A Second-Grade Probability and Graphing Lesson." *Arithmetic Teacher* 30 (March 1983): 23–24.

Artist–Author and Title Index